TROUBLE ON MAIN STREET

ALSO IN THE
History *of* Canada Series

TROUBLE ON MAIN STREET

MACKENZIE KING, REASON, RACE, AND THE 1907 VANCOUVER RIOTS

Julie F. Gilmour

General Editors
MARGARET MacMILLAN and ROBERT BOTHWELL

ALLEN
LANE

ALLEN LANE
an imprint of Penguin Canada Books Inc., a Penguin Random House Company

Published by the Penguin Group
Penguin Canada Books Inc.
90 Eglinton Avenue East, Suite 700, Toronto, Ontario, Canada M4P 2Y3

Penguin Group (USA) LLC, 375 Hudson Street, New York, New York 10014, U.S.A.
Penguin Books Ltd, 80 Strand, London WC2R 0RL, England
Penguin Ireland, 25 St Stephen's Green, Dublin 2, Ireland (a division of Penguin Books Ltd)
Penguin Group (Australia), 707 Collins Street, Melbourne, Victoria 3008, Australia
(a division of Pearson Australia Group Pty Ltd)
Penguin Books India Pvt Ltd, 11 Community Centre, Panchsheel Park, New Delhi – 110 017, India
Penguin Group (NZ), 67 Apollo Drive, Rosedale, Auckland 0632, New Zealand
(a division of Pearson New Zealand Ltd)
Penguin Books (South Africa) (Pty) Ltd, 24 Sturdee Avenue, Rosebank,
Johannesburg 2196, South Africa

Penguin Books Ltd, Registered Offices: 80 Strand, London WC2R 0RL, England

First published 2014

1 2 3 4 5 6 7 8 9 10 (RRD)

Copyright © Julie F. Gilmour, 2014

Manufactured in the U.S.A.

LIBRARY AND ARCHIVES CANADA CATALOGUING IN PUBLICATION

Gilmour, Julie F., author
Trouble on Main Street : Mackenzie King, reason, race,
and the 1907 Vancouver riots / Julie F. Gilmour.

(History of Canada)
Includes bibliographical references and index.

ISBN 978-0-670-06512-7 (bound)

1. Race riots—British Columbia—Vancouver—History—20th century.
2. Racism—British Columbia—Vancouver—History—20th century.
3. Vancouver (B.C.)—Race relations—History—20th century. 4. Vancouver (B.C.)—
Emigration and immigration—Social aspects—History—20th century.
5. Vancouver (B.C.)—Emigration and immigration—Political aspects—History—20th century.
6. King, William Lyon Mackenzie, 1874–1950. 7. Canada—Foreign relations—1867–.
I. Title. II. Series: History of Canada (Toronto, Ont.)

FC3847.4.G54 2014   971.1'3303   C2014-900032-4

eBook ISBN: 978-0-14-319191-9

Visit the Penguin Canada website at www.penguin.ca

Special and corporate bulk purchase rates available; please see
www.penguin.ca/corporatesales or call 1-800-810-3104, ext. 2477.

For Jeff

CONTENTS

INTRODUCTION TO THE HISTORY OF CANADA SERIES

Canada, the world agrees, is a success story. We should never make the mistake, though, of thinking that it was easy or foreordained. At crucial moments during Canada's history, challenges had to be faced and choices made. Certain roads were taken and others were not. Imagine a Canada, indeed imagine a North America, where the French and not the British had won the Battle of the Plains of Abraham. Or imagine a world in which Canadians had decided to throw in their lot with the revolutionaries in the thirteen colonies.

This series looks at the making of Canada as an independent, self-governing nation. It includes works on key stages in the laying of the foundations, as well as on the crucial turning points between 1867 and the present that made the Canada we know today. It is about those defining moments when the course of Canadian history and the nature of Canada itself were oscillating. And it is about the human beings—heroic, flawed, wise, foolish, complex—who had to make decisions without knowing what the consequences might be.

We begin the series with the European presence in the eighteenth century—a presence that continues to shape our society today—and conclude it with an exploration of the strategic importance of the Canadian Arctic. We look at how the mass movements of peoples, whether Loyalists in the eighteenth century or Asians at the start of the twentieth, have profoundly influenced the nature of Canada. We also look at battles and their aftermaths: the Plains of Abraham, the 1866 Fenian raids, the German submarines in the St. Lawrence River during World War II. Political crises—the 1891 election that saw Sir John A. Macdonald battling Wilfrid Laurier; Pierre Trudeau's triumphant patriation of the Canadian Constitution—provide rich moments of storytelling. So, too, do the Expo 67 celebrations, which marked a time of soaring optimism and gave Canadians new confidence in themselves.

We have chosen these critical turning points partly because they are good stories in themselves but also because they show what Canada was like at particularly important junctures in its history. And to tell them we have chosen Canada's best historians. Our authors are great storytellers who shine a spotlight on a different Canada, a Canada of the past, and illustrate links from then to now. We need to remember the roads that were taken—and the ones that were not. Our goal is to help our readers understand how we got from that past to this present.

Margaret MacMillan
Warden at St. Antony's College, Oxford

Robert Bothwell
May Gluskin Chair of Canadian History
University of Toronto

INTRODUCTION

Few characters in Canadian history are viewed with such extremes of both respect and ridicule as William Lyon Mackenzie King. Alternately portrayed by historians as an anglophile, an "American," a brilliant political mind, a naive spiritualist, a man of reason, and a racist, King was in fact all of these things, and it is this combination that makes him such a fascinating subject. In order to understand his later state-craft, we have to understand King, his world view, and his philosophy of government. To do this, it is necessary to examine his early professional life on its own terms before he became prime minister—in its international context, for King was an international man. He left his family home in Toronto for Chicago in the fall of 1896. While pursuing a master of arts under the supervision of eminent sociologist and political economist Thorstein Veblen, he also threw himself into the world of urban reform. He dabbled in settlement work at Jane Addams's Hull House for a time until the pressures of school drew him back to labour studies and his thesis. He was content in the United States and rather than returning to Canada after submitting his master's paper, he began pursuing a PhD at Harvard. However, King was not just a North American in his outlook. He was, after all, a Canadian subject of the British Crown, raised in the British Empire, and so when an opportunity arose to study at the London School of Economics, he accepted without reservation. He had therefore lived, worked, and studied in Canada, the United States, and Great Britain by the fall of 1899. He was not yet twenty-five years old.

King seems to have embodied the very struggles facing twentieth-century Canada since both he and his country self-imagined at various times as important or insignificant, as American, British, or something else altogether. King and Canada were in the midst of huge changes in direction. In King's case, the first decade of the century transformed him from an aspiring freelance civil servant into a member of Parliament and a fledgling diplomat with a recognized track record of successful international diplomacy. Canada was experiencing a shifting cultural landscape in which the importance of North American identities was growing clearer and the nation's older transatlantic links with Great Britain were receding. This change was obscured by the formal political links that still bound Canada to Britain, but it was nevertheless a cause for concern among those who valued the British connection. These developments were amplified by the changing ethnic composition of Canada. The years before the First World War were extraordinary for the increase in immigration to Canada's west and the shift away from British and American settlers to immigrants from regions previously considered "less desirable" but now necessary for the economic goals of Canadian business. But immigrants could lower wages by expanding the workforce, a point of concern for labour unions, particularly if the immigrants were not white Europeans and thus did not even resemble the workers who faced what they perceived as unequal competition—from those whom they considered to be unequal people. Among these new immigrants were workers from China, Japan, and India who were often set apart for particular abuse by those who feared the rise of non-white immigration to Canada.

Fears of Asian immigration took a violent turn in Vancouver during a September 7, 1907, protest march. A crowd of demonstrators formed a mob, destroyed businesses in Vancouver's Chinese and Japanese neighbourhoods, and caused great distress to the communities and embarrassment for the Laurier government in Ottawa, which was called upon to mitigate the damage to Britain's relations with both Japan and China. Fortunately for Laurier, he had the able young deputy minister of labour, W.L. Mackenzie King—a natural conciliator itching to take on more responsibility—to carry out some of this work. King was quickly linked with these events and engulfed in the diplomacy that followed, and this experience influenced his thinking about Asia, Britain, the United States, Canada, and immigration for years to come. His international, political, reform-minded, and well-documented life gives us a fascinating window into Edwardian Canada and its place in the world. The riots were therefore both locally interesting and international in their implications, raising questions far beyond Vancouver and Ottawa about Canada and its diplomatic relationship with Britain and its allies.

King is both personally and metaphorically at the centre of this story. He was present as the riot was investigated; became an acknowledged expert on the questions associated with it; and struggled with the politics of nation and empire that framed it. He travelled extensively to consult with officials from many countries at the highest levels of government, and he would eventually become the prime minister who oversaw the dismantling of the anti-Asian immigration legislation that was produced prior to and as a result of the riots themselves. I have therefore used King's diaries extensively throughout this book, particularly when referring to the period 1908–1909. During this time, King kept meticulous notes about his missions to London, Washington, India, China, and Japan. He reported extensively about his meetings and often recounted these conversations almost verbatim. King was in the habit of returning home after a day's work and sitting down with his secretary, Francis W. Giddens, to type up his notes. On learning that King was going to meet American president Theodore Roosevelt, one of Roosevelt's friends emphasized to him the importance of keeping very good notes: "to be sure to record everything with care for my own protection, as if later on there was a difference of opinion the President would simply say I lied."[1] While it would be a mistake to suggest that King's diaries tell the whole story, we can with confidence state that this story could not be told without them. And this is an important story about Canada and its place in the world before the First World War.

The man responsible for putting King in the middle of this tale, and who most immediately faced the challenges of the days after September 7, 1907, was Sir Wilfrid Laurier, King's superior, mentor, and prime minister. The aging and worldly Laurier was a French-Canadian Liberal with imperial sensibilities. As his biographer (later the undersecretary of state for external affairs) O.D. Skelton observed, Laurier "would not enter into dangerous and entangling new imperial commitments, but he would faithfully and punctiliously perform the obligations of the existing bonds."[2] He had overseen an enormous expansion of Canadian immigration to the new prairie provinces; had weathered the Alaska Boundary Dispute that placed Canada uncomfortably against the interests of both the United States and Great Britain; had navigated the government through the perilous shoals of the British war in South Africa; and had just returned from the 1907 Imperial Conference, where he had asserted Canada's mistrust of efforts to create an Imperial Federation, as well as his faith in the imperial status quo of dispersed power. Laurier supported the continuation of conferences between "government and governments," assuming that London would continue to lead and the dominions to follow.[3] He was therefore anxious to assure London that Canada was not going to diverge from British policy toward Japan and would not endorse any legislation that would unfairly target Japanese subjects. However, Canada was a long way from London and the electoral politics of British Columbia weighed heavily on the prime minister. The Liberals had been drubbed in the province in the 1904 dominion election, and were about to take a beating in the upcoming October 1908 election in BC from candidates who called for the outright exclusion of all Asian workers, including the Japanese with whom Britain was allied and the Indians who were British subjects.

After a decade of increasing scientific and cultural exchanges, Japan and Great Britain entered into the Anglo-Japanese Alliance in 1902. The agreement allowed Japan to go to war with Russia without fear of British intervention, and it ensured that British interests in the Pacific were protected while the bulk of the Royal Navy was concentrated in the North Sea to face the growing German threat. This was not a popular move on Canada's Pacific coast, where the fear of war with Japan was much more prevalent than in London or even in Ottawa. Nevertheless, Canada's foreign policy, particularly in the area of military decision making, lay with London, and Laurier and his government were forced to work within the limitations set by existing Empire policy.

Liberals of the Progressive Era believed in the power of government to improve social conditions and relied on experts of many kinds to show the way. In this case, Laurier chose King as his expert to oversee the investigation into the causes of the riot and the assessment of the damages it caused. He was selected because of the importance of managing the local politics, labour issues, and international implications of the violence. King had proven himself to be a reliable functionary in the Department of Labour. He had a background in labour mediation and could be trusted to understand the implications for the Liberal Party in the province. In fact, the riots were a career opportunity for King. He was thrust out of the backrooms of the Department of Labour and the Liberal Party in Ottawa into a much larger diplomatic world. This appointment began a period of intense activity for the young deputy minister and created the conditions under which he was increasingly linked to Canadian policy on the questions of labour unrest, Asian immigration, and the opium trade. The riots thus created a chance for King to develop both expertise on the issues associated with Asian immigration and passionate opinions on the government's responsibility to manage its relationship with Britain and the flow of labourers at home and abroad.

This is therefore a Canadian tale, with King a very Canadian protagonist, set on an imperial and international stage. While the anti-Asian riots of Labour Day weekend 1907 occurred in one Vancouver neighbourhood, they echoed from coast to coast and across the Canada–United States border, the Atlantic, and the Pacific. The riots and the various responses to the disorders teach us about Canada's relationship to its neighbours and to the great powers of the time. We see in Canada's response to the riots how both these international relationships and local conditions could define what was possible in the policy realm. In Canada's attempts to avoid further trouble on "Main Street," particular local economic woes, irrational fears of difference, and the desire to control labour conditions coloured provincial politics, national immigration policy, and even great power diplomacy between 1905 and 1914. Indeed, this is a story of how two days of trouble on Westminster Avenue in 1907 set the contours of Canada's immigration agenda and gave shape to a set of systems and institutions that resisted change for the next several decades and whose assumptions, issues, and concerns are still present in some of our immigration debates today.

Historians of the city of Vancouver will be quick to point out that, in fact, no street called "Main" existed when the riots took place. In 1907 Main Street was still Westminster Avenue, so that when the violence broke out it was actually at the corner of Westminster Avenue and Hastings. The street was renamed in 1910 and has been called Main ever since. For a hundred years, Main has been at the centre of memory of these events. And so the riots and the spectre of irrational violence anywhere in Canada were very much the trouble on "Main Street" that King feared. This metaphorical Main Street was often invoked by politicians and public intellectuals when they considered the implications of immigration for electoral politics, order, and even the future of British Columbia within Canada. A direct and explicit relationship thus existed among local BC politics, Canadian immigration policy, and global affairs. This book investigates this relationship and shows how, during the period 1907–1910, local interests, individual approaches to politics, and serendipity were translated into national policy or sometimes hijacked along the way. It reveals the struggles Canada faced as it tried to exercise its fledgling powers as a nation abroad in the councils of empire, in the corridors of the White House, and among the great powers of Asia.

Canada's position at the northern end of North America, on the edges of two historic empires, and atop thousands of square kilometres of underpopulated land makes it a fascinating case for the study of empire and immigration. As we wrestle with the current implications of global economic crises for the Canadian economy and national security, as well as the demographic challenges of governing a country more blessed in resources than manpower, it is instructive to examine the ways we managed similar and related questions in another age—the ways we defined success and failure, and the impact our choices then had on the formation of Canada and its relationships with the world.

ONE

The Riots

In 1907 Vancouver was a city of untapped potential—a city on the rise. The Klondike Gold Rush had brought people and business opportunities to the city and, together with the wheat boom, contributed to a growing demand for both housing and the local forest industry's products. New construction downtown and in the new bedroom communities transformed the city of wooden shopfronts and unpaved streets into a bricks-and-mortar outpost of the British Empire. However, those who wished it would become the centre of British identity on the west coast saw danger in the city's habit of cozying up a bit too closely to Washington State or becoming a Pacific city with real and abiding ties to China and Japan.

These ties were not merely economic or geographic. A significant percentage of the people arriving in Vancouver were originally from China, Japan, and increasingly, India. The population of Vancouver in 1901 (which was still clustered along the south shore of the Burrard Inlet and did not include Point Grey and South Vancouver) was 26,133.

More than 20,000 of this number were of British origin and 2,840 were from either China or Japan. By 1911 the total population had risen to 100,401. Of these, 46,488 were English, 29,131 Scottish, 3,871 Chinese, 2,486 Japanese, and 726 from India—or "Hindu," per a misleading Canadian style of race reckoning adopted from the British.[1] The number of Asian residents of Vancouver counted in the 1911 census may well have been higher but for the events of September 1907.

Canada's demographic and economic links with Japan and India received several important boosts in the 1890s and 1900s. First, in the years after Victoria's Diamond Jubilee celebration in 1897, an increasing number of Sikh veterans of the British army had chosen to settle in British Columbia and had spread the news of economic opportunities for East Indians in BC to their friends and family back home. Second, Japanese connections had a new institutional framework in the 1894 Anglo-Japanese Treaty of Commerce and Navigation. Laurier and his government were interested in increasing Canada's economic links with the Pacific, but until 1905 the prime minister was reluctant to sign on to the treaty if it was going to have the effect of opening Canada's borders to increased Japanese immigration. Japan's consul general in Ottawa, Tatsugoro Nossé, had spent enough time in Canada to grasp Laurier's dilemma. He understood the explosive potential of the question of Asian immigration in British Columbia. In order to reassure Ottawa that it could become a signatory to the treaty, Nossé promised that his government would limit the number of Japanese entering Canada to fewer than three hundred per year. Although Laurier would later discover that Nossé had made this assurance without the proper authority from his government, in the meantime this would allow Canada to both sign the treaty and spare Ottawa the problem of standing between the interests of London and Vancouver.[2] Laurier had only the consul general's word that this right would not be abused, but since Nossé was well known in Ottawa circles and a genial sort of man, the question was set aside for another day. Laurier was hopeful that the Japanese would be able to control their own emigration, and that he could have both the treaty and relative quiet in British Columbia, where fears of Japanese competition in a number of industries, including fishing and fruit growing, were leading to an increasingly hostile public. Unfortunately the coast did not remain silent for long. Despite Nossé's promises and Laurier's assurances, Vancouverites were seeing ever-increasing numbers of Japanese faces arriving at the port of Vancouver in July 1907.

It did not matter to the average Canadian that the migrants disembarking from the *Kumeric* in July had come from Hawaii rather than Japan. To many, these were still Japanese immigrants who had come in violation of both the Japanese agreement and Laurier's promises that Asian immigration would not increase. These views were reinforced by the growing influence of Vancouver's Asiatic Exclusion League (AEL). The AEL, founded by trade union activists as the Japanese and Corean Exclusion League in San Francisco in 1905, was a binational organization, whose purpose was to rally public opinion against Chinese, Japanese, Korean, and Indian migration. It organized branches up and down the Canadian and American Pacific coasts, including in both Vancouver and Seattle. Since Vancouver was less than 230 kilometres from Seattle, the exclusion organizations were closely tied to each other. Such groups were increasingly popular as the Canadian economy slowed along with shifts in the global economy. The sharp economic downturn of 1907 had been an important factor in the discontent among workers in BC that fall. Until then, the economy had been relatively strong, generating jobs and, if not exactly contentment, at least toleration of recent immigrants. The BC economy relied heavily on global markets for the natural resources that it had in abundance. The dominant and even record-setting BC industry in 1906–1907 was mining, followed by a strong forestry sector, salmon fishery, and Okanagan Valley fruit-growing industry.[3] While the period 1896–1913 is usually described as an economic boom time, 1907 was considered a year of relatively high unemployment and a general economic slowdown compared to

1906.[4] The details are perhaps less important than the fact that British Columbia shared the perception widely held across North America that an economic crisis was at hand.

In addition to the problem of unemployment in BC during the summer of 1907, it had become clear that a variety of factors were bringing more Japanese workers to Canada despite Nossé's promise. During the summer of 1907, Japanese who had been imported as workers into the Hawaiian Islands over the previous twelve years responded to a health crisis, changes in US immigration policy, continued low wages, and job insecurity by buying passage to BC, where they were told wages were higher and jobs plentiful. Passage on the June 20 sailing of the *Kumeric* direct to Vancouver was sold to interested workers through the Boarding House Keepers Union in Honolulu for thirty-six dollars—more than a month's wages in Hawaii and six dollars more than the usual ticket price for passage on a tramp steamer between Hawaii and Vancouver. And so, in July the *Admiral,* the *Jauréguiberry,* the *Kumeric*, and the *Indiana* brought a total of 1,750 Japanese from Honolulu to Vancouver without firm offers of employment or accommodation.[5] A fertile ground was therefore waiting for the arrival of members of Seattle's Japanese and Korean Exclusion League when they arrived to assist the Vancouver AEL in organizing its September 7 protest march.

Asian immigrants concentrated in the neighbourhood along Dupont Street (now Pender) had become a pebble in the shoe of some of Vancouver's most vocal citizens over the years, since the city's incorporation in 1886 and the completion of the transcontinental railroad. On the one hand, Vancouver was now a critical point on a long line of communication connecting London to the length of the Dominion and then by steamship to Britain's Pacific interests in Hong Kong, Singapore, and India. On the other, the fact that it was the railway terminus also made Vancouver a logical stop for former employees of the Canadian Pacific Railway and other transients looking for seasonal work. A few thousand of these workers were Chinese. Attempts had been made to exclude Chinese from the city, but a combination of federal intervention in provincial politics and the pull of real and imagined economic opportunities encouraged Chinese workers to come to Vancouver anyway. Most were single men and most lived close together in Chinatown.

In the 1890s and 1900s the city's fast growth had put pressure on the existing sewer system, drinking water, electricity, housing stock, and transport. Vancouver was not alone in this problem. Across North America and in Europe reformers sought solutions for the social ills of their cities, which were suffering from overcrowding, poverty, and disease. The international wave of moral and civic reform movements, such as the US Progressive Movement and the Social Gospel movement in both Canada and the United States, had their effects in Vancouver. Civic improvement was therefore generally on the minds of city officials who sought to minimize the impact of health crises, crime, and other moral failures on the city's development.

Chinese workers had moved into a neighbourhood of unregulated rooming houses and shacks that was a poorly serviced, often squalid part of the city that already had a reputation for immorality and disease because of the large number of poor white working men that had previously called it home. Even when city officials had made attempts to clean up the streets, lingering fears of difference and prejudices against Chinese immigrants contributed to a lasting impression that Chinatown was irredeemably filthy, unhealthy, and morally suspect. In response to the perceived crisis on the west coast, some people organized themselves into groups such as the AEL. These exclusion leagues met and organized protests against what seemed to them to be policies that encouraged waves of unassimilable "oriental" immigrants to settle in Chinatowns up and down the Pacific coast.

When the Japanese began to arrive in significant numbers after 1890, they were seen as a tidy, civilized community and yet still very much outside of "Canadian" society and even a threat to mainstream British Vancouver because of their perceived inability to assimilate and their talent for competing economically. Most Japanese workers were drawn to the fishing industry along the coast. While there was a decline in the number of men arriving just before Japan's war with Russia, in the years after 1905 the number of Japanese in Vancouver began to increase again. "Little Tokyo" arose adjacent to Chinatown and just down the street from City Hall, which in 1907 was located at the corner of Westminster Avenue (today's Main Street) and Hastings.

In the 1890s Japan's minister of war (and future prime minister), Terauchi Masatake, had travelled to Vancouver and had felt that Japanese and Canadian workers were bound to clash eventually over labour conditions.[6] The Japanese government was therefore aware that tensions on the west coast were rising. A special envoy, Kikujirō Ishii, was sent to Canada from the Japanese consulate in Seattle. Aged forty-one, Ishii was an experienced, professional diplomat, respected for his skill. Soon he would become vice-minister of foreign affairs in Tokyo, and eventually minister of foreign affairs—and a viscount to boot— but for the moment his job was to investigate anti-Japanese feelings in North America, to study the living and working conditions of Japanese immigrants along the Pacific coast, and to make recommendations. The increase in Japanese migration from Hawaii to ports on the North American mainland had caused tension in the relationship between Washington and Tokyo. Ishii's selection for this fact-finding mission was an indication that the Japanese government attached importance to its relationships with the two North American countries and to the impact migration was having on the diplomatic climate. Japan did not wish to further antagonize the United States or appear weak in the protec-tion of the rights of its citizens and so the envoy's mission was delicate. Ishii's original schedule had slated him to visit Seattle on Saturday, September 7, but the plan had changed: he would spend the weekend in Vancouver. His tour had not gone unnoticed by the exclusion leagues— itself a measure of its significance and Ishii's importance. A march had been planned to coincide with Ishii's visit to Seattle, and there is evidence that, when he left for Vancouver, the protest march was reorganized to follow him there.[7]

A number of speakers from the American-based anti-Asian groups travelled north to attend an organized labour parade and demonstration in Vancouver. They included A.E. Fowler, the secretary of the Anti-Japanese and Corean League of Seattle.[8] A well-known and enthusiastic agitator against Asian immigration in the United States, Fowler was considered the "brains" of the organization, and his supporters felt he would make great strides in the movement to achieve Japanese exclusion.[9] He was scheduled to give a rousing talk at City Hall on Saturday night, and he undoubtedly played a role in the eruption of violence that followed. Vancouver was plenty agitated to begin with on that hot evening. Unemployment was high and the economy was struggling. Workers and politicians were looking for someone to blame and "cheap oriental labour" had become a regular target. There was, therefore, a certain amount of irritation with Ottawa, distrust of Tokyo, and fear for the future simmering among the people gathered at the Cambie Street grounds at seven o'clock to march to City Hall for an evening of speeches and protest. Nevertheless, the crowd was festive and enjoying the holiday atmosphere.[10]

There is no question that this event was an exclusionist event from the beginning, although no one seemed to have planned for an outbreak of violence. On September 3, Alderman Stewart requested the use of City Hall "for a mass meeting dealing with reclusion of Orientals." His request was voted on and granted by the city council and entered into the minutes.[11] The Vancouver Asiatic Exclusion League aimed to show its support for exclusion by marching publicly as a group to City Hall for the event. While the Vancouver AEL has been characterized as a labour organization, the league was in fact more: it had members from not only Vancouver's unions but also its churches and veterans' associations, and also welcomed some of the province's politicians, including the president of the city's Conservative Association, C.M. Woodworth, and even the mayor, Alexander Bethune. While the event was clearly intended to target Asian immigration policy, it is unlikely that the mayor would have endorsed an event that was intended to lead to actual law-breaking in his town.

The parade route passed along some of the main streets in the heart of Vancouver: Georgia, Granville, Hastings, ending at Westminster Avenue (Main Street) and City Hall. While the original City Hall building no longer stands, one can still see its neighbour, the Carnegie Library, on the corner of Main and Hastings. Like the library, City Hall was a two-storey building with a tower, albeit less prominent than the library, and built of a darker stone. The Hastings side of the building had a small balcony accessible from the second-floor windows, from which one could address people waiting on the street below.

By nine o'clock, a huge crowd was gathering on Hastings. They had arrived following the parade marshal, Major E. Brown, who led the formal procession of cars, workers, banners supporting the protection of "a White Canada,"[12] and bands playing "Rule Britannia" and "The Maple Leaf Forever."[13] When the program was scheduled to begin, the hall, which could hold around two thousand people, was filled and, according to the *Manitoba Free Press*, at least seven thousand protestors thronged the streets nearby. The crowd was starting to get excited as it burned the lieutenant-governor of British Columbia, James Dunsmuir, in effigy. Dunsmuir had become a flashpoint for anti-Asian immigration activists since he had used his position as the king's representative in the province to disallow provincial legislation aimed at excluding Asian immigrants. While he did so with the full support—indeed at the request—of the federal government in Ottawa, his actions smacked of hypocrisy and self-interest as he himself was a well-known employer of Chinese labour. And so, as his image burned, the crowd "cheered lustily."[14]

Inside City Hall, a standing-room-only crowd listened intently to the invited speakers, who generally advocated moderate political action, but who did so within the racist framework so common in British, American, and Canadian culture at the time. Indeed, the racial hierarchy that placed Britons and other Anglo-Saxon whites at the top of a continuum of racialized categories was so prevalent that it had taken on the impression of being natural, scientific, and even logical across all of the white-settler colonies located in the British Empire and in the United States. Asian immigrants were therefore much less desirable than white settlers and had been formally recognized as less than citizens by the BC government when their right to vote was taken away. In a society in which Asian immigrants had been disenfranchised, politicians had been able to defame the Chinese, Japanese, and Indian communities with impunity. There was therefore nothing new in the speeches at City Hall. The crowd had heard these arguments against Asian immigration before, but they were energized by the scope of the resolutions that called on the government to completely exclude Asian immigrants and demanded that the national governments in Washington and Ottawa finally take action to protect the communities of white citizens on the Pacific coast.[15]

Meanwhile, thousands of supporters had packed themselves into the narrow side streets around City Hall. A bonfire added a carnival-like atmosphere to the event and the crowd was energized. We do not know the content of Fowler's speech precisely, but several sources suggest that he may have used tales of his own recent experience across the border, in Bellingham, to incite the mob to the violence that immediately followed. The British Foreign Office (FO) was certainly convinced of the role of American "interference" in Canadian anti-Asian activities.[16] A Foreign Office report even named Fowler as the individual "who proposed a march through the Chinese and Japanese quarters" and "the same person who led the attacks on the Hindoos at Bellingham." The report further claimed that Fowler instigated the mob violence directly, avowing that "it was some boys directed by Fowler who threw the first stones."[17] When he had finished his official speech indoors, Fowler addressed the overflow crowd on the street. He reminded them that only days earlier the residents of Bellingham, Washington, had taken it upon themselves to run a number of Sikh workers (or "Hindoos," as he called them) out of town. Whatever the immediate cause may have been, or the particular role of individuals from the United States, the crowd shed its previously festive mood and began to march along Dupont Street into Chinatown, which was unfortunately only a block away. One correspondent described the moment after the mood turned: "the crowd was wrecking all that was movable and breakable in Chinatown."[18] While Chinese shopkeepers and their families hid in the backrooms of their businesses, white men and boys threw stones and bricks through the storefront windows until every pane of glass in the area was shattered.

Reports of the events of that night agree that the residents of the Chinese quarter initially put up little resistance to the violence; however, King's investigation into the damages suffered by the Chinese uncovered the fact that the Chinese community had spent a great deal of money on firearms after the initial act of violence in order to defend themselves against possible further acts. Accounts differ in their explanations of why the Chinese victims put up little fight at the outset. English-language newspapers tended to see this as a result of the weaknesses stereotypically attributed to the Chinese: passivity, fear, and cowardice. More recent scholarship has expanded our understanding of the riots through the study of Chinese-language press accounts, and suggests another explanation: that the Chinese took a moral stand to meet violence with non-violence.[19] Materials published by the Chinese Benevolent Association explained the choice, saying,

> Our country [China] uses culture and civilization to deal with enemies. The Analects of Confucious say, "Use uprightness to treat resentment; use kindness in return for kindness." Improve ourselves in order to wipe away this humiliation [that the riot has brought to Chinatown]; face upward and feel free.[20]

In any case, the Chinese residents' decision to respond in this way was contrasted in the English-language press with the more active resistance organized by the Japanese in the evening hours of September 7 when "Little Tokyo" became the centre of the mob violence. Sometime around ten o'clock there was a shift in direction and the mob began to move northward toward Westminster and Powell, into the Japanese neighbourhood just north of City Hall. The residents organized themselves to resist the mob, and by many accounts they were ready to battle openly in the streets. An arsenal of available materials had been collected and stored on the roofs of Japanese homes. These included broken sake and whisky bottles, "knives, stones, clubs, [and] bricks."[21] And, to the surprise of the rioters, organized waves of shouting Japanese defenders threw themselves at the threatening crowd. The combination of this unexpected and effective defence and the arrival of the Vancouver police convinced most of the rioters to disperse by the time they reached the newly built Japanese Methodist Church at the corner of Powell and Jackson, which therefore escaped damage.

R.G. Chamberlain, a former inspector of the Dominion Police (the institutional predecessor to the Canadian Security Intelligence Service), was Vancouver's chief of police in September 1907 and in command of a fairly small force of men. In June of the same year, when Chamberlain took over the job, he gave the city council a strength report of sixty-two officers of all ranks, including jailers and the fire warden. Only twenty-six were constables with "beats" on the street.[22] This was a small force to police the entire city of Vancouver on a good day and completely inadequate during the riot.

When the crowd began to get out of hand, Chamberlain dispatched his available officers and called in the city's fire truck. The police used the fire crew in two significant ways. First, with the fire brigade close by, Chamberlain could act quickly to prevent any buildings from being destroyed by fire, but he could also use the department's truck, hoses, ladders, and personnel to assist with crowd control. A truck was placed across Carrall Street and was used to prevent curious onlookers from joining the rioters in Chinatown and adding to the crisis. The fire truck was damaged in the melee when the crowd overturned it, causing injuries among the crew.[23] The crowd also intervened whenever the police tried to make an arrest. As officers reached for a rioter, the crowd would pick him up and carry him overhead into the centre of the crowd, far from the reach of the police. While individuals in the police force may very well have been sympathetic to political aims of the rioters, they did draw the line at violence and arson and worked hard during the night to bring order to the city. It took some time for a disturbance of this size to lose momentum, but the police force was praised in the press and in official communications at the highest levels for their work under difficult circumstances.

A recent historical study has made the tantalizing claim that Chinese-language accounts of the riots provide evidence of more extreme violence. Some of these papers reported that several Japanese deaths resulted from the clash with shopkeepers in the Japanese neighbourhood.[24] However, the English-language press reported no fatalities, and unequivocal evidence one way or the other has yet to be found. It seems unlikely that Mayor Bethune would insist that there was "some damage to property but none to person,"[25] if any of the rioters or victims of the rioting had been killed. In addition, no record exists of any arrests or prosecutions for manslaughter or murder related to the events of September 7. The account of the Japanese consul in Ottawa, Tatsugoro Nossé, submitted to the governor general, was based in part on a telegram from the special envoy from Japan, Kikujirō Ishii, who had been the object of the American anti-Asian activists' plans. His report emphasized property damage rather than personal injury. As Ishii later recalled, despite the efforts of the authorities, the riots continued into the night:

> Towards midnight the fourth attack was made by the rowdies on the Japanese quarters. Later, twice again they tried to attack the Japanese stores, but on account of the utmost vigilance kept by both the Japanese

and city police force, and also of the late hour of the night, the number of rioters gradually decreased, and by 3 o'clock Sunday morning (the 8th) they scattered everywhere, and the tranquility was restored by dawn ...

Of the 56 stores, all the windows and door glasses were smashed, and two Japanese were wounded. At about 10pm Monday night (the 9th), the rioters, numbering from 600 to 700, came marching towards the Japanese quarters, but were dispersed by the mounted policemen, and half-an-hour later the rioters set the Japanese Primary School on fire, but the building was saved by the Japanese from destruction.[26]

Many newspaper accounts also describe injuries of the sort caused by bottles, knives, and bricks being hurled in a brawl. Ishii was a direct witness to the riot as he himself was caught up in the midst of the violence. *Harper's Weekly* magazine reported that he and the Japanese consul at Seattle, Saburo Hisamidzu, "withdrew to safety amid a shower of stones and bottles."[27] Ishii made it back to the Japanese consulate safely in time to send an urgent midnight cable to Tokyo to inform his government of the attacks on Japanese subjects.

The Vancouver authorities largely managed to restore order by daybreak, although the Japanese themselves were taking no chances and had assigned individuals to patrol the neighbourhood and were prepared to continue their defence. In 1961 H.H. Sugimoto interviewed a retired member of the Vancouver police who had been on patrol that Sunday morning. In his words, Sergeant Kuner saw "a brash young man, who, disregarding the Sergeant's good advice, was about to enter the 'guarded zone,' whereupon the policeman pointed out to him the 'men on sentry duty' on the other side. The man beat a hasty retreat!"[28] In this way the police and Japanese sentries were able to keep most of the curious and the mischievous out of the neighbourhood and avoid looting.

In the morning, Mayor Bethune, Police Chief Chamberlain, Japanese consul Kishiro Morikawa, and the special envoy, Kikujirō Ishii, met to discuss the crisis. Each had his own perspective on the pressing issues.

The mayor wanted to see the Japanese stand down and cease their attacks on "whites" who entered the zone; the Japanese consul wanted protection for the property and persons of Japanese subjects; and Ishii was also calling for compensation for losses sustained during the disturbances.[29] It is significant that no representative from the Chinese government was present at the meeting. While Canada had an official treaty relationship with Japan as a result of the 1894 Anglo-Japanese commercial treaty it had signed in 1905—not to mention the Anglo-Japanese alliance of 1902, renewed in 1905—its diplomatic relationship with China was much more distant. China had signed treaties with Great Britain that arguably assured the protection of Chinese subjects on British territory (the first of the "Unequal Treaties": the Treaty of Nanking, 1842, and the supplementary Treaty of Bogue, 1843). But since these treaties had been negotiated and signed decades before Confederation and since China and Canada had no diplomatic relationship outside of the one with Britain, the Canadian government was unaware of the implications of these treaties for Canada until King travelled to China in 1909. If the situation were not problematic enough, Laurier also tended to dismiss the Chinese as a weak state. O.D. Skelton, his future undersecretary of foreign affairs, put it this way: "In the case of China there was no complication of alliance and no menace of military power."[30] Despite the lack of Chinese representation in Canada, the Chinese government was kept informed of events in Vancouver through telegrams sent to Peking (present-day Beijing) by the Chinese Association of Vancouver. When an official was eventually dispatched in October to oversee the treatment of Chinese in Vancouver, he was sent from the office of the Chinese consul general in San Francisco.[31] One might reasonably conclude that the establishment of China's first consul general in Ottawa in 1909 was a consequence of the activism of the Chinese community in the face of these events.

While city officials and foreign representatives strategized, shopkeepers emerged to board up their broken windows and curious

Vancouverites came to see the damage in the less heavily defended Chinese quarter. According to the *Vancouver Daily World*'s account, the visitors to Chinatown were "curious sightseers, whites, Hindoos, and Japanese, men, women and children."[32] This description lends support to the contention that the violence was directed at property for the most part rather than at Japanese or Chinese individuals. A curious aspect to these events is the fact that even at the height of the violence on Saturday night, some Asian workers could move through the crowd unharmed. The day remained tense, but further outbreaks were avoided on the Sunday evening.

Monday brought new tensions in the form of a Chinese general strike in protest of the violence. No Chinese went to work on Monday morning, and their absence was keenly felt throughout the city and the surrounding area. Chinese lumber workers left their camps and came to town. Household servants failed to arrive at their employers' homes. Laundries, restaurants, and shingle mills were shut. The situation continued to simmer on Monday evening when a group of whites attempted to burn down the Japanese-language school, only to be repelled by the Japanese sentries. By Wednesday, after a few tense but relatively quiet days, the Chinese were back to work and the crisis seemed well and truly over. Twenty-four people had been arrested and were quickly charged with the crime of "riotous conduct." Police court reports for September 1907 reveal that only twelve of these individuals were committed for trial; the other twelve had the charges dismissed or withdrawn.[33] This marked the end of the disturbances and the beginning of an important period of response and reaction.

Among the first to weigh in were British diplomats seeking to understand how to react to such violence in this dominion of the British Empire. Sir Claude MacDonald, ambassador to Japan, emphasized the importance of the American Executive Order of March 1907, which excluded Japanese labourers from travel to the continental United States, and the order's impact on the number of Japanese migrants arriving in Canada.

When the United States began to turn Japanese away from the ports of San Francisco and Los Angeles after March 1907, those leaving Hawaii due to labour disputes and fears of the plague found themselves travelling in large numbers to Vancouver instead. The result was a huge number of "Japanese" immigrants arriving (via Hawaii) despite Japanese assurances that they would restrict the numbers of permits for travel to Canada. The Hawaiian Japanese had been abroad since the 1880s and 1890s. There was no reason to expect the Japanese government would have the power to control their movement, and yet this was the feeling in Vancouver.

James Bryce (Viscount Bryce after 1914), the British ambassador in Washington, provided his own interpretation of the September 7 events based on a set of reports coming from the British vice-consul at Seattle. The Foreign Office was in fairly close contact with Bryce on the question because of the involvement of anti-Asian activists in the mistreatment of Sikhs in Bellingham who were "natives of British India." The ambassador was painfully aware of how complicated the situation had become and how "far-reaching" it was in its implications.[34] He understood that Indian communities in North America had been and could again be used by groups seeking an end to the Raj; if the British wished to maintain their position in India, it was dangerous to add fuel to the argument that British freedoms were an illusion and Empire immigration laws were discriminatory.

There had been, according to Bryce, irritation in the US government over the Anglo-Japanese Alliance, which brought Great Britain into a close relationship with a state that President Roosevelt greatly mistrusted. But while Bryce could accept that there was pleasure in some quarters over the thought of a rift between Japan and Great Britain, he was unwilling to attribute to the US government any active policy designed to encourage disorder in Vancouver. He wrote to Sir Edward Grey in the Foreign Office:

> It would be incautious at present, and it would probably prove incorrect to infer any deliberate policy on the part of any American authority to

embarrass the relations between Great Britain and Japan. But it would not be too much to say that there has evidently been no feeling of regret that the anti-oriental agitation in British Columbia, with its expected effects on Anglo-Japanese relations, has been greatly aggravated by American agency.[35]

Bryce acknowledged the role of agitators such as Fowler and reported on the American's activities in Vancouver leading up to the violence. In Ottawa, the governor general, Earl Grey, likely reporting the same opinions he read in this British account of the riot, felt there was "good reason for the belief that the Vancouver riots were fomented by agitators coming from the United States."[36] This revealed more about British distrust of the Americans than it did about the larger causes of the riots, but it does show clearly that Fowler was at the centre of events.

In the immediate wake of the disorders, the political focus was on whether it was short-term irritants that led to the violence, such as the actions of individual "rowdies" and American agitators like Fowler, or the longer-term perception that increasing numbers of Asian immigrants were arriving at the port of Vancouver. Bryce's commentary was more perceptive than most, but it still generally emphasized the role of particular individuals.

The Department of the Interior, however, headed by Frank Oliver, was more concerned with the impact of Asian immigration on the eruption of disorder in Vancouver. On September 14 he sent T.E. McInnes as an undercover agent of the department to Vancouver "to investigate the trouble in connection with Asiatic immigration into British Columbia, and, in particular, to ascertain whether the present Japanese, Hindoo and Chinese influx into the province be spontaneous or induced by direct agencies ..."[37] From the department's perspective, it was the recent growth in Asian immigration that had disrupted BC society and required monitoring and possibly further control. Oliver was equally concerned with immigration from each of these areas, but he recognized that the forces bringing migrants differed depending on the country of origin and that the resulting problems would require different solutions.

On the other side of the country that Saturday, the deputy minister of the Department of Labour, William Lyon Mackenzie King, was returning to sleepy, leafy Ottawa. He had been visiting family and friends and taking in the Canadian National Exhibition, which always marks the end of summer in Toronto. While he had enjoyed his visit and the short holiday, the ambitious King had plenty of work to occupy him in the nation's capital. Despite his advanced degrees from the University of Toronto and the University of Chicago and his ongoing PhD program at Harvard, he was not interested in pursuing an academic career; nor would he settle for a life in the civil service. Rather, King and his mother hoped that he, the grandson of the rebel William Lyon Mackenzie, would one day take his place in the House of Commons, with the goal of becoming a cabinet minister and, ultimately, perhaps even prime minister.

King therefore took his opportunities to work with the prime minister, Sir Wilfrid Laurier, very seriously. To this end, King got a jump on the fall parliamentary session and arranged to meet with Laurier over the weekend of September 7. Saturday morning's agenda included a meeting with the grand old Liberal Party leader at 11:15 to discuss party strategy for a by-election in North Oxford, Ontario, that King was considering campaigning for himself. King did not feel the interview had gone well, as he later confided to his diary: "I feel like leaving the Service all together, my plan though is to hold on, smile at misfortune (which I cannot do) and wait patiently for other chances, and prepare better for them."[38] King's priority was not Sir Wilfrid's. King desperately wanted an opportunity to run in the first possible by-election, become a member of the cabinet, and become a minister rather than merely a civil servant. What could he do now that would advance his career and give him the credentials that would be necessary to move Laurier and get that all-important political job? What the young Mackenzie King could not realize was that his opportunity to shine in the service and represent his government was being created at that very moment across the country on Westminster Avenue, in the city of Vancouver, where the trade union march protesting against Asian immigration had flared out of control.

TWO

Eyes on Vancouver

It was clear that Laurier was going to have to act quickly since the eyes of the world were on Vancouver. He needed to put an end to the idea that Canada had become dangerous for Asian, particularly Japanese, migrants, or that it had abdicated its responsibilities to the Empire's global diplomacy. By December, the prime minister had appointed Rodolphe Lemieux, Canada's postmaster general and minister of labour, to negotiate directly with the Japanese in Tokyo to find a way to limit Japanese immigration to Canada. In addition, he had named Lemieux's deputy minister, W.L. Mackenzie King, to lead a commission in Vancouver to assess the damages of the riots. The tasks Laurier set for these men were not simple, as they had to be performed not only with Canadian interests in mind but also within the context of a web of international relationships with London at the centre.

King, like most of the rest of the world, was reading about the west coast violence in the press. The riots were extensively reported in the

United States, Great Britain, and Japan, and Canada's violence became a point of embarrassment for the British. It was an unacceptable affront to the Japanese to have such aggression directed at Japanese subjects by an allied nation, and it put a strain on the important relations between Britain and Japan. The Chinese made official complaints to Britain about the behaviour of Canadian citizens and sent a special envoy to Canada to defend the rights of its subjects. If that was not enough to trigger the interest of the Foreign Office in London, the violence in the British dominion was an unexpected boon to the Americans, who sought to use it to discredit the ongoing British criticism of American "oriental" immigration policy. As Vancouver business owners in Chinatown and the Japanese quarter swept up the broken glass and other debris left by the rioters, Laurier's government began to face the extent of the necessary diplomatic cleanup. By 1907 Britain had placed Japan at the centre of its plans to contain both Germany and Russia. After Japan's impressive defeat of the Russian navy in 1905, it had become a powerful force in the Pacific and Britain was eager to renew the 1902 Anglo-Japanese Alliance in order to both protect its own interests in Asia and allow it to defend itself against the potential threat of a growing German navy in the Atlantic. Britain's diplomatic concerns were therefore initially with the potential implications for its relationship with Japan, rather than with the Chinese, who were the first to bring the problem to the Foreign Office's attention.

On September 9 Ch'en I-fan (Ivan Chen), Chinese chargé d'affaires in London, called at the British Foreign Office to personally communicate his concerns about the violence against Chinese in Vancouver. Chen had lived in London for some time. He spoke English fluently, was known in social circles, and had a reputation as both an accomplished scholar and a witty after-dinner speaker. He was in the process of finishing an English translation of the *Hsiao Ching, The Book of Filial Duty*, written around 400 B.C.E. by an unknown student of one of Confucius's disciples. However, Chen was likely in no mood for pleasantries on September 9, as he had received a telegram from the Chinese Association in Vancouver, outlining the extent of the violence perpetrated against the Chinese community there. When he arrived at the FO, Chen was polite and diplomatic, but he made it clear to officials that he wished Britain to intervene diplomatically to ensure that the property of Chinese subjects in Vancouver was secure and that China's people would be protected from further mob violence. Since responsibility for Canada lay in another branch of the government, the Colonial Office (CO), this branch was subsequently notified on September 10. The FO reported that Chen had word of "a demonstration against Chinese and Japanese ... on the 7th ... when much property had been destroyed, and that the lives and property of the Chinese residents, were in danger."[1] It was clear that the situation was urgent, so the CO moved swiftly. The colonial secretary, Lord Elgin, sent official notice by telegraph that evening to the governor general of Canada, adding his own hope that the Dominion government had taken "all necessary steps."[2] On the evening of September 11, the CO received assurances from Canada that the situation was in hand.

At the same time as Ivan Chen was rushing to the FO in London, official Ottawa was taking its own steps to get as much information as possible, to communicate to Vancouver its anger at the situation, and to assure Britain that the government had control of the city. On Monday the 9th, the governor general and Prime Minister Laurier discussed the matter by telephone. Laurier was happy to take advantage of the constitutional chain of command in this case. Earl Grey was a much more imposing figure to the conservative majority of British Columbians than the Liberal prime minister, and was therefore an ideal choice for the purpose of overawing even the kind of citizen predisposed to riot in Vancouver's streets. The result was the following message directed to Mayor Alexander Bethune: "His Excellency the Governor General has learned with the deepest regret, the indignities and cruelties of which certain subjects of the Emperor of Japan, a friend and ally of His Majesty the King, have been victims and, he hopes that peace will be promptly restored and all offenders punished."[3]

Naturally Laurier too was incensed by the lawlessness in Vancouver. He was irritated that Canada's treaty obligations were being flouted so publicly and was concerned about the implications for Canada's foreign relations with Britain and Japan. But neither he nor the governor general mentioned at all the approximately 3,500 Chinese residents of Vancouver who had been victims of the riots.

Nevertheless, Ivan Chen and the Chinese government continued to take an interest in the situation in Vancouver in the months following the riots. First, Chen remained in communication with the FO to ensure that Chinese subjects in other parts of Canada were being protected from possible violence. Once the FO had received assurances from the governor general that this was so, it informed Chen that steps had been taken in the matter. Having addressed this immediate concern, Chen informed the British that the Chinese wished to ensure that Chinese losses would be compensated and the offenders punished.[4] To this end, a Chinese consular official from San Francisco was going to travel to Vancouver in order to make his own inquiry into the Chinese losses.[5]

By September 10 Laurier had received word from Robert George Macpherson, the Liberal MP for Vancouver City, that the situation was calming. This may have been overstating the case, as only the night before the Japanese community had been forced to defend the Japanese primary school against arsonists. Nevertheless, Laurier shared this new information and his anxieties with the governor general. "In this later rioting the Japs showed fight, turned upon their assailants and routed them. This is at once a cause for rejoicing and for anxiety. Rejoicing because the rowdies get a well deserved licking; anxiety because this may make the Japs very saucy and render an adjustment of the trouble more difficult."[6] Laurier's comments reflect the attitudes of his time. He did not fully trust the Japanese presence in Canada and did not particularly want a large number of Japanese immigrants entering the country, but he was embarrassed by the disorder and boorish behaviour in Vancouver and felt compelled to send an official apology to the emperor of Japan on behalf of the Dominion of Canada.

On September 20 Laurier wrote to Sir Claude MacDonald, the British ambassador to Tokyo, requesting that he communicate Canada's apologies to the Japanese emperor.

> His Excellency the Governor General particularly desires me to ask you to convey to the Government of H.M. The Emperor of Japan his deep regret for these deplorable occurrences, as well as the assurance that the Canadian Government will faithfully adhere to the obligations devolving upon them, not only from the law prevailing amongst civilized nations, but especially from the requirements of the treaty existing between the Emperor of Japan and His Majesty the King ...
>
> Such occasional troubles should not however be considered as in any way marring the good relations which we are most anxious to have with Japan, and His Imperial Majesty may rest assured that every possible means will be taken to protect the persons and property of his subjects in this country.[7]

The governor general felt that this letter should not have been sent without approval from the Foreign Office, but he need not have worried. Despite Laurier's unorthodox, direct approach, officials in the FO were grateful for his prompt action, as revealed in the following exchange:

> "[Strictly speaking] such a communication should have been sent via CO and FO but in the circs I think the CO did right to sanction it being despatched to Tokio [sic] direct. It should have all the more effect on the Japanese."
>
> F.A.C. 26/9 (Sir Francis Campbell)
>
> "I agree: it is well that the Canadian Govt should accept responsibility for this our Treaty obligations" E.G. (Edward Grey)[8]

Sir Francis Campbell and Sir Edward Grey were prominent members of the Foreign Office. Campbell was a professional diplomat and the assistant undersecretary of state between 1902 and 1911. He was acknowledged to be an expert on Asia, and it was standard practice to forward him materials relating to the region. Edward Grey, the governor general's cousin, was a Liberal politician and the foreign secretary from 1905 to 1916. His generous attitude toward Canadian diplomacy and Canadian interests was reflected in the conversations he would have with King in the coming months about the possibility of Canada sending its own representatives to the Asian capitals. And so despite the official channels that Canadian foreign policy was expected to travel—via the governor general to the secretary of state for the colonies and back—we see here a certain amount of latitude on the part of the Canadian government in its international relations. This tendency to streamline communications and take action when national interests were clear grew in the first decade of the century. Canadians were beginning to insist that their government act in a national rather than a colonial style.

Canada's interests were not always those of Great Britain. This divergence was clearest when the United States was involved in the equation. In addition to the diplomatic ramifications of the September events for Britain's relationship with China and Japan, Canada needed to keep the United States firmly in mind with each decision. In September 1907 President Theodore Roosevelt was not slow to spot an opportunity in the Vancouver riots. The incident would, he hoped, poke a hole in British complacency on the question of race in North America. Britain had been very critical of American immigration policy aimed at the Japanese and of the actions of the San Francisco school board in insisting on segregating Japanese students in October 1906, which led to violence in the spring of 1907. Roosevelt was torn on the issue. On the one hand, he understood very well that Japan was a great power, and great powers needed to be treated with respect. On the other, Roosevelt believed in the rule of law, detested mob violence, and thought stopping Japanese immigration altogether was the only way to eliminate the conflict. Moreover, the president was concerned about conciliating with Canada, to compensate for bruised feelings over the nation's loss of a boundary dispute to the United States in 1903. In the final analysis, Roosevelt hoped for English-speaking solidarity, and a common front on Asian immigration was as good a place as any to start.

Like Canada, the United States had been involved in discussions with Japan on the question of labour migration. Following the San Francisco earthquake in 1906, there was an increased demand for cheap labour and limited space in the city's schools. Large numbers of Japanese workers were contracted to come to California from Hawaii, and as a result, local pressure to keep Japanese children out of public schools was rising. In October 1906 the San Francisco school board passed the "Separate School Order," which made segregation official policy in the city schools. This was not received well in Tokyo, and the Japanese made this clear to American diplomats, raising fears in 1906–1907 that a war between Japan and the United States was a real possibility.

In a quid pro quo, Roosevelt agreed to stop school segregation in San Francisco in return for a voluntary restriction on Japanese labour migration to the continental United States—the so-called Gentlemen's Agreement of 1907–1908. In March 1907 the president further supported legislation intended to restrict the number of Japanese entering the continental United States from Hawaii. A limited number of migrants were issued identification documents, which were more than merely passports—they also amounted to permission to leave one's home prefecture in order to settle at a particular destination. These documents, issued in Japan or by Japanese consular authorities when documents had been lost or destroyed, gave the holder permission to both leave home and land in a particular destination: Mexico, Canada, Hawaii, or, the most coveted destination, the United States. Despite Japan's close control over emigration, the passports and the restrictions on labourers who wished to land in the continental United States only reduced the rate at which Japanese (or Hawaiian Japanese) arrivals increased, and tensions between the United States and Japan continued to rise. By spring, flashes of violence directed against Japanese migrants worsened the situation.

Roosevelt was angered by the May 1907 violence against Japanese in San Francisco.[9] From his perspective, the tensions caused by this kind of extremist activity made the situation even more tense and only made his job of avoiding war with Japan more difficult.

The president was quite convinced that Japanese immigration into Canada needed to be reduced, if not eradicated completely. While he did not support the methods used by the mob in San Francisco, he was, at root, sympathetic to their logic. He shared the white Canadians' attitude toward Japanese workers and understood their frustration with rising competition in the tough economic times that followed the 1907 Wall Street panic. Roosevelt was puzzled by Japan's concern about his attempts to limit Japanese migration, as he felt the same type of restrictions were applied to Americans (and to Chinese) who wished to work in Japan. He was convinced that the "total number of passports" available to Japanese migrants had to be reduced if he was to avoid "trouble."[10] The president feared further violence in San Francisco and, more important for a politician perhaps, feared agitation in Congress for exclusionary legislation based on the model used to exclude Chinese workers, which would only further alienate the Japanese state—a country that he believed was a real military threat to US Pacific territories such as the Philippines, Alaska, and Hawaii.

It was therefore a convenient state of affairs for Roosevelt to be able to point to similar examples of anti-Japanese attitudes among the citizens of one of Britain's own dominions. As he wrote to his friend Senator Henry Cabot Lodge of Massachusetts on the Wednesday after the riots:

> ... I have precisely the same feeling you have had over the Vancouver incident. It is only a few months since the English papers were commenting with complacency upon the effects of our Constitution, the lawlessness of the national character, and contrasting it with the British Empire. Now a much worse outbreak has occurred in Vancouver than anything that has occurred in San Francisco. It will do

good in two ways. In the first place it will bring sharply home to the British public the fact that the British commonwealths along the Pacific will take precisely the same attitude as the American states along the Pacific; and in the next place, it will bring Japan toward a realization of the fact that in this matter she will have to face the same feeling in the British Empire which she does in the American Republic. Of course in San Francisco and California the action of the mob was indefensible, tho[ugh] I prevented such outrages as occurred in Vancouver by the fact that I was much quicker to take preventive steps than the British officials were; but the attitude which is back of the movement is in each case sound.[11]

Roosevelt, as chief of a large and powerful independent republic, had no one to answer to but himself—though of course he assiduously courted public opinion. Laurier was not so fortunate. As the prime minister of a parliamentary democracy within the British Empire, he faced the constant danger of a vote of "no confidence" in the House, the ire of provincial Liberal Party members in BC, and the censure of the British. The Canadian prime minister was therefore forced to balance local demands with the larger concerns inherent in Canada's position as a member of the British Empire and as a neighbour to the United States. Since 1901 the United States and Great Britain had been engaged in the process of building the "special relationship" that would define the nations' interactions for much of the rest of the century. One by one, long-standing diplomatic irritants between the two powers were being smoothed over, and Canada's position both on the North American continent and in the Empire frequently placed it on the agenda. In 1903 the British government had sacrificed Canada's local interests to the cause of Anglo-American harmony in the conclusion to the Alaska Boundary dispute, reasoning that Canada would be better protected if the Americans felt no sense of grievance toward Canada and the British Empire. Laurier was naturally upset that Britain had set aside the interests of its imperial partner, but he had no option but to swallow hard and live with the result, which, it must be said, was not all that unfavourable.

Laurier knew Canadian actions reflected back on London and were assessed by outside parties within this context of Empire. From Roosevelt's perspective, Canada's difficulties were Britain's problems. And, at a time when Britain was intent on improving its relationship with a United States that was increasingly important on the world scene, the details of Canada's diplomatic relationships took on a new meaning. On the one hand, any success Canada had in creating mechanisms to limit Asian immigration was viewed positively by the United States, as the number of Asian immigrants entering the US via Canada would be reduced and, perhaps more important for US diplomats in the midst of negotiations with Japan, legal precedents for controls might be set and reproduced. On the other hand, Canadian, as well as Australian, New Zealander, and South African, attempts to exclude "orientals" caused the British headaches in India, where they were already dealing with a growing nationalist movement, as well as causing serious strains in their relationship with Japan.

Although he did not have a treaty with the Japanese to consider, Roosevelt was struggling with some of the same dilemmas. He too had an active exclusionist community on his country's west coast that was not above using violence to make its feelings about Asian immigration known. A quick survey of the president's correspondence from the summer of 1907 puts the Japanese question at the centre of his concerns and shows the links he drew between events in California and those in British Columbia.

Roosevelt spent the summer of 1907 at his family home at Oyster Bay, New York. While he made a point of taking his daily ride with his wife Edith, matters of state were never far away from his thoughts. Uppermost in his mind was the possibility of war with Japan. Reports from his friend Baron Speck von Sternburg, the German ambassador to Washington, and his own ambassador to London, Whitelaw Reid, were full of German and British rumours of a coming war between the United States and Japan. Perhaps more disturbing than these rumours' ubiquity was the fact that they predicted an American defeat. It was felt that if the Russian navy could be sunk, then the Americans were surely vulnerable. In his correspondence, Roosevelt tried to convince himself and others that he did not believe war with Japan would occur. He felt there was no real pretext for war, but should it happen, he was confident in the United States' chances of victory. However, this did not stop the president from doing what he could to build up the navy or doing everything he could to maintain peace with the Japanese government. As he wrote to Elihu Root, his secretary of state, "I am more concerned over this Japanese question in all its bearings than over any other, including that of the trusts."[12]

As an ingredient in his overall policy, Roosevelt was reaching for ways to convince Japan to more effectively reduce labour migration to the United States. When he was informed that Greece was in negotiations with Japan to limit immigration, he was delighted. A European precedent would be a weakness in any Japanese claim that limits were impossible to manage by treaty.[13] The president's strategy was to remain courteous and fair toward the Japanese government and to do as much as he could to protect its subjects living in the United States. In his personal correspondence with Speck von Sternburg, Roosevelt made it clear that he was prepared to use force to combat racial violence in the United States while building up the American navy—a useful combination of soft and hard power.

> I shall treat them [the Japanese] not only with justice but with every courtesy and consideration, and have gathered enough troops in the neighborhood of San Francisco to be able to take prompt action should there be [so] much rioting and violence against the Japanese that the municipal and State authorities could not protect them, at the same time I am keeping the fleet exercised and trained ...[14]

And so, in a fashion that became emblematic of his presidency, Roosevelt advocated the maintenance of peace with Japan through the practice of justice and fair play, supplemented by the exercise of strength, his "big stick." In addition to keeping troops ready to stop any violence that might arise in California, the president set in motion the logistical organization required to send the entire US navy, the Great White Fleet, around the world on a Pacific cruise intended to show Japan and the world that the United States would not be bullied.

In addition to dealing with immigration questions and Japan more generally, Roosevelt was also struggling with a sharp economic contraction in the late summer and fall of 1907. While his domestic critics blamed the crisis on his attempts to investigate the behaviour of large financial institutions and pass anti-trust legislation, the economic decline beginning that summer was much more widely spread than just a Wall Street panic. Uncertainty was on the rise after the Russian defeat in the Russo-Japanese War. The stock markets in Paris and London were struggling, and even blue chip Canadian railroad securities were selling at a lower price. These changes were amplified in the minds of financiers, politicians, and labourers across the globe by the contrast with the previous years.

Because of the links between this difficult economic climate and anti-Asian racism, Laurier remained fearful of further outbreaks of racial violence on the coast despite Mayor Bethune's assurances. In his letter to the Canadian embassy in Tokyo, the prime minister spoke directly about this possibility, writing, "... it should not be forgotten that race prejudices are slow to die out and that it is not impossible that the mischievous agitation which, there is reason to believe is still secretly carried on by the parties responsible for the late outrages, may yet produce some similar incidents."[15] Both the Japanese and British governments were satisfied with Canada's swift apology and assurance that the riots did not reflect Canada's official feelings toward Japan, but concerns remained and thorough explanations were required. In addition to Laurier's candid assessment of racial prejudices in British Columbia, official explanations from Britain and Canada in 1907 followed two dominant themes—that the riots were either the result of unusually high levels of Asian immigration to Vancouver or the outcome of the work of American agitators. These explanations seem to have been largely shared by the Japanese.

On October 2 Ambassador Claude MacDonald sent a memo from Tokyo assuring the British government that relations with Japan had not been seriously threatened by the events in Vancouver and that the Japanese press had been "distinguished for its moderation" on the question.[16] Further, the Japanese were reported to have been pleased "at the prompt action taken by the Canadian Government and the local authorities of Vancouver, and at the tone adopted by the British and Canadian press."[17] This response contrasted with the Japanese irritation regarding the American situation; nevertheless, the Japanese press was eager to find a "remedy" for the anti-Japanese feeling in Canada.

The racial and economic conditions that created the situation leading to the riots were largely still present in the weeks and months afterward, so when the riots ended the federal government was intent that the potential flow of Chinese, Japanese, and South Asian migrants be stopped. Unfortunately for Laurier, ships carrying workers from India, as well as Japanese from Hawaii, were still on their way to Canada's Pacific ports. In Ottawa, opinion was divided. The governor general, Earl Grey, was one of the British officials advocating for the fair treatment of Britain's "East Indian" subjects in British Columbia. (Grey had spent time in India and was aware of the delicate politics of Britain's Indian Empire.) In his mind, there was no question about how Canada should treat those migrants who were fleeing violence in Bellingham and elsewhere. They were, he reminded Laurier, entitled to "sanctuary of Canadian soil," and he hoped that they would "experience the advantage of being subjects of the King" upon their arrival.[18] Laurier's concerns were much more practical. There had just been a riot against Japanese and Chinese residents of Vancouver and there was no money designated to establish hygienic, comfortable camps for these refugees on the Canadian side of the border.[19] More critical perhaps was the fact that Laurier was convinced that Indian migrants were "an element to which the people of B.C. have a still greater aversion than to the Japs ..."[20]

The governor general's commitment to the advantages of Empire did not mean that he advocated the free and frequent movement of South Asian migrants to BC. On the contrary, Lord Grey recognized that Laurier had local politics to take into consideration and that Indian migration was negatively perceived and therefore needed to be carefully controlled. Laurier had warned him, writing,

> The situation with regard to the Hindoos is far more serious; and to speak frankly I see no solution for it, except quietly checking the exodus from India. We are sending a special officer to B.C. to find out who are [sic] bringing those poor people to our shores. If we can find that out, the problem will be very near solution.[21]

The governor general was pleased at the Japanese response and hoped that the Indian government could do the same. Writing to Laurier, he commented,

> I think I may congratulate you on the way in which the puzzle is solving itself out—Now that the Jap government have agreed to restrict the outflow of Japs from Japan to Canada at a figure to which even the Western Miners Federation cannot reasonably take objection. There should be no further serious difficulty from that quarter—and I am inclined to agree about what I understand is your view that the best chance of settling the more difficult Hindu problem is for the Government of India to take a leaf out of the book of the Government of Japan—As soon as you are in a position to make a definite recommendation on this subject I will cable home—the BC position is being anxiously watched in England, but at present I am just marking time with the authorities of the C.O. [Colonial Office], F.O. [Foreign Office], and I.O. [India Office]. I fully recognize the difficulties you have to encounter from the temperament which appears to pervade not only B.C. but the West generally, and I sympathize with you most sincerely.[22]

Lord Grey's attitude toward Asian immigration reflects the position held widely in the Empire—a position that officially distinguished among Asian migrants, affording more importance to those from other parts of the Empire. This attitude conveyed a defence of British liberties, a respect for Britain's international agreements, and a powerful distrust of "native" migration to the white settler colonies. The mindset was most acute in Australia and South Africa, where the governments had spoken openly about their desire to exclude or control the movement of non-white British subjects, and indeed had taken steps to do so. Canada was beginning to find itself faced with similar challenges as the number of British subjects from India began to rise. Despite the obvious racism aimed at "orientals" in general, Indian, Japanese, and Chinese migrants were not in the same administrative categories, nor were they treated in the same ways by the British government; hence the involvement of the Colonial, Foreign, and India offices.

South Asian immigrants were relative newcomers to Canada. A group of Punjabi Sikhs serving in the British Hong Kong Regiment passed through Canada during the celebration of Edward VII's coronation.[23] Their visit received quite a bit of positive press. And, when their regiment was disbanded later that year, many chose to go to Canada rather than to India. South Asian immigration to Canada really began with these soldiers. The Sikhs from the Punjab at the turn of the century had been living lives that "pre-adapted" them for immigration—a tradition of mobility, independence, relative freedom from caste and tradition, and relative prosperity under the British after 1858.[24] And so others with ties to these men followed in a familiar pattern for immigrants, coming once they had heard about the opportunities available in Canada and seen for themselves that the first migrants had been successful.

Because of the community's origins in the army, the kinds of work available in BC, and Canadian restrictions on the movement of women and children before 1919, most of the South Asians in BC and in neighbouring Washington State were male Sikhs and Muslims from the Punjab, who were working in the lumber mills with the intention to send money home to India and to return once they had made their fortune. Like the Chinese, these bachelor communities were considered suspect by white settler society. The close community ties that supported migrants through the tough times were seen to be insular and signs of "the Hindoos'" unwillingness to assimilate. The long hours sojourners worked at the mill and the money they sent home confirmed their separation from Canadian society. However, Indian immigration could not be prevented at Canada's borders. Despite being "orientals," these workers were British subjects, and as such, they were legally entitled to freedom of movement within the Empire. That neither the British nor the Canadian governments were comfortable with large numbers of South Asian settlers in the white self-governing dominions was insufficient in itself to stop this kind of immigration without trampling on the "British Liberties" that were so highly esteemed among the advocates of the British civilizing mission. Any attempts to restrict Indian migration caused public relations problems for the British in India and increased criticism from Indian nationalist groups, which were always looking for new ways to discredit the British administration.

After Laurier's government raised the head tax on Chinese workers from one hundred to five hundred dollars in 1903, there was a huge decline in the number of Chinese looking to travel as steerage passengers on Canadian Pacific steamships. Chinese immigration had almost ceased completely, and it was reported that the company replaced the lost Chinese fares by encouraging Indian workers from Hong Kong to look for work in Canada.[25] Fearing new waves of violence, Laurier responded by seeking advice on ways to control "inflows of Hindus."[26]

The matter was pressing because even as the mob rioted in Vancouver a passenger ship called the *Monteagle* was approaching the port of Vancouver carrying nine hundred more British subjects from India who were looking for work, and, according to Mayor Bethune, they were arriving with neither "accommodation nor employment."[27] Bethune's concerns about housing for the new arrivals were based both on the reality of Vancouver's housing shortage and on racist assumptions about the causes of the difficulties faced by South Asian immigrants in finding a place to live. There is no doubt that housing was hard to come by as the city grew between 1900 and 1911. In a market that favoured landlords, immigrants who were considered "undesirable" were often turned away.

When Laurier received Bethune's telegram warning of the arrival of nine hundred homeless and jobless migrants, he thought deportation could be a solution. Canada's immigration law provided the government with the right to deport those immigrants who became indigent. However, Bethune was not convinced that these workers were "paupers," and so another solution needed to be found if Canada was to turn them away. While Laurier and the governor general were convinced that South Asian workers were unsuited to life in Canada,[28] there is evidence that workers who came to Canada from India were quite willing to take on the challenge of adapting. Although Canadian immigration and municipal authorities were focused on the problems of hygiene and accommodation promised by the large number of indigent arrivals, those aboard the ship seemed to have had a fairly optimistic outlook and were building social connections that would help them get by in Canada. One young man was excited and optimistic about his new life in Canada despite the difficulties ahead:

> We learned about Canada from relatives of people in the village. In 1907 eleven of us set out together for Canada. I was nineteen. Most of us were pretty young, but one fellow was at least fifty.
>
> It took us over two months to get to Canada. The most dramatic part of the trip was the long voyage from Hong Kong to Vancouver aboard the "900 boat" [the *Monteagle*]. With so many people travelling together there was a great anticipation of what we were to experience in Canada; no one you met on board had actually been there, so all kinds of rumours circulated. Some said that we would be rich in no time. Others said that we might freeze. Generally, though, people were pretty realistic. They were willing to work hard, and thought of

Canada as being a place where opportunities were available to make good use of hard work. Few of us had such opportunities in India.[29]

These migrants were about to start a new chapter of their lives, and their arrival—and that of thousands of others—was to start a new chapter in the life of William Lyon Mackenzie King. When Laurier turned to his star civil servant for help in resolving the crisis, he did so knowing that King combined intelligence and a thirst for collecting evidence, and for reaching reasoned conclusions based on the facts. To that extent, King was a man after Laurier's own heart, although unlike the prime minister he also had a strong streak of religiosity that permeated his private reflections and writings. But Laurier had hired King as someone who knew how to ask questions and get answers. His record showed he could do it. King had extensive experience finding the delicate balance between the needs of employers and the concerns of workers. He had worked extensively in labour negotiations and had recently completed some very complicated work to resolve the 1906 Lethbridge, Alberta, coal strike. Not only did he facilitate a settlement when one was far from certain, but he went on to codify the procedures he used in the 1907 Industrial Disputes Investigation Act. If that was not enough to recommend him for the job, he was also familiar with some of the individuals most closely involved in the crisis, particularly the Japanese consul, Tatsugoro Nossé.

At the beginning of October, Nossé contacted the dominion government to request that immediate steps be taken to account for Japanese losses in Vancouver and to ensure that the victims would be compensated. He also requested that solutions be found in Ottawa, rather than through the Foreign Office in London. He framed the whole exercise within the context of his "hope that in view of the cordial and friendly relations existing between Japan and Canada, the case may be settled at Ottawa independent of the British Government and without going through the usual diplomatic channels."[30] And so on October 12, 1907, the first commission connected with the riots in Vancouver was announced; soon it would be open for business. This commission, headed by King, was charged with assessing Japanese damages caused by the rioters. However, King was not satisfied with the narrow scope of this commission. Eventually he managed to expand the project to include the causes of the riot and would even receive commissions to study Chinese losses, Indian immigration to Canada, and the opium trade as well.

The first indication that King was considering the broader implications of Asian immigration to Canada and Japanese immigration in particular appears in his diary on September 18. According to his own account, King arrived at the prime minister's office that afternoon around five o'clock and was shown a telegram sent to Laurier by the Trades and Labour Congress. A resolution passed by the congress had sharply criticized Canada's participation in the Commercial Treaty with Japan. When Laurier asked him what he would do, King made the following recommendation: "a Commission to investigate the effect of the Oriental immigration on conditions in B.C. ... would reveal the truth which was necessary for intelligent action on the part of parl[iament] ... [And] further that an immediate inquiry into the cause of the recent influx & the source etc. was desirable."[31] From this early date, then, King was focused on the question of an inquiry into the causes of Japanese immigration to Canada rather than fixating purely on damage assessment. Laurier seemed to have this in mind on October 4 when he suggested in cabinet that King conduct "an inquiry into the methods by which ... Oriental labourers [had] been induced to come to Canada during the present year" rather than simply recording damages.[32]

As the deputy minister of labour, King had been involved with the draft of the Privy Council resolution that would appoint a commission to study Japanese losses. He had recommended that Chief Justice Gordon Hunter be responsible for the investigation, but when Minister of Labour Lemieux showed King a draft on October 11, he discovered it was he, not the chief justice, who had been chosen to study the question. King therefore had two separate investigations on his agenda by mid-October. And so, though he had hoped he might be part of the delegation heading to Tokyo, he would not be making the trip. As he saw it, King was given "the next best thing":

> When I saw the draft of the Order-in-Council, I observed that it had been made out in the first instance appointing the Chief Justice of B.C. the Commissioner, that in Council it had been changed by naming myself. The appointment of Commissioner for this purpose was my own suggestion both to Sir Wilfrid & Earl Grey and Mr. Lemieux. I have urged it strongly with Lemieux all week, & in each case have suggested the Chief Justice. I was inclined at first to say I thought it would be better to have the C.J. then it occurred to me that this might not come with good grace, and that it was best to seize opportunities as they come.[33]

Once he received the appointment, King was surprised to find that the investigation was to focus only on the riots' effects on the Japanese community rather than on the experience of "all orientals."[34] King felt so strongly about the inclusion of Chinese losses in the inquiry that he even raised the issue with the prime minister. The two men had a lengthy discussion in which King advocated the payment of damages to Chinese victims as well as Japanese, for a variety of reasons. He felt that since the Canadian government had characterized the riots as anti-Asian rather than anti-Japanese, the optics of not recognizing the claims of other groups would reflect badly on the state. While Laurier thanked him for his candour and promised to consider the matter, he felt that Canada's treaty with Japan put that country's subjects in a different position with respect to claims. For the time being, there would be no investigation into Chinese claims.[35]

Despite his differences with the prime minister and a nasty head cold, King got to work at once preparing the Japanese Commission. On Monday morning, October 14, he made a point of visiting the Japanese consulate in Ottawa to see Nossé. The men spent two hours together discussing the planning details for the commission and reviewing the claim forms received by the Japanese government. King assured the Japanese consul that the claims would be judged fairly and that payments would be made directly to members of the Japanese community seeking damages, in exchange for a receipt. This, according to King, seemed to assure Nossé that the commission would not require further Japanese government involvement. King then left Ottawa and headed west toward Vancouver.

While in Toronto, King met one evening with a respected friend of his father, Goldwin Smith. Smith was a former Oxford history professor who, after years of teaching at Cornell University, had retired and settled in Toronto. The acquaintance between the two men was a long-standing one from which King had previously benefited. Since Smith was a friend of King's father and a scholar with a global reputation, King was fortunate to have received letters of introduction from him that had opened doors for King at Harvard. King was grateful for the opportunity to discuss his latest project with the knowledgeable older man. Smith had made no secret of his belief that Canada's future would involve a union with the United States, thus creating a larger Anglo-Saxon nation. He had written extensively on the idea that Canada was an unnatural state, preserved by political interests when all of its natural economic connections were to the south. The two men discussed the situation on the west coast. Smith's assessment, as it was reported by King in his diary, was that "the Orientals [would] some day possess the West Coast of Can[ada]" and that Canada's East would be annexed to the United States.[36] With this dire prediction ringing in his ears, King boarded a train for Vancouver. He arrived on the evening of October 20 and set to work with his stenographer, Francis W. Giddens, and his translator, T.I. Nagao.

Within an hour of his arrival, Kishiro Morikawa, the Japanese consul in Vancouver, visited King at his hotel, where they met together for half an hour in the parlour. King again apologized on behalf of the Canadian government for the treatment Japanese subjects had suffered at the hands of the mob and assured him that the nature of the riots was anti-Asian generally rather than anti-Japanese particularly. King also arranged with Morikawa to use the offices of the consul to meet with claimants, in the hope that it would be "convenient" for the Japanese of the city to meet in a familiar location.[37] The Canadian government had requested that King advertise to Japanese community members the commission's plan to meet over four days, contact potential claimants, and prepare the Japanese claims for presentation to the government. All of this was now complete.

That afternoon, King lunched with Chief Justice Gordon Hunter, whom he had previously favoured for the role as commissioner. Hunter was named chief justice for BC in 1902 and had a reputation for competence and wit. In the years to come, it would be the Liberal Party loyalist Hunter who would rule in favour of Indian immigrants seeking to enter the country on the *Panama Maru*, leading to the decision to charter the even more famous *Komagata Maru* to sail to Canada and challenge Empire-wide controls on Indian migration in 1914. But these events were still years in the future. In the meantime, Hunter shared with King his views about the reparations, "points of procedure," and Asian immigration more generally. When pressed about popular opinion and "oriental" immigration, he was perhaps in the minority in BC since, according to King, "He [Hunter] said that the intelligent feeling in the Province was all against the exclusion of the Japanese." Another judge with whom King spoke that Sunday afternoon similarly blamed the exclusion movement on the activity of "labour unions and politicians"—both evidently low on his list of valued members of society.[38]

Early Monday morning, King met with the local Liberal MP for Vancouver City, Robert Macpherson, who convinced him, for "tactical" reasons, not to hold the commission in the Japanese consul's offices. Instead he arranged to have King meet with petitioners in Pender Hall at 804 Pender Street. Macpherson was loyal to his leader Laurier, but, like most of the BC Liberals, disagreed with him wholeheartedly on the question of Japanese immigration into British Columbia. He viewed the prime minister's stand on the Japanese as defined by part of Laurier's misguided loyalty to Britain, rather than as considered policy. King felt that if it were not for party discipline, Macpherson "would come out openly and lead a strong movement for the exclusion of the Japanese."[39]

King met with Morikawa in his offices after breakfast. He used the now rather convenient excuse of the small size of the consular office and the possibility of a future investigation into Chinese damage claims to suggest that it would be preferable to arrange for the commission to meet in Pender Hall rather than at the consulate. King also gave a special press interview in order to both publicize the commission and reassure concerned residents of BC that Lemieux's trip to Japan would not begin with the minister receiving instructions in England. This was a Canadian mission with Canadian goals. A flurry of editorials had expressed concern that he would be starting his negotiations with consultations in London and that this reflected a blind faith in Empire politics rather than care for Canadian interests. Since Lemieux's trip was not starting in London, King had no trouble giving straightforward assurances that Lemieux never intended to travel to London at all, and King could therefore dodge the question of British interests completely.

King sat down on this visit with the Vancouver chief of police to get his views about the riot, but it was during his next encounter with Chamberlain that King formed a strong impression that the police could not be relied on to enforce order in the future if the number of Japanese immigrants continued to increase. He believed he understood Chamberlain's position with regard to Vancouver's Asian population and he made a point of sharing this information with Laurier, saying,

Chamberlin [sic] ... was not to be counted on in the matter of assistance he would give in preventing a struggle. My own feeling was that he was quite prepared to encourage a revolt against the Japanese if he thought it would be the means of cleaning them out; that he had said to me quite distinctly that he could not, with his force, attempt to keep any order as long as their [Japanese] numbers were increasing.[40]

King also met with the city solicitor and Chief Justice Hunter and then went on a tour of the Japanese quarter with Morikawa. He finished the day in a rather civilized style, enjoying champagne served by Mrs. Morikawa at the family home. After taking care of some final details, he had a night's rest, knowing the difficult work of the commission was about to begin.

King met with Japanese claimants, witnesses, and their counsel continuously from Tuesday, October 22, to Tuesday, November 5. He had set up the commission at Pender Hall for the purpose, and it was open from 10:30 in the morning until 4:30 each weekday afternoon. Morikawa gave a statement about the Japanese claims as the hearings began, but after this presentation he remained silent, observing each day's session as a quiet representative of the emperor's government. According to the official report prepared by King, the commission heard from 80 witnesses and adjudicated 107 claims. The total "actual damages" was assessed to be $1,553.58, and "consequential losses" were $9,036.00. King also provided for $1,600.00 in legal costs incurred by the Japanese government in preparing the claims. Although this sum was eventually returned by the Japanese government, the offer was a grand gesture on King's part. The assessments King made on damages were lower than Nossé's, but not completely out of line. Nossé had originally estimated Japanese claims to be $2,405.70 for actual, and $11,113.75 for consequential, losses.[41] King noted that although most Japanese claimants presented fair assessments of the damages they suffered, the difference between his and Nossé's assessments was

to be accounted for by somewhat exorbitant claims made by one or two merchants for alleged losses in business, and more or less excessive claims made by some of the Japanese boarding-house keepers, who claimed indemnity for a time exceeding that for which it appeared reasonable to make an allowance, or who, in hiring guards for the protection of their property during the time of the riot and the days immediately succeeding, failed to exercise reasonable judgment in the amounts they expended on this score.[42]

This passage reveals that the Canadian government was much more willing to accept the damages associated with broken windows and smashed goods than it was to compensate businesses for lost income or for the cost of hiring security during the period when Japanese businesses were threatened. The government also had a much narrower understanding of the duration of the disorder. The presentation made by counsel for the Japanese, Howard J. Duncan, suggested that Vancouver's Japanese community felt under threat for as much as two weeks rather than just during the weekend.[43] Nevertheless, after communicating with Ottawa about his findings, King was given permission to pay these claims. A Bank of Montreal account in Vancouver in King's name was credited with the necessary funds, and King paid the Japanese directly within days of the conclusion of the commission's hearings once a receipt discharging any further rights to compensation had been signed.

While King was absorbed in the process of interviewing witnesses, Minister of Labour Rodolphe Lemieux had travelled across the Pacific and arrived in Japan on November 13. Upon his arrival in Tokyo, he received a note from Nossé, who was worried about the growing scope of King's investigation. Nossé insisted that King was complicating Canada's relationship with the Japanese government and that he was overstepping his mandate by looking into the causes of Japanese immigration.[44] He was mistaken on both points. King absolutely had the authority to examine the question of Japanese immigration and, in the end, his commission and its findings were well received by the Japanese government, which accepted the terms decided by the commission and expressed official thanks through the Japanese consul in Vancouver on November 19: "I cannot too strongly express the satisfaction and approval of my government in your award and adjustment of the losses and damages sustained by the Japanese residents here, a feeling, I am sure, shared by every claimant." Morikawa also made a point of making his personal feelings about King's style and the impact of his work in Vancouver known:

> I would assure you that the great skill, unvarying patience and urbanity which marked your conduct of the Commission, has done much to restore the feeling of my countrymen here that the Canadian government and the people of Canada are opposed to every element whose purpose is to defy the ordinary rules of decency in life, and the wider laws which bind nations in friendly accord.[45]

Morikawa and King had worked effectively together to investigate the claims and come to an agreement that would go far toward repairing some of the damage done by the rioters. It would not, however, erase King's long memory of the violent way Canadians could react to Asian immigration.

On November 5, the last day of the investigation into Japanese losses, King was officially commissioned to convene a second investigation. Between November 11 and 13, King collected testimony from 101 witnesses on the question that had personally drawn him from the start: "the Methods by which Oriental Labourers have been Induced to come to Canada"—in other words, the factors King interpreted as the causes of the riots. From the outset, King interviewed individuals from Japan, China, and India living in Victoria and Vancouver, as well as the firms that managed contract labour and their counsel. He targeted the activities of private firms such as the Canadian Nippon Supply Company, which arranged labour contracts for workers from Japan, China, and India.

King's report on this question, produced in July 1908, reveals his position on the matter and his approach to the question of Asian immigration in the wake of the riots. King clearly supported the idea that uncontrolled immigration from Japan to BC was the cause of the rioting. His report addressed the immigration statistics between 1900 and 1907 and concluded that "it [was] not a matter of surprise" that if there were, at most, 7,500 Japanese living in Vancouver in 1906, and 8,125 Japanese (even if they were from Hawaii) arrived in the first ten months of 1907, that "the residents of Vancouver, should have experienced some concern" and that "consternation should have been felt in many quarters." King also suggested that the increased tension was worsened by "the simultaneous arrival from the Orient of Hindus by the Hundreds [the *Monteagle* alone brought 900] and Chinese in larger numbers than those of immediately preceding years. It was an alarm at numbers, and the cry of a white Canada was raised."[46] King overstated his case, particularly in his interpretation of Chinese arrival numbers and his assessment of the number of Japanese migrants. Chinese arrivals had been significantly reduced by the head tax, and concerns about impending arrivals were largely based on rumours. In the case of the "Japanese" arrivals, he might be forgiven, however, since it was this very mistaken interpretation of the numbers arriving that fuelled the anti-immigration sentiment in the first place. The 8,125 Japanese migrants he pointed to, and to which rioters reacted, represented all of the Japanese arrivals on ships landing at Vancouver, including those from Hawaii, those proceeding to the United States, returning residents, and those refused entry by either government. By his own reckoning, only 1,641 Japanese from Japan entered Canada in 1907.[47] King found evidence that Japanese workers were moving in large numbers from Hawaii[48] due to a significant reduction in their wages and fears of a plague epidemic. After interviewing migrants from Hawaii, King concluded that in addition to the closure of the continental US ports to Japanese workers, "it was in the efforts of the Planters' Association to lower the wages of the Japanese resident in Hawaii, that we find the beginnings of that unrest which has led to Japanese coming in such large numbers from the Hawaiian Islands to British Columbia during the past year."[49]

King's interviews and meticulous examination of the documents provided by the Canadian Nippon Supply Company and the Japanese Boarding House Keeper's Union of Vancouver did reveal that despite public resistance to Japanese immigration, some BC businesses continued to negotiate the movement of more Japanese workers to their work sites. It was generally felt among employers that Japanese workers were far less likely than British workers to strike, and that they would work for a lower wage and seemed content to do the most dreary and dangerous tasks. Among the most notable employers of "coolie" labour was the lieutenant-governor; King reported that Dunsmuir had indeed arranged for contracts of Japanese workers for the Wellington Colliery Company in his capacity as company president.[50] The agreement was for the Canadian Nippon Supply Company to provide five hundred Japanese coal miners and approximately forty other labourers to the Wellington Colliery Company, for which the supply company would receive five dollars per miner once the workers had successfully completed one month in the mine and avoided all strike activity. However, the contract was dropped because there were not enough workers willing to work in the mines. Japanese immigrants preferred to work on the railway or elsewhere.[51] That said, despite initial assumptions that the Grand Trunk Railway was intending to import large numbers of Japanese workers, King was unable to find any evidence that this had occurred.

It should also be noted that King was impressed by the business practices of the Canadian Nippon Supply Company, commenting that "[a]s an arrangement between corporations and large bodies of inexperienced foreign labourers, it is doubtful whether a more perfect system could be worked out to the advantage of all parties concerned."[52] However, this statement should not in any way be interpreted as an endorsement on King's part of Japanese immigration to the province. Despite the effectiveness of the immigration officers and the supply company, King's conclusion was that the preservation of harmony between the several classes in the province of British Columbia, no less than the furtherance of friendly relations between this country and Japan demands that there should be an effective restriction of the number of Japanese who shall be admitted to Canada each year.[53]

In the same report, on the subject of Indian migration, King was skeptical of the Canadian Pacific Line's ability to protect Indian customers from moneylenders and others looking to make a dollar from their hardships. He would clarify his position later, after consultation with London and after travelling to India himself, but in this report he concluded:

It will be apparent from the brief review here given of a part of the evidence, that the immigration from India, and the methods by which it has been carried on, besides occasioning unrest in the province of British Columbia, has resulted in great hardship and injustice to many of the Indians themselves. Apart altogether from the question of whether or not they are suited to this country, it is clear that without some supervision on the part of the authorities which will protect the natives from false representations, it is within the power of a few individuals to create a situation not only prejudicial to the lives and fortunes of hundreds of well-meaning and innocent persons, but of grave concern to the British Empire itself.[54]

King's conclusion, then, was that the activities of a number of small firms and the Canadian Pacific Line created an untenable influx of Asian workers in the summer of 1907, leading to fear and disorder among the white settler population.[55] He proposed solutions consistent with his outlook as a rational social scientist, a liberal, and a social reformer. The government should, according to King, use better statistical methods to chart the number of immigrants actually remaining in Canada. It should ensure increased representation of the immigration service on the west coast so that immigration could be monitored accurately, and it should pass legislation designed to control the flow of Asian workers into Canada.

At the end of November, the Chinese were still waiting for their commission. It would eventually begin in May 1908, but in the fall the Canadian government still had little interest in including the Chinese in discussions about compensation, as there was no treaty binding them to do so.[56] Sir Edward Grey disagreed with this stance and encouraged the Canadians to reconsider, arguing that the Chinese had been allowed to enter the country and establish their livelihoods, and this was enough to allow them the expectation of protection from the Government of Canada.[57] Sir Edward was supported in this position by his cousin, Earl Grey, who, when hearing that the Chinese were not included in King's commission, commented,

> It has been presented to me that Mr. Mackenzie L. King's [*sic*] Commission does not enable him to adjudicate upon claims for compensation put in by Chinamen who have suffered loss.
>
> I am not aware of any reason why the Japs should have a preference over Chinamen or white men, and conclude, if the representation made to me is correct, that there has been an error in the drafting of the Commission?[58]

The issue of Chinese damages was an important diplomatic point for the British in 1907. Rather than being grounded in a theoretical point of honour, the British interest in having the Canadians pay damages to the Chinese was motivated by practicality: the hope was to establish an important precedent since Chinese pirates had been attacking British ships along the Canton River for years. This resulted in a terrible strain and a high cost to the British for doing business in the region, and the Foreign Office was seeking compensation from the Chinese government for the damages. In fact, the FO wished to link the two cases in a quid pro quo by withholding Chinese compensation until British claims had been paid. As a result, the FO wished to be kept informed about Canadian plans to pay compensation to Chinese riot victims in Vancouver.

Sir Francis Campbell wrote a confidential memo to the Colonial Office, which documented this position clearly:

> It will be observed that Sir J. Jordan [Britain's ambassador in Peking] has taken the opportunity to call the attention of the Chinese Government to the fact that His Majesty's Government have in certain instances failed to obtain compensation for the loss of British lives and property in China.
>
> Sir E. Grey is of the opinion that the quest of compensation for the losses sustained by Chinese subjects at Vancouver may perhaps afford a useful lever for obtaining redress from the Chinese Government in matters of an analogous nature, such for instance as the pending claims arising from piratical attacks on British vessels on the Canton River.
>
> I am accordingly to request that Lord Elgin [the secretary of state for the colonies] may be so good as to communicate with Sir E. Grey in the event of the question of payment of any compensation to Chinese subjects being raised by Mr. Mackenzie King.[59]

Campbell's memo clearly shows that the British wished to ensure the Canadians did not pay too quickly, as this would remove the pressure on China to pay the far greater British claims. Although the FO was firm in its insistence that Canada pay real damages to Chinese subjects, it was equally clear that no "consequential damages" were required, as the Chinese government would never make such payments to the British victims of piracy on the Canton River.[60] However, in the final reckoning, Britain expected Canada to "pay reasonable damages for actual losses sustained."[61] It was hoped that the Canadians would not go too far in paying the Chinese because, as Earl Grey's private secretary, Charlie Jones, suggested, "Great Britain herself had had to make good some damage of a similar kind which was done by her subjects towards Chinese in other parts."[62] Accordingly, King and the Canadian government were warned that they were not to make any statements promising damages to the Chinese until they communicated with the Colonial Office in London and received word that they could proceed.

So, while the British were willing to let the Canadians take the lead in the Japanese case, British concerns in another part of the world imposed different limits on Canadian action on Chinese losses.[63]

The question of restitution for losses in Vancouver was thus an Empire-wide matter. Even before King's commission was established, the governor general advised the prime minister to consult with an Empire expert on the topic. He suggested Laurier contact Judge P.M. Laurence of the Cape Colony. Laurence had been working on the matter of public compensation for Boer War losses in South Africa as the chairman of the War Losses Compensation Committee, and, although Earl Grey found him "a dull and ponderous fellow," he also considered him "a learned and accurate encyclopedia."[64] By coincidence, Laurence happened to be staying nearby at the Russell House in Ottawa and was playing golf with a mutual friend that afternoon, so he was consulted. It was thought that some of the lessons learned in South Africa about compensation could be applied to the Canadian case—although, once the commission had gathered all its evidence, the amount of damages asked for and granted to the Japanese victims of the Vancouver rioters turned out to be fairly low.[65] This made it simpler for London to be more forthcoming with respect to the question of Chinese damages.[66]

Canadian actions in the immediate wake of the riots were generally quite effective. Laurier's quick apology, addressed directly to the emperor of Japan, was well received. King's work investigating and compensating Japanese damages was similarly positive in its effect on Canada's relations with Japan. Morikawa communicated both with King and with the Japanese Foreign Office, praising King's even-handedness and the swiftness with which the commission's investigation was completed. Most important, each of these responses was managed within the requirements of Empire policy, without complaint from London. Canada had demonstrated its willingness to participate in the wider project of Empire policy in Asia, even if Laurier remained careful about how policies sympathetic to Japan would be received in BC and in the House of Commons. Maintaining this balance would become more complicated once Lemieux's mission was underway. Now London, Ottawa, and Washington could turn their eyes to Tokyo.

THREE

Lemieux in Tokyo

Sir Wilfrid Laurier was at his wits' end with BC politics and politicians. Not only had the Liberal Party struggled there (and would lose most of its seats in the 1908 federal election), but the continued resistance to Asian immigrants from the BC members of his own party, and even within his cabinet, had complicated his position. Robert G. Macpherson, the Liberal MP for Vancouver City, was particularly vocal on the question of Japanese immigration. He had published his opinion in July 1907, declaring that it would be best if the Japanese were kept out in order to preserve Canada "as a white man's country."[1] He was not alone in this opinion. Ralph Smith, another member of the Liberal caucus, and William Templeman, the minister of mines and inland revenue, had also parted ways with their leader on the question of Asian immigration during the summer. Laurier recognized the potential importance of the Japanese market for Canadian goods and, more important, he realized how much the British government valued

Canada's continued goodwill toward the Anglo-Japanese Alliance. He reminded Macpherson of this:

> I would like you and our friends to remember that Japan is an ally of Great Britain and that we have a treaty of commerce passed with that country recently with the approval of everyone in Canada and that moderation of language would at the present time be more than useful.[2]

Laurier liked to have his elections every four years, in the fall, and by his political calendar one would be due in fall 1908. However, where BC was concerned, the prime minister and his advisors were convinced that the Liberals were not in a position to carry the province. They were correct. Given the BC provincial stand on Asian immigration, it was almost impossible to find a Liberal candidate who would be politically consistent with both the national and provincial platforms. Ottawa had been warned, or perhaps threatened, directly by Templeman, who was convinced that the Liberal Party would become irrelevant in BC if nothing were done to demonstrate the party's willingness to stop Japanese immigration. Aside from the difficulties this division caused for his electoral prospects, Laurier remained concerned about the possibility of future disorder initiated by Canadian opponents of Asian immigration. Both his source within the Asiatic Exclusion League in Vancouver and common sense warned him that anti-Asian organizations would continue to press the government for increased restrictions on Japanese immigration if boats continued to arrive from Hawaii, and that their calls could be popular in the west. He therefore needed a solution that would quiet the west, console the Japanese, and allay the concerns of the British. If that goal were not complicated enough, the Americans were negotiating immigration controls with the Japanese government at exactly the same time. In October, Roosevelt had appointed Michigan lawyer Thomas J. O'Brien ambassador to Japan.[3] It was initially thought that O'Brien should negotiate a hard limit on Japanese migration to the continental United States, but by October 18, 1907, when William Howard Taft, the US secretary of war and future president, travelled to Tokyo himself, he realized that the US might be best served by leaving the negotiating up to the British via the Canadians.

In the meantime, after some reflection and consultation on how Laurier could both set limits on Japanese immigration and maintain good relations with Britain, the United States, and Japan, Laurier decided to send two of his most experienced and capable men—Rodolphe Lemieux, the postmaster general (and minister of labour) and Joseph Pope, the undersecretary of state—directly to Tokyo. Lemieux was an able public speaker, lawyer, journalist, and Laurier Liberal—that is to say he was a conciliator by nature. The son of a postal clerk and Liberal activist, Lemieux married Berthe Jetté, the daughter of Louis-Amable Jetté, the lieutenant-governor of Quebec from 1898 to 1908.[4] His letters home to his father-in-law give us a sense of his experiences and his impressions of Japan. While Pope was the junior member of the delegation, he brought his own set of skills to the mission. Pope was born to a respectable Tory family from Charlottetown and had been the trusted private secretary of Prime Minister John A. Macdonald. His marriage to Marie-Louise Joséphine Henriette Taschereau of Rivière-du-Loup, Quebec, brought him into Laurier's personal orbit as well. His "discretion" and diplomacy were therefore well known in Canada's highest circles, and when the Department of External Affairs was created in 1909, he was made its first undersecretary.[5]

As Lemieux's subordinate in the Department of Labour, King was involved in the prime minister's deliberations about whether to send a representative, who it should be, and to what end. He initially recommended himself to Laurier as the person best suited to travel to Japan on a fact-finding mission to assess these causes. He vowed that he would agree to the assignment, if asked. As we know, he was not, and he quietly ceded the role to Lemieux. Since the focus of the mission had shifted to negotiating immigration limits, it was important for the mission to include someone who could speak for the dominion government. Lemieux had a certain standing as a cabinet minister that King was all too aware he himself lacked. Lemieux also spoke French, the European language of choice for most Japanese diplomats, a skill King had not mastered. At forty-one, Lemieux was the youngest member of cabinet, which worked in his favour as no problems of health or age could be allowed to interfere with his undertaking a long and arduous journey. Both King and Lemieux were involved in drafting both the order-in-council sending Lemieux and Pope and the statement of intentions that Lemieux would present upon arrival. This statement identified rising immigration numbers as its primary concern. In the words of his mission memorandum, Lemieux's trip was undertaken with

> reference to the recent largely increased influx of Japanese immigrants to Canada, which, in view of the negotiations between the two countries during the last few years ... was quite unlooked for on the part of the Canadian Government. This unexpected volume of immigration has unfortunately given rise to certain disturbances and to a strong racial prejudice in the Province of British Columbia, whereby a number of Japanese residents have recently suffered maltreatment.[6]

The Canadian mission's official task, as set by order-in-council PC 2256 on October 12, 1907, was

> to discuss the situation with His Majesty's Ambassador at Tokyo and Japanese authorities, with the object, by friendly means, of preventing recurrence of such causes as might disturb happy relations which have under the said Treaty existed between the subjects of His Majesty the King, in Canada and elsewhere, and the subjects of [the] Emperor of Japan.[7]

Although unstated in the order-in-council, the goal was always that Lemieux would seek to negotiate limits on Japanese migration that would reduce the number of Japanese workers coming to Canada to less than four hundred per year—fewer if possible. Laurier dispatched his mission and asked the governor general to inform the Colonial Office of its general aims. On October 13, two weeks before Lemieux sailed from Vancouver on the twenty-eighth, Governor General Grey advised the CO that some sort of credentials were required to show that Lemieux's mission had British approval. This telegram contained no concrete information about the "nature of the proposals." However, from the governor general's telegram, the CO understood the mission's goal to be the limitation of Japanese emigration to Canada.[8]

It was too late to send Lemieux his written credentials directly. Instead, a telegram was rushed to Sir Claude MacDonald, the British ambassador in Tokyo, asking him to present Lemieux and Pope to the Japanese authorities with "the approval of His Majesty's Government" and to give the Canadians any assistance they might need.[9] Again, no mention of immigration questions was made, but MacDonald would have made the same assumptions as his superiors at the FO, who knew by this time that Lemieux intended "to press for *restriction* of Japanese immigration."[10]

In preparation for his visit, Joseph Pope requested printed copies of the confidential reports on treaty negotiations between Britain and Japan in the period 1894–1905 that involved Canada.[11] There was some concern in the FO about the advisability of sending sensitive materials out of the department, but copies of the "volumes of confidential print of Japanese Treaty Revision Series for the years 1894–1905 inclusive" pertaining to Canada were sent to Tokyo and set aside for Pope to consult with on the understanding that they would remain in "his personal custody" and would be returned at the end of the negotiations.[12] And so with the best wishes of the prime minister, letters of introduction from the governor general, and a promise of help from the British Foreign Office, Lemieux, Pope, and the rest of the Canadians left Ottawa to start their long voyage to Japan.

After an extremely stormy and unpleasant winter crossing on the *Empress of China* between October 29 and November 13,[13] the

Canadians arrived in Yokohama. Lemieux was well taken care of by the British ambassador; as he and his wife disembarked at the port of Yokohama, they were met personally by the British consul general, sent by MacDonald to inquire about Lemieux's needs and, perhaps more important, his plans. The entourage arrived in Tokyo the next day, November 14, and MacDonald presented them to Count Tadasu Hayashi, the Japanese foreign minister, that very afternoon. Hayashi was the preeminent Japanese diplomat of his time. He spoke English; had served in St. Petersburg, Peking, and London; and most important, had been closely involved with the diplomacy behind the Anglo-Japanese Alliance, meaning that he was associated with the political faction that set store on good relations with Great Britain and its empire. He was known to be a shrewd negotiator, and Lemieux was far less experienced, perhaps even out of his depth.

Lemieux's position was, however, improved considerably by the presence of Sir Claude MacDonald at each of the meetings. MacDonald also treated Lemieux on several occasions to social events at the embassy, where he might meet the "right" people and learn from their experience. MacDonald impressed Lemieux with his stories of his time in China during the Boxer Rebellion and with his library. On the whole, Lemieux felt that MacDonald and his wife were "charmants." And why not? They had arranged for a grand dinner on November 19 to introduce the Canadians to many of the most influential members of Japanese society.[14] MacDonald was a sympathetic ear on the question of the Canadian desire to limit Japanese immigration. In fact, once convinced of the Canadian case, he was an important ally. On November 15, in a private meeting, Lemieux presented MacDonald with the details of his government's proposals. They were, in short, that because of the unexpected rise in Japanese immigration to Canada—despite previous agreements with Japan regarding limits on the number of exit visas available to that country's citizens—Canada was seeking further assurances that the numbers negotiated by Japanese consul Nossé and Laurier would be observed: that is, that no more than four hundred Japanese would be allowed to enter Canada in any given calendar year. In MacDonald's confidential addendum to Sir Edward Grey in London, he wrote,

> There is no doubt that the assurances given in the name of his Government by Mr. Nossé are very definite. The first was given in 1903. On that occasion Mr. Nossé stated that "it was not the desire of the Japanese Government to force their people into British Columbia, and they were willing to conclude an Agreement with the Canadian Government by which, in the event of their present policy of rigid restriction being considered unsatisfactory by the Canadian Government, they might bind themselves."
>
> In 1904 and 1905 similar assurances were given, and the adherence of Canada to the Treaty was without doubt due to these assurances.
>
> I therefore venture under the circumstances to request your permission to support the Canadian Government's proposals, which I do not think Count Hayashi will object to in principle, though before his written acceptance is obtained considerable pressure may be required.[15]

Thus, when Lemieux arrived in Tokyo, the key points of the negotiations had already been identified: Canada's strong desire to limit Japanese migration, Nossé's assurances that Japan would voluntarily limit the number of emigrants, the conditions under which Canada had ratified the 1894 Commercial Treaty in 1905, and the difficulty of having these limits expressed in an official treaty agreement. As Lemieux would come to discover, the Americans were also struggling to convince Foreign Minister Hayashi to sign a revised immigration treaty, and the Japanese press was "up in arms" at the thought of more "concession[s] to the American anti-Asiatics."[16] US ambassador Thomas O'Brien came to Lemieux in person on November 18 with the request that the United States join the British and Canadian negotiators in the hope that they would make a "common cause." Demonstrating a firm grasp of diplomatic protocol and Canada's position as a British dominion, Lemieux reported to Laurier that they had "of course, declined."[17] After this he made a point of "carefully" avoiding O'Brien despite his social invitations, knowing that the ambassador was likely to have made them in order to press for information about the talks.[18]

The Americans had already approached the Japanese government with their own diagnosis of the immigration-related problems on the US Pacific coast. In the fall of 1907 Taft, acting as Roosevelt's secretary of war, was sent on a grand tour of the Pacific states, the Philippines, and Japan. He arrived at Yokohama on September 28, just weeks after the rioting in Vancouver. During this visit, Taft discussed several points of contention in the Japanese and American relationship, including immigration, and reassured his Japanese counterpart, the minister of war, that the anti-Asian violence in San Francisco was "local and due to [a] bitterness of feeling not shared by [the] country at large." Further, he theorized "that the occurrences at Vancouver, B.C., showed it was impossible to control local riots growing out of labor-organization."[19] Taft telegrammed Roosevelt that his Japanese counterpart agreed that labour tensions were to blame and that he had seen evidence in Vancouver ten years previously that led him to believe there would someday be problems between "the low class of Japanese immigrants" and Canadian workers.[20]

The question of Japanese immigration to North America arose again during Taft's luncheon with the Japanese foreign minister, Count Hayashi, on September 30. Taft characterized Hayashi's position in the same confidential telegram to the US president:

> that only [a] small part of Japanese people was interested in [the] mere question of immigration; that Japanese people would be entirely satisfied with complete restriction of immigration by treaty if it applied equally to the immigrants from all the countries, European and Asiatic; that chief interest in it was taken by syndicates who were engaged in the business of furnishing Japanese coolies for a commission; that these syndicates had influence politically and had carried on a campaign to rouse the people on the subject ... that they bitterly resented a treaty based on inequality between Japanese and Europeans; that he had sent

Itchit [Ishii] to examine [the] question of immigration in the United States and Canada and was waiting for his report, before formulating a policy.[21]

On another occasion, in October, Taft noted that Hayashi made the link between immigration concessions and the Vancouver riots: "... the very serious situation in Vancouver, B.C. ... made it necessary for them [Japan] to take further steps to prevent additional immigration into that country ..."[22] Taft concluded that attempts at treaty negotiation between the United States and Japan should be stopped. He felt that because of the Japanese relationship with Britain, it would become possible to leave the control of Japanese migrants to the Japanese government, which would be more sensitive to an ally's needs. Rather than expose the United States to censure by implementing exclusionary legislation or pressing for a treaty that would prove embarrassing to Japan, he advised Roosevelt that the United States should just wait for Britain to manage the crisis.[23]

Taft was on the right track as there was movement in the negotiations between Japan and Britain, and the outcomes of these discussions would have real and explicit effects on both Canada and the United States. In November, while the Canadian mission was in the midst of discussions, Count Hayashi was also in communication with the US ambassador. On November 27 Ambassador O'Brien cabled Secretary of State Elihu Root the following:

> In an interview today Japanese Minister for Foreign Affairs promised reply to your proposed measures as soon as statistics could be verified and said that the same restrictive measures would be applied with respect to British Columbia as with respect to the United States; also that Japanese Consul General at Honolulu has no power [to] issue passports. Emigration Hawaii restricted two hundred and fifty in November. Will consider further reduction as suggested. Assured me of the utmost confidence in our good intentions. Pleased with our attitude and will cooperate in every reasonable way.[24]

The links between the parallel negotiations are evident in this telegram. Though Lemieux had rejected US requests for the countries to negotiate together, the simultaneous discussions were still defining the realm of the possible in both. The United States wanted to avoid legislation back home that openly excluded Japanese nationals, and it therefore demanded a reduction in the number of Japanese leaving their home prefectures for the US. Canadian negotiations were indirectly having this desired effect since fewer Japanese entering Canada would mean fewer Japanese passing from Canadian ports into the United States. Canadians were concerned about Japanese leaving Hawaii and, of course, it was the US government, not the Japanese, that had the most significant influence on those numbers, so the US negotiations with Japan were in this sense critical to the achievement of the Canadian goal.

By November 20 the Colonial Office had authorized MacDonald "to support the proposals made by the Canadian Commissioners."[25] The sticking point was going to be negotiating the Japanese concession to provide a treaty or public written assurances. The Canadians were in Japan to get documents they could produce in Parliament to show the exclusionists in British Columbia and elsewhere that the Canadian government had taken action to restrict the movement of Japanese migrants, while at the same time preserving the honour of the Japanese government and the terms of the 1894 Anglo-Japanese Treaty of Commerce and Navigation. After Canada signed on to the treaty in 1905, the Canadian government was required to allow for certain kinds of free movement of Japanese subjects on Canadian soil: "… the subjects of each of the two High Contracting Parties shall have full liberty to enter, travel, or reside in any part of the dominions and possessions of the other Contracting Party, and shall enjoy full and perfect protection for their persons and property."[26] This was something that may have seemed reasonable to the British since the British Isles were so far from Japan, but it had a completely different resonance for Canadians perched on the edge of the Pacific, where the riots had put the safety of Japanese subjects and their property in question. But the Canadians in Tokyo received good news from Vancouver on November 18: King sent word to Lemieux that, after an extensive investigation and public hearings, the Japanese claims had been assessed and all parties were content with the results.

As we saw earlier, Lemieux's brief was intended to communicate to the Japanese that the "disturbances" in Vancouver were due to what were perceived to be high levels of Japanese immigration.[27] According to this document, British Columbia's physical isolation from the rest of Canada and its small population left the province vulnerable to influence from the United States, "where the same question is agitating the public mind, and threatens to combine all classes, irrespective of boundaries, in one common cause ..."[28] This explanation for the Vancouver riots was apparently accepted in Ottawa. Earl Grey told the Colonial Office about "the strong racial prejudices" among "people on the Pacific Coast," which were "to be regretted yet ha[d] to be taken into consideration by all who desire[d] to cultivate best relations between Canada and the Orient."[29]

Lemieux was doing his best to build relationships with his Japanese hosts and took the opportunity to socialize, travel, and see some of the most remarkable sites in Japan. In the process, he learned to recognize the high level of Japanese culture and the importance of face and honour from the Japanese perspective. As a representative of one of the British dominions, he was treated with extraordinary hospitality. He was presented to members of the royal family during the Chrysanthemum Festival, where he was led on a tour of the royal gardens. He was invited to a formal dinner hosted by Prince Fushimi Hiroyasu and his wife; had tea with the French-speaking chief judge of the Supreme Court in his chambers; and watched military training exercises at a Japanese high school. He also had his first experience eating sushi with a wealthy art collector and was taken on a trip to a Buddhist temple that he described as one of the most extraordinary moments of his life.[30] The group came upon the monks in the middle of a service and the chanting and the sacred silence afterward impressed Lemieux and reminded him of the Franciscan and Trappist monks of his own tradition. Lemieux and his wife, Berthe, had a few anxiety-filled minutes days later when an earthquake struck Tokyo in the early hours of November 22. The experience made Lemieux both anxious and eager to conclude his mission. As he wrote to Laurier, he wanted to return home "to God's own country, Canada, notwithstanding the many and many courtesies showered upon us every day since our arrival in Japan."[31]

While Lemieux's experience as a guest of the Japanese government was beyond reproach, the process of negotiation was not easy. On November 25, after a lunch and likely a cigar and a chat with MacDonald at the British embassy, the delegation travelled together for Lemieux's first meeting with Hayashi at two o'clock. MacDonald had received official permission from London to support the Canadian proposal, so it was time to begin in earnest. Lemieux and Pope were accompanied by MacDonald and F.O. Lindley, the second secretary of the British embassy. On the other side were Hayashi and his vice-minister for foreign affairs, Baron Sutemi Chinda. Hayashi had made an intelligent choice in including Baron Chinda in the discussion since he was a diplomat with extensive experience in North America, having been a student in the United States and served previously as the consul in San Francisco.

The two sides went back and forth several times over two points: the question of an official note of understanding that could be communicated to the Canadian people, and the issue of Japanese migration via Hawaii. On the first matter, the Canadian side would leave with no less than a written statement explicitly restricting the number of Japanese workers and artisans to a proposed limit of three hundred. This number was not intended to include students, merchants, wives, or returning Japanese. On the Japanese side, as conveyed in Count Hayashi's communication with the Americans, his government could never agree to any document that would publicly recognize that Canada was treating the Japanese people differently from any other. The second question was equally troublesome. While Canadians considered migrants from Hawaii to be "Japanese," there was, according to the Japanese government, nothing they could do to control the movement of ethnic Japanese who had lived in Hawaii rather than Japan.

After dinner on December 3, Lemieux and Hayashi shared coffee, cigars, and conversation. Lemieux felt that it was a very productive discussion and that they had come to an understanding that would satisfy both the Canadian prime minister and the Japanese government. The next day, at an informal meeting between Lemieux, MacDonald, and Ishii, the group sat down and drew up an outline of an agreement that resembled the existing one with the United States. It included an assurance from the Japanese government that Lemieux could announce in public regarding the limitation of emigrants from Japan, as well as detailed instructions to be sent to local prefectures prohibiting the exit of Japanese for Canada, except for those already resident in Canada, domestics to be employed by existing residents, contract labourers acknowledged by the Canadian government, and workers for Japanese who owned farms or mines. It did not, however, limit the number of workers to three hundred, and as such was seen as "worthless" by Joseph Pope.[32] The group agreed to leave it until the next morning at ten, when they were all next scheduled to meet at the Foreign Office. Since he did not have the authority to act alone, Lemieux sent a copy of the Japanese proposal to Laurier in Ottawa for approval.

Lemieux was coming to a deep understanding of the Japanese position as it was presented to him and had a great deal of respect for the men with whom he was dealing. He wanted Laurier to understand the real difficulties Japan faced in complying with the request for public documentation of any agreement, and underlined the importance of the Japanese concessions, saying, "I do not think it possible to get better terms than these."[33] After cabling Laurier, Lemieux wrote a quick note to MacDonald asking that he also inform his government of the terms proposed by Hayashi so that they could move quickly to accept the terms at the next meeting with the Japanese delegation on December 9. Lemieux was confident and pleased when he sat down to write his father-in-law that evening. Under the agreement as it stood that night, he had received both a general declaration he could make public and a secret note placed with the British ambassador outlining the details of the Japanese commitment as a sign of good faith. Lemieux was proud of this plan to leave a note of understanding with MacDonald since it was his own idea.

Sir Edward Grey at the FO responded that the British were committed to the Canadian decision, writing, "If the Canadian Govt accepts, the matter is settled."[34] And so on December 5, Lemieux, the British legation in Tokyo, the governor general, the Foreign Office, and the Colonial Office were all convinced that an agreement had been reached. But Laurier proved to be an obstacle. When the governor general telegraphed Laurier with congratulations on Lemieux's "success,"[35] he received Laurier's refusal in return.

On the afternoon of December 9, the Canadians arrived to some fanfare by special railway car at the town of Nikko in Tochigi Prefecture. An official car carried them from the station and the flags of Great Britain and Japan had been hung in their honour at the beautiful and famous Hotel Kanaya. They were greeted by the deeply bowing hotel staff and were taken to see the nearby waterfalls, temples, and scenic drives. It was upon his return to Tokyo that evening that Lemieux received Laurier's telegram that demanded his swift return home.[36]

While the new rules proposed to limit Japanese immigration might have been acceptable, Laurier did not view them as reliable enough for his own political needs. He explained his position to the governor general, declaring, "I feel pretty sure that it will not satisfy the people of BC who are full of the idea that the province is to be[,] as a result of a deep plot and design, taken possession of by a quiet, persistent and systematic Japanese invasion."[37] He was convinced that the Japanese government had not adhered to the previous agreement as stated in the

British and Canadian treaty with Japan, and now he wanted assurances they would remain faithful to the existing terms. Otherwise, he told the governor general, the "invasion" feared in British Columbia would continue,[38] and the Canadian government would have to reconsider its participation in the treaty when it came up for renewal in 1911.

Lemieux was struggling to find a way to explain to the prime minister that, for the minister to accomplish his goals, he would have to act indirectly. The Japanese were not going to publicly admit to a policy that would limit immigration just because Nossé had made personal promises. As Hayashi had told Lemieux, "We must save face with our people."[39] But the Japanese government had made significant concessions, including the promise that, should Canada decide to control the movement of Japanese via Hawaii under the existing Alien Labour Act, they would not object. Lemieux was convinced that the agreement would do indirectly all the things Laurier and King were seeking, and that if only he had ten minutes in person with Laurier he could convince him of this fact. In an attempt to save the process, Lemieux clarified the terms agreed to by the Japanese for the prime minister:

Japanese Government agree to prohibition of all labour emigration except following:

1. Resident Japanese returning for the second time;
2. Bona fide domestic servants for Japanese residents only;
3. [Those] brought in under contract approved by Canadian Government in each case;
4. Agricultural labourers for work on farm owned by Japanese under same restrictions as those provided for by their arrangement with United States, namely, from five to ten labourers per 100 acres.

Will give written assurance in general terms to be made public ... Present object of our enforcing Alien Labour Law against Hawaii.[40]

MacDonald shared Lemieux's conviction that the Japanese had adhered to the essence of their consul's promises, and yet Laurier was not convinced. He saw no reason to change his position and wrote back to Lemieux, "I confirm my cable of yesterday. Think any departure from arrangement made with Nossé must produce deplorable effect. It would be looked upon as a breach of faith. Conditions now are the same as last year and no reason can be given for not adhering to our agreement."[41] Laurier had taken the advice of the superintendent of the Federal Immigration Branch, William Duncan Scott, that Canada could not accept Japan's proposal. Fearful of Japanese expansion, Scott looked at the experience of California fruit growers falling behind Japanese migrants and expected that the same would happen to BC agriculture. At the same time, Laurier had great trust in Lemieux, Pope, and MacDonald. He was therefore willing to believe that they had access to information that he had not received in the mission's telegraph correspondence. As he confided to Earl Grey,

> Perhaps they fail to appreciate objections which seem so very clear and peremptory to us ... The way would be clear if Japan would carry out the assurances which we received from their Consul [Nossé], and on the faith of which the treaty was ratified, and we should still press for this. If they fail in this, I think Lemieux should come back, taking Japan's proposal with him, for discussion here, with all the information which he would bring back and which would assist us to reach a conclusion.[42]

Despite previous optimism, as Christmas approached, the situation seemed bleak. It came to London's attention that the assurances that Nossé, the now former Japanese consul general, had given in 1903 about Tokyo's willingness "to bind themselves" to a low number of emigrants were given without the authority of his government.[43] In fact, Nossé had since been recalled to Tokyo, and London was unaware of whether he had departed "in disgrace or to advise the Japanese Government ..."[44] In the meantime, Lemieux began to organize his travel home via the Trans-Siberian Railway and continued to attend social events organized by the British embassy and the Japanese government. He even arranged to host a dinner for sixty-two honoured guests on December 17. Lemieux was thrilled that the toasts to the emperor and the king were enthusiastically followed by shouts of "*Banzai!*," but he and his guests remained preoccupied with the fact that the negotiations had reached an impasse. The Foreign Office, surprised by the Canadian refusal, warned that a "breakdown" in the process was imminent.[45] However, Sir Edward Grey remained optimistic that "it [would] come right in time" as long as the Canadian and Japanese governments were willing to show some "goodwill" toward each other and toward the process.[46] By December 19 the Canadian representatives' position had shifted only slightly: they now desired to limit labourers (domestics and agriculturalists) to four hundred and they continued to require a statement that could be read into the public record. MacDonald was convinced the Japanese could agree to the number and to a public document in general terms.

On December 21 MacDonald and Hayashi met and agreed to the terms as he and Lemieux had outlined them. Both sides felt that they had accomplished Canada's goals and Hayashi had the Japanese Foreign Office type up an official document. However, MacDonald was also convinced that the Canadian cabinet had a serious "misunderstanding" of the terms. He telegraphed Earl Grey in the hope that he could communicate with Laurier and convince him that the general statement and confidential memo were in earnest, solemn, binding, and realistically the best they could do without abandoning the 1894 treaty and excluding Japanese immigrants altogether.[47] Laurier remained unconvinced. On December 24 he decided that no firm decision could be taken until Lemieux returned to Canada and demanded that the minister leave Japan immediately. MacDonald arranged a meeting that very night for Lemieux with Hayashi to lay out the circumstances of his departure and a plan to move forward in his absence. Lemieux even left a signed copy of the documents with the British embassy so that as soon as the

Canadian cabinet had agreed, it could be signed by the Japanese and put into effect without delay.

On Boxing Day, as Lemieux left for Canada, MacDonald was waiting for the Canadians' final decision on the agreement. Though the negotiations had stopped during Lemieux's absence, MacDonald assured London that they were merely "interrupted" rather than broken.[48] The British hoped that after Lemieux had discussed the details of the negotiations with Laurier in person, he would agree to the terms that were, in fact, not far from the Canadian demands. Hayashi was willing to make a "public declaration to the effect that the Japanese Government 'will take efficient means to restrict Japanese emigration to Canada,'" that could be "laid before the Dominion Parliament."[49] The difference between this offer and what the Canadian government insisted on was slight, but real in diplomatic terms. The confidential memorandum, produced as a favour to Great Britain, would never be published. The Japanese would never be required to explain how these restrictions would be implemented, and they would never have to lose face internationally by being subject to restrictions not applicable to other favoured powers. The distinction between this public declaration and the desired written assurances would arise as a question again in Parliament when Lemieux reported on the success of his mission to Japan. But Lemieux and MacDonald were so confident that the terms would be accepted that the papers were signed, sealed, and left in Tokyo for the hoped-for moment when Laurier's government would telegraph their official agreement to the terms.

In the end, Lemieux took passage across the Pacific rather than via Europe in order to return home more quickly. Mackenzie King left a letter for Lemieux at Victoria welcoming him home from his "momentous" trip and suggesting that due to Lieutenant-Governor Dunsmuir's "somewhat compromising position" in the area of Asian migration he would be better to avoid meeting with him and come back to Ottawa directly.[50] Upon arriving in the capital, Lemieux immediately submitted an extensive, confidential memo to the cabinet, arguing strongly for the acceptance of the negotiated terms.[51] The cabinet—meaning Laurier—now fell in line.

The Conservative Party leader, Robert Borden, had some concerns about Lemieux's conclusions. He was most upset at the idea that, rather than acting to control its own borders, Canada had given the power to make decisions about Japanese immigration to the Japanese. He was reacting to the public memorandum written by Hayashi that reasserted Japanese citizens' rights under the 1894 treaty: "full liberty to enter, travel and reside in any part of the Dominion of Canada."[52] As Borden stated in the House, "The real object of [Lemieux's] mission was to induce Japan to exercise that control over immigration into Canada which we should be able to exercise ourselves."[53]

Despite Borden's opposition, Parliament—or at least its Liberal majority—agreed to Japan's terms. In the end, this agreement is what has come to be known as the Gentlemen's Agreement of 1908, or the Hayashi-Lemieux Agreement. Under its terms, Japan agreed to limit emigration to Canada to a trickle of no more than four hundred workers a year, and Canada agreed not to pass any legislation aimed directly at Japanese subjects as it had against Chinese workers. It was the kind of agreement the United States had sought, and it was also the kind of strategy London hoped could be negotiated with India, although dealing with British subjects would make this task much more complicated.

FOUR

The Man in
the Middle

The new year, 1908, found William Lyon Mackenzie King tired but, as he told his faithful diary, committed to continuing his work. Perhaps he had overextended himself in the work of the commissions, but he was resolved to "strive again, & again, & again" to do the right thing and stay "on the path of right and duty."[1] The year ahead would bring new challenges and responsibilities for the thirty-three-year-old King, including a flurry of trips to Washington, DC, to meet with Theodore Roosevelt, a fact-finding trip to London and Asia, his first electoral victory, and his subsequent emergence as the rookie Liberal member of Parliament for Waterloo North.

At the beginning of January 1908 Lemieux had returned from Tokyo; the Canadian government was in the process of officially agreeing to the terms of the nation's Gentlemen's Agreement with Japan, now known as the Hayashi-Lemieux Agreement; and the commissions that King had chaired in Vancouver on Japanese losses and the causes of Asian immigration had largely finished their work. Although the reports had yet to be officially written and submitted, Japanese victims of the riot had been awarded their damages. However, the questions surrounding Japanese immigration to the United States, Indian immigration to British Columbia, and Chinese reparations for damages from the riots were still open. Each question brought local BC politics onto the national stage and each had implications for Canadian, North American, British imperial, and international affairs.

Despite the positive feeling Lemieux brought home about the negotiations in Tokyo, there was still work to do before cabinet, Parliament, and the Canadian public would be sold on the agreement. Lemieux's ambiguous credentials and authority to speak for the governments of Canada and Great Britain became a point of contention in the House. Laurier sought to reinforce the strength of Lemieux's position in Tokyo by publishing some of the Canadian government's telegraphic correspondence with the Foreign Office during the period leading up to his mission. These communications were published in the hope that they would prove that the mission had Ambassador Claude MacDonald's enthusiastic assistance and the green light from London to negotiate limits on Japanese immigration to British Columbia. In other words, Laurier's, Lemieux's, and King's efforts had been blessed, even sanctified, by a higher power—high enough, at any rate, to override nativist prejudices in British Columbia or Conservative leader Borden's reservations.[2]

Admittedly, some loose ends remained. Although the targets of Vancouver's riot were primarily Chinese and Japanese businesses, the question of Indian migration was an unavoidable part of the "oriental problem" that needed to be addressed in the wake of the disorder. It was generally acknowledged that in view of the racist attitudes of many white inhabitants of BC and elsewhere in Canada, a rise in the number of South Asian migrants would also be destabilizing. In addition to the changes included in the Gentlemen's Agreement that Lemieux brought home,[3] the Canadian government sought to limit the number of Asian immigrants arriving on the west coast through a piece of legislation known as the "continuous journey regulation." Laurier signed an order-in-council on January 8, 1908, that could, if the Ministry of the Interior deemed it necessary, prohibit the entry of those who had not travelled from their country of birth or citizenship directly on a ticket purchased in advance and via a "continuous journey."[4] This regulation was designed to solve the problem of Japanese workers coming in large numbers from Hawaii, as they would be required by the new rules to return to Japan to buy a valid ticket. It also had the effect of preventing most Indian immigration to Canada since there were no Canadian Pacific Line ships that sailed directly from Indian to Canadian ports. The order-in-council had a few loopholes that needed to be closed, but it did have the effect desired by its authors.

What should be done next was now King's problem. Without really intending to, he had become Canada's expert on Asian immigration. Members of the US State Department who watched immigration matters recognized his expertise, and when Roosevelt wanted Britain's ear, King was summoned unofficially to the White House through a mutual friend from Harvard, Colonel John James McCook. McCook was a New York lawyer and a supporter of the president. He had sent a personal invitation to King as a fellow Harvard man to attend the Gridiron dinner in New York in January 1909. When Roosevelt heard King was coming, he got McCook to extend the invitation for a quick trip to Washington.[5] Roosevelt likely saw an opportunity to send a message to the British and the Japanese without having to create a formal paper trail. Fortunately for King and for future historians, McCook took King quietly aside and warned him to keep accurate notes of his discussions with Roosevelt in order to protect himself from the president's tendency to reframe the content of conversations as it suited him.[6]

The result of McCook's intervention was a series of meetings between King, the president, and relevant members of both the State Department and Commerce and Labor in January and February

1908. King had opportunities to discuss Japanese immigration with the individuals most closely tied to the question in the United States, including Roosevelt's secretary of state, Elihu Root, and Oscar S. Straus, secretary of commerce and labor. King arrived in Washington for his first visit on January 25, 1908. His first meeting was with Straus. Presumably at the president's request, Straus inquired casually about the details of the Canadian agreement with Japan. He must have hoped that the young and inexperienced King would give up details that Lemieux had kept close to the vest in Tokyo. He suggested to King that as the US and Canada had "common interests" in the matter it would be helpful to know what was agreed to behind the closed doors of the Japanese Foreign Office. King ably sidestepped the question, using the chain of command to free him from responsibility and referring Straus to Lemieux, the minister in charge.[7] When that line of questioning did not work, Straus moved to flattery and announced that he and his government were pleased with the potential of the new continuous journey regulation. Once these preliminaries were over (and the details of the conversation reported to the president), King had his chance to meet with Roosevelt himself.

Over a long lunch of oysters, bouillon, eggs, beef, and pumpkin pie, the president and King had an opportunity to share their views about the Asian immigration question. Heeding McCook's warning, King made a point of taking very detailed notes when he returned to his hotel that evening, so we may read quite extensively about the conversation in his diary. When asked about the Canadian situation, he replied that the government had come to a "satisfactory" arrangement with Japan, but that the problem was larger than the immediate tensions of labour competition and "had become a race problem." King had indeed come face to face with the racism in the Canadian west and recognized that a solution like Lemieux's, which reduced Japanese immigration, would be irrelevant if the public did not perceive this reduction. The problem was not that workers were arriving—it was that they were Japanese.

In response, Roosevelt emphasized the common ground between the western US states and British Columbia:

> This may seem a strong statement, Mr. King, but I believe that if the people east of the Rockies in the United States were indifferent to the situation and the British were indifferent to the feelings of the people of British Columbia, there would be a new republic between the mountains and the Pacific, that the peoples of the two countries felt their common interest in this so strongly ... If you were going to England, I would give you some strong messages to take to Sir Edward Grey. I would have you tell him that in the present situation he could do much for the cause of peace, not that we want to ask the help of the British, but the Japanese must learn that they will have to keep their people in their own country.[8]

Roosevelt had fallen under the spell of the idea of racial zones championed by historian Charles Pearson in his 1893 book *National Life and Character*. The basic idea was that the world would be divided into zones inhabited by one racial type: whites would occupy the temperate areas, blacks the tropical, and so on. Roosevelt hoped to one day organize a convention at which world leaders would agree to such a division and legislate it into existence, but in the meantime he wished to keep North America white. However, he feared for the future of a white Pacific Northwest. Roosevelt had hoped that because of these shared interests in the Pacific, King would take the American cause to London, where, given their alliance with Japan, the British could convince the Japanese government to voluntarily limit emigration to the continental United States.

Of course, once Roosevelt had made this request, King needed to inform the prime minister and the governor general that his visit to Washington had turned out to be much more than a social call. King returned to Ottawa and sat down with Laurier on January 28 to report the details of his visit. King's commentary on Roosevelt's unorthodox request and on the extent of American fears of war with Japan shocked

Laurier. After a moment's pause, Laurier agreed that despite petty differences between his administration and Roosevelt's, it was in Canada's interest to maintain its friendship with the US and to provide help where it could—all the more so because Canada and the United States shared a mutual interest "in keeping the yellow man out."[9] While on a political level Laurier respected Canada's international obligations and had impressed the Japanese with his supportive position on the Anglo-Japanese relationship during his term in office, he in fact held much the same race-related beliefs as the BC Liberals and saw "little hope of any good coming to this country from Asiatic immigration of any kind."[10] Laurier asked King to return the next day, to give the prime minister time to consider his options.

King was justifiably convinced that avoiding war between the United States and Japan was vital for the survival of Canada as a nation, even if the president did overestimate the likelihood of such a war occurring. Canadians would be sorely divided if the Japanese navy arrived on the American Pacific coast. While Canada would officially be allied to Japan through its connection to Great Britain and the 1902 Anglo-Japanese Alliance, it was clear that Canadian sympathies would lie with the US navy, its main hope for domestic defence. King put it this way:

> If it came to actual hostilities between the United States and Japan, it would be very doubtful if some small local conflict would not take place in Vancouver or some parts of British Columbia, and it is also probable that thousands of the people of British Columbia would go over and join the American forces. If England endeavoured to help Japan, I am not sure that there might not be a movement started for the separation of British Columbia from the British Empire.[11]

It was clear to both Laurier and King that passing along the US request for British intercession was one way Canada could show that it was friendly to its southern neighbour and perhaps earn some capital that could be traded later for concessions on an irritant such as pulpwood duties. The next day, Laurier agreed to the plan. It would not have been seemly for a Canadian to represent the United States abroad, so King proposed a cover story for his trip to London, to which Laurier agreed.

> I then said: "Sir Wilfrid, in regard to the other matter—the Japanese question—should it appear that the President was desirous of having me or any other person go to England, it would be necessary to conceal the purpose and have some ostensible reason to give to the public for going." Sir Wilfrid replied that certainly that would have to be done, but we could easily find some good reason. I suggested that possibly some point in connection with Hindu immigration might be discussed; Sir Wilfrid replied, laughingly: "We might trust to your fertile imagination for a good reason." and then asked me if I was going to Washington today, and I said "Yes."[12]

King hurried immediately over to Government House, where he met with the governor general at 3:30 to make sure that he was in agreement with Laurier's position. In addition to requiring Earl Grey's input due to his position as the British Crown's representative in Canada, King was personally concerned about his opinion. Grey was a mentor to King and represented both the new imperialism and the British liberal tradition that King admired so much. He was deeply enmeshed in the world of British imperial policy through his business dealings, his role as governor general, and his family connections. The two family members that were perhaps most relevant for King's travels in 1908–1909 were Earl Grey's cousin Sir Edward Grey, the British foreign secretary, and the Earl of Minto, who was Grey's predecessor as governor general, the current Viceroy of India, and his brother-in-law.[13]

Once Earl Grey had given King permission to carry Roosevelt's message directly to Sir Edward Grey in the Foreign Office, King sped off to catch the 4:45 train to New York City. King arrived in New York at nine the next morning and met Secretary of State Elihu Root just after noon at the State Department in Washington, where he told Root that he had discussed Roosevelt's proposal with Laurier and that the prime minister had agreed to send King to London under the pretext of the need to consult on changes to Indian immigration controls. According to King, Root was pleased that King was going since he would "share the real nature of the situation" with the British. He also tried to appeal to King's racial prejudices and loyalty to the Empire.

> You are familiar with the conditions, and you could do much to aid the British authorities in understanding the real nature of the situation. Having been among the people of British Columbia, you know how little the people in the East really appreciate the seriousness of the situation. You know, too, that it is precisely the same in the United States, the people along our Atlantic seaboard have hardly yet begun to realize just what the situation is ... By going to England, you would render a great service to the British Empire, and secondarily to this country also. This question affects the Empire, not only in regard to Canada, but also to Australia and other colonies. It is not without its significance in India. It is the big question of alien peoples and new lands. It is natural that they should seek to better their conditions, but there is sure to be friction where they come in contact with peoples of a higher standard of civilization.[14]

King had several fairly intimate discussions with Roosevelt on this and other matters on this second trip to Washington, and the president set out his feelings on the Japanese question in several extended formal and informal interviews. He felt there had been a significant shift in the possibilities for American negotiations with Japan since the Vancouver riots. In his opinion, while the Japanese had previously tried to "play off the United States against Great Britain," in the wake of the Vancouver riots they "had been forced to realise that it was no longer possible to try to take advantage of the one as against the other. That the feeling was really one of common objection to their gaining a foothold on this continent."[15] Roosevelt wanted the British to understand the seriousness of the North American predicament since westerners (and the president himself) believed that "The Japanese [would] get possession of the passes of the mountains" and "[white America would] never get them out of there in a hundred years of fighting."[16] He concluded that the movement of Japanese workers had to be stopped and that the result of continued Japanese immigration, even the immigration of Japanese under contract to American firms, would be disastrous and "bricks [were] sure to fly."[17]

Roosevelt even had his staff show King the details of the US negotiations with Japan so that he would "be able to speak with full knowledge to the Imperial authorities."[18] King was sent to see Huntington Wilson, who had recently returned from a series of diplomatic postings in Tokyo and was now the third assistant secretary of state. Wilson had been charged with keeping track of "affairs in the Orient" and had been compiling statistics on Japanese immigration to the United States.[19] Among the documents he had produced—but was not willing to show King—was a collection of the complete diplomatic correspondence between the United States and Japan on the question of Japanese immigration since 1892. The collection was confidential in February, but King suspected that it would be prepared for printing and distribution to Congress once the US fleet arrived in San Francisco in June, if the Japanese failed to live up to their agreements on restricting emigration. If this dissemination occurred, it "would be a direct challenge to Japan."[20]

The president himself asked King to consult with the British ambassador in Washington, James Bryce, and gave King a list of British government and opposition leaders in London he should see on his behalf.[21] On the firm advice of Bryce, Earl Grey, and Laurier, King decided that meeting with these individuals was a mistake, but he did agree, with their permission, to take on the mission to aid Roosevelt. Rather than communicating with Roosevelt's contacts, King was asked to have his dealings through the Foreign, Colonial, and India offices as, according to Earl Grey, "it would be impossible for [King] to get away from the fact that [he] was connected with the Government of Canada and an official, and whatever form the mission might take, it was nevertheless an official mission."[22]

King spent an evening with Bryce, recounting his many conversations with the president and his staff and explaining Roosevelt's position. Bryce was taken by surprise in all this. Despite diplomatic protocol, neither Roosevelt nor Root had informed him of their plan to send King as their messenger to London. The reasons for this secrecy are murky but are probably connected with the politicians' intention to keep the request unofficial. Bryce had a heated private discussion with Roosevelt about King's mission after dinner that evening and needed King's clarification about the origins of the idea to send a Canadian on Roosevelt's behalf to London. King assured him that despite the tone of Bryce's conversation with the president, this was Roosevelt's idea and not Laurier's. As King noted in his diary, "He [Bryce] said from the way the President spoke to him that he thought the President was anxious to have it appear that I had come with a message from Sir Wilfrid. I said that I had no doubt that he felt some delicacy about admitting that he himself had sent for me."[23] There is little reason to conclude that King was mistaken on this point. First, Roosevelt's own papers reinforce the fact that he was worried about war with Japan and that he believed Britain had influence with its allies. Second, the continuous journey regulation had already been passed in January, and there was no legal reason for King to travel to London to consult with London on its form. And third, despite a number of important discussions King had about other means to control Indian immigration, his trip to London did include conversations with Sir Edward Grey about Roosevelt's concerns. He was to do what he could to explain to the British the dilemmas of Japanese immigration on the west coast and make sure they understood what was at stake. As he put it to Laurier on February 4, after this second whirlwind trip to Washington,

> The United States is desirous that Japan should be made acquainted in a friendly way through her ally that the United States can have only one policy toeard [*sic*] her in the matter of her keeping her promises for restricting emigration, that the United States is not anxious to have any

trouble if it can be avoided, but that it rests with Japan to avoid it. The United States does not wish to convey this information through any formal communication. They wish nothing to be on record.[24]

King was working and travelling at a brutal pace. His trip home to Ottawa on February 3 was exhausting as it was delayed by a blizzard and the rather prudish King was forced to spend the evening surrounded by what he considered the shocking behaviour of his fellow travellers—a fun-loving theatre troop.

While King was away, Laurier and Grey had been discussing his activities. The governor general had been worried about how Bryce might feel about the Canadians behaving in such an irregular fashion, and Laurier had grave doubts about the president's sincerity since he had denied initiating King's mission. King perceived this skepticism and felt sure that Laurier doubted that the Americans had sent for "our little … Canada,"[25] but once King told Laurier about his meeting with the US ambassador, the prime minister felt sure that it was indeed true that King's trip was at Roosevelt's request, and Grey was reassured because Bryce had given his blessing to King's (and Canada's) actions.

Laurier and Roosevelt may each have been managing different sets of constraints, but they shared a distrust of alterations in the ethnic composition of North American cities. We can see this common ground clearly in Laurier's correspondence with Roosevelt, which seems to suggest that although the prime minister supported British policy, and was also motivated by local pressure to restrict Asian immigration, he was personally also wary of Asian immigrants, blaming their arrival for the tension that followed. We can also see that, for Laurier, the situation was largely, although not completely, a question of labour relations. It was Asian *labourers* that were the problem for Laurier (and King), not Asian *gentlemen*, as the prime minister noted in a letter to Roosevelt:

> Unfortunately we know, from experience, that wherever on this conti-
> nent, as well as in other lands, labourers of Asiatic races come in

competition with labourers of the Caucasian races, serious troubles immediately arise, and that for many years, and perhaps many generations, the only way of preventing those troubles is to restrict, to the narrowest limits possible, the contact of those races in the labour market of our continent.[26]

It follows, then, that since the Asian community was firmly established in BC and this "contact" between workers was going to continue, Laurier was anticipating more violence. When King advised Laurier on February 18 that he should have "a couple of secret service men" sent to Vancouver to investigate and keep Ottawa informed, he was told that this kind of work was already "going on."[27] The Canadian minister of the interior, Frank Oliver, had quietly dispatched an agent under an assumed name to British Columbia on October 14, 1907. The minister asked this agent, T.R.E. McInnes (sometimes known as W.E. McInnes), to "investigate the trouble in connection with Asiatic immigration into British Columbia, and, in particular, to ascertain whether the present Japanese, Hindoo, and Chinese influx into the province be spontaneous or induced by direct agencies."[28] McInnes's reports were read with great interest in Ottawa and London: his November assessment of the situation in BC emphasized the effects of labour migration from Hawaii, private companies bringing Japanese contract labour, the role of the Canadian Pacific Line, and Chinese Guild operations. His assessment of the danger that Japanese immigration posed to Canada's west coast communities provides a sense of why an agreement limiting Japanese immigration was so important to Canadian politicians of this time. McInnes saw the danger as primarily due to the arrival of Japanese migrants, rather than Chinese or Sikh workers. From his perspective, it was

... caused by the presence of Japanese in numbers that were never anticipated. The attitude of the people of the province toward the Japanese is one of fear—the whites are afraid of what the near future threatens from these people. The Japanese do not confine themselves to certain limited and subordinate occupations as do the Chinese and Hindoos.

The Japanese are competing with white merchants for white trade; they are competing with white artisans and clerks for work and employment in every line of activity.[29]

McInnes recognized in the potent combination of economic pressure, racial prejudices, and changing demographics the possibility of renewed violence. He combined these fears into fairly standard racialized descriptions of these immigrant groups and the "dangers" they posed to the community. In one instance, he assessed Sikh workers by using the Chinese and Japanese as a foil: "The Hindoos are not aggressive like the Japanese nor adaptive like the Chinese, they are physically unfit for the climates of British Columbia; they work in a very listless manner; they are handicapped by religious customs and prejudices ..."[30] According to McInnes, because these fears remained commonplace on the west coast, the Asiatic Exclusion League and its agenda remained a danger in BC. A February 1908 memo to the Canadian minister of the interior, sent during the Conference of Asiatic Exclusion Leagues of America in Seattle, reported that the league aimed to influence the "immigration policy of Mexico, the United States and Canada and [would] attempt to entangle Western Canadians with Americans in the expected struggle with Japan."[31] While with hindsight his claims of the AEL's growing influence seem alarmist, his ideas were taken seriously in both Ottawa and London. He was dismissive of the lowly origins of the officers of the league, but he suggested that "the mass of the people are giving a quiet support to it ..."[32] and that any solution to the question of Asian immigration would have to include discussions with the league. He even recommended that Lemieux meet with its members before departing for Tokyo to assure them that their concerns were taken into account in his negotiations.[33] McInnes's conclusion was that if such demands for increasing restrictions on Japanese immigration were not met, "premeditated riots [would] occur [that] winter after the white lumbermen return to town out of work; and there [would be] a danger that a slight incident, such as a street fight between a white and a Japanese, [might] at any time lead to a spontaneous outbreak."[34] This, according to McInnes, was the outcome that the exclusionist groups in the United States were hoping for.

In December 1907 the Japanese and Korean Exclusion League officially changed its name to the Asiatic Exclusion League in response to the public demand to work toward the exclusion of East Indian migrants as well. At the same meeting, a call went out for an international conference of exclusionists. This international meeting was held in Seattle on February 3, 1908. McInnes attended under a false name and reported back to the Department of the Interior on the attendees, the discussions, and the goals of the organization. He claimed that 163 members attended the convention, "from Utah, Colorado, Nevada, Idaho, and Montana, as well as from the three Coast States of California, Oregon, and Washington ... one from Mexico City and one from Vancouver."[35] Initially fourteen delegates from Vancouver, Victoria, and New Westminster planned to attend, but according to McInnes,

> ... influence was brought to bear through various channels upon the selected delegates, and the idea of co-operating with the Americans was presented in such a light that in the end there was not a single Canadian delegate who would attend ... except S.J. Gothard, of Vancouver, and he went at his own expense ...[36]

Although Gothard went alone, Vancouver remained important to the group's planning: Gothard was elected vice-president of the organization, the next meeting was scheduled to be held in Vancouver in March 1909, and McInnes was present for a conversation in which Gothard was asked "if Vancouver could not 'stir itself up again' about the time the American fleet reached San Francisco."[37] Gothard is reputed to have "volunteered to 'deliver a riot' ... on the second Monday in March" (March 9, 1908) if the AEL wished it to happen.[38] McInnes was not content to remain an observer. According to his own account, he was actively trying to thwart Gothard's plans and to discredit him among the members of the Victoria and Vancouver Asiatic Exclusion leagues.[39]

In response to McInnes's report, Frank Oliver recommended that the American fleet, which was on its way around the world to Japan, not be invited to land at the port of Vancouver and that the disallowance of BC's newly passed Natal Act, which attempted to control Asian immigration through language testing, be held over until after March 9 in order to avoid giving the AEL an excuse to resort to violence. By mid-February, McInnes had reported that the official link with the now more radical American wing of the league had been rejected by the Canadian branches. His claim to have been responsible for this step away from American influence may or may not be true, but it is clear that the importance of the exclusion leagues in BC was declining—certainly the March riot that Gothard had promised and the president of the San Francisco League had hoped for did not occur. This was probably more attributable to the fact that Ottawa seemed to have been taking action to restrict immigration from Japan and violence seemed an inappropriate response to political cooperation.

Nevertheless, February also brought another attempt by the legislature of BC to control its own immigration from Asia when it passed its own version of the Natal Act designed to provide legal means to refuse the entry of immigrants without adequate (European) language skills. King and others were fairly certain that, like earlier attempts, this one would be struck down by the Supreme Court of Canada as ultra vires—beyond the jurisdiction of provincial legislation. And so, while there was no concern that the provincial law would remain on the books, the federal government was required to explain it to Britain and the United States as well as to mop up any difficulties that arose as BC tried to implement the policy in the meantime.[40] Governor General Grey telegraphed the Colonial Office on February 9, promising to protect any Japanese in BC in the interim: "... my Government will, as formerly, disallow act with least possible delay, and in the meantime will take all necessary legal proceedings to protect Japanese subjects from effects of it."[41] (Under the British North America Act, Canada's constitution, the dominion government, and indeed the imperial government in London could disallow—render null and void—any provincial act.) A number of Japanese were arrested under this new legislation and convicted by a BC magistrate before disallowance occurred. These actions, according to the governor general, were evidence of a conscious strategy on the part of the BC government. At the federal level, it was hoped that if the courts could overturn the convictions before the disallowance, the BC legislature would be prevented from trying to pass a similar bill again. The Canadian government therefore held off on disallowance and argued, successfully, that the convictions were invalid because they conflicted with Canada's existing treaty agreement with Japan.[42] Grey was very anxious that the strategy be communicated to the Japanese government so as to avoid the impression that the Canadians were ignoring their treaty responsibilities. While the colonial secretary, Lord Elgin, was pleased at the success of this effort, the problem of Chinese, and particularly British Indian, subjects remained. They were still vulnerable under the terms of the provincial Natal Act and could be deported.[43]

Though Japanese immigration to Canada and the United States was definitely on the agenda for King's trip to London, the Canadian government's stated purpose in sending King was to get British input on the brand new continuous journey regulation intended to avoid future outbreaks of anti-Asian violence by controlling both Japanese and Indian immigration to Canada. While Chinese immigration had been largely controlled by the head tax, and Japanese immigration by the Hayashi-Lemieux Agreement, it was generally acknowledged that in light of negative Canadian attitudes toward any kind of Asian immigration, a rise in South Asian migration to the region could be destablilizing. In April 1908, in response to a meeting of South Asian immigrants in Vancouver on March 22, McInnes filed a report to Ottawa specifically on "Hindoo" (South Asian) immigration, which was dutifully sent by cablegram to Lord Morley, the secretary of state for India, and passed on to the Colonial and Foreign offices.

This meeting had, according to McInnes, been organized by an employee of the American Immigration Office, Taracknath Das. According to the dossier compiled by the Indian government, Das had been engaging in political activity since his student days in Calcutta, even participating in the establishment of a revolutionary society during a nationalist uprising in Bengal between 1905 and 1906.[44] McInnes described him as a "Hindu nationalist agitator" who "extract[ed] tribute from other Hindus here"[45] and published nationalist articles in the *Press Hindusthan* that McInnes felt were aimed at a Canadian audience rather than the immigrant community. According to McInnes, they were "for whites to read ... to create the impression among Canadians that there will be serious danger to the Empire if Hindus are shut out of Canada as they are shut out of Australia. It seeks to make the Government hesitate in any policy of exclusion or even restriction by threat of revolt in India."[46]

This call for exclusion was exactly what many had in mind as the number of Sikh immigrants was perceived to be growing. In part, the Vancouver riots were an expression of fear of the possibility that the Sikhs driven from Bellingham by Fowler and his associates would settle in BC. Local politicians communicated to Ottawa these fears of future, unscheduled arrivals. Laurier certainly took this and the more general fear of increased numbers arriving from abroad into account as he strategized how to balance the demands of empire with local politics. In the governor general's correspondence with Laurier and the Colonial Office, we see how the desire to reduce fears of Indian immigration to BC was transmitted to London in November 1907: "In view of the anticipated outbreak at Vancouver on the arrival of the next steamer importing Hindus Sir Wilfrid Laurier desires to give people of B.C. an assurance that the inflows of Hindus will be regulated."[47]

But how could British subjects be restricted in their movement throughout the Empire? In 1907 Canada was one site in a broader global struggle between supporters of various kinds of Indian independence on the one hand and British imperial rule on the other. Those seeking independence, or at least attempting to discredit a variety of British policies toward the subcontinent, saw the Dominion of Canada as a place where legal attempts to place controls on the movement of Indian "natives"[48] within the Empire might be challenged. And so, when Canada sought ways to limit the movement of "Hindoos" into British Columbia through its continuous journey regulation, Laurier, King, and others believed that London should be informed directly. Therefore, Laurier was not merely seeking an excuse that could explain King's visit to the Foreign Office, although it clearly had strategic value.[49] He reminded King that, "Were you in England and a question were asked in the House as to why you were there, if it were known that you had gone in connection with work for the United States there would be serious trouble. This whole matter will have to be kept very secret and confidential."[50]

The matter was so confidential, in fact, that Laurier declined to send his response to Roosevelt's letter in the post, preferring to send messenger King personally back to the White House on the February 22 afternoon train. The travel was starting to take a toll on King's (and his secretary's) health. He was not sleeping well and was suffering from back trouble when he woke on the twenty-fifth to meet with the president and his staff. Whether it was due to experience or irritation, this time King was less inclined to give Roosevelt the benefit of the doubt. Laurier, King, and Grey had all been disappointed by the way the president had misrepresented to American advantage the chain of events leading to King's mission to London. King had felt it smacked of "sharp practice" and Laurier had seen it as "a smart Yankee trick."[51] This time King arrived at the White House on his guard and viewing his treatment with a critical eye.

Roosevelt made him wait in an adjoining room and proceeded to dictate letters and meet with visitors within earshot of King, who found his "free and easy manner ... undignified, and in matters of state, really improper."[52] Eventually Roosevelt did meet with King and Root, and reaffirmed the same message he wished to communicate to the British: that he would continue to treat the Japanese with politeness, but that if they failed to live up to their agreements on immigration, he would be willing to use force. This done and other officials met, King returned to Canada, arriving in Toronto on the twenty-sixth, where he visited with his parents and proceeded on to Ottawa on the twenty-seventh.

While in Ottawa, King met regularly with Laurier and Grey. He updated Laurier on the twenty-seventh about his latest conversations with Roosevelt and his plans for the upcoming trip to London while the prime minister dined casually on a very light lunch of two boiled eggs, bread, butter, and tea. For his part, Laurier was pleased because events had made the cover story of Indian immigration all the more plausible. The *Monteagle*, a Canadian Pacific ship, was about to arrive in Vancouver the next day, carrying British Indian subjects whom Canada was preparing to deport. Thus, when King finally got his opportunity to travel to London in March 1908 he was ostensibly and credibly "on [a] mission to England to confer with the British authorities on the subject of immigration to Canada from the Orient and immigration from India in particular."[53] The order-in-council appointing King, which he drafted himself,[54] publicized the problem in the following way:

> That notwithstanding the regulations for the restriction of immigration from the Orient, certain classes of immigrants, in particular British East Indians, are being induced to come to Canada under circumstances which may necessitate refusal of their admission to our shores;
>
> That experience [had] shown that immigrants of this class, having been accustomed to the conditions of a tropical climate, are wholly unsuited to this country, and that their inability to readily adapt themselves to surroundings so entirely different inevitably brings upon them much suffering and privation; also, that were such immigration allowed to reach any considerable dimension, it would result in a serious disturbance to industrial and economic conditions in portions of the Dominion, and especially in the Province of British Columbia ...[55]

The document further stated that since the movement of Indian subjects involved Empire interests, it was felt that King should consult with the British government. Indeed,

> the whole subject of Oriental immigration is one of the first concern to Canada, and affecting, as it does, the relations of the Dominion with foreign Powers, and the relations of our people with fellow British subjects in India, involves consideration of the highest importance, not only in Canada, but to the British Empire as a whole.[56]

This was not just diplomatic frippery. King recognized that the action of the Canadian Pacific Line in bringing Indian workers to Vancouver was potentially disruptive, and he was equally uneasy about the treatment of South Asian immigrants by the Canadian government in 1908 once they had arrived. In February he had managed to bring Laurier around to the idea of paying Chinese victims of the riots for their losses, but the two men still diverged on the issue of the British Indian subjects on the *Monteagle*, whom Canada had turned back. King protested to Laurier that he "felt humiliated as a British subject, to witness the kind of treatment which these men had had to endure, that in sending them back to India, they had not been given a flat deck to lie upon, but were stowed away along the ship's sides and its interior encasements, that it could not do other than help to provoke the strongest resentment."[57] He was therefore highly motivated to find a way to ensure that there would be no further misunderstandings about the policy regarding the immigration of Indian subjects to the dominion, and thus no further embarrassment to the Canadian government as it sought ways to close the nation's doors to Indian migrants. And so, armed with a public and a private agenda, King prepared to leave for London. He had been there before and had a circle of friends waiting for his visit, but this time he was a man on a mission. The importance of it pleased him.

FIVE

The Mission to London

It might be tempting to think of King's trip to London as a "trip abroad," but in a significant sense it was more akin to a trip from the provinces to one's own capital. Not only was London the cultural, economic, and political metropolis to Canada's hinterland, but there was a Liberal, and thus likely sympathetic, government in power under Prime Minister Henry Campbell-Bannerman. His cabinet included the coincidentally Canadian-born colonial secretary, Lord Elgin (who was assisted by his undersecretary, Winston Churchill); John Morley, the secretary of state for India (who was about to become Lord Morley upon Campbell-Bannerman's resignation due to ill health); and Sir Edward Grey in the Foreign Office. These men were influential, powerful, and in high demand. There would usually be no reason for them to give privileged access to a young civil servant from abroad, except that this particular civil servant was Canadian and therefore their responsibility, a Liberal and therefore ideologically familiar, and in possession of strong letters of introduction from Earl Grey, which indicated King was a gentleman of promise. Having been to London previously, in October 1899, King had many personal connections in London society and was fairly familiar with the city and its social scene. As a Canadian civil servant, he was very knowledgeable (if at a distance) about the department of the British government that managed the dominions' affairs—the Colonial Office, as well as those managing Britain's relations with Asia—the Foreign and India offices. When King sailed from Saint John, New Brunswick, on the *Empress of Ireland* on March 6, he was carrying letters of introduction to Lord Strathcona, the Canadian high commissioner to Great Britain (and not coincidentally one of Canada's richest men), Lord Elgin, Morley, and, as Roosevelt had hoped, Sir Edward Grey. The Colonial Office had prepared in advance for King's visit, informing the Foreign Office of his arrival and anticipating joint meetings that Grey, as the senior minister, was invited to attend.

King landed at Liverpool on Saturday, March 14, and after a brief scrum with English reporters, made his way to London. King's first stop was a visit required both by protocol and common sense with Canada's high commissioner. King met with Lord Strathcona on Monday afternoon, informing him of his mission and the government's position on immigration, and outlining the departments with which he would be consulting over the course of his four-week visit. Strathcona made King feel at home, asking after his father and complaining about his rheumatism. However, there was still business to be conducted and Strathcona took King to task for having spoken with reporters in Liverpool. Even if he had been misquoted, the Canadian representative had inadvertently reinforced an already pernicious perception of British Columbia as dangerous and the Canadian economy in a depression. In the future, King had best remember "it was better to say nothing."[1] After this somewhat rocky start, King rose to the challenge set by his first mission to London and was later praised by all of the officials with whom he met for his competence, his intelligence, and his commitment to the work. In order to understand why this was so, it is best to examine in turn each of the two areas in which he was working—North American relationships with Japan and the movement of British subjects from India throughout the Empire. First on the agenda was the growing conflict between Roosevelt and the Japanese.

Having paid his respects to Lord Strathcona, King made his first visit to the Foreign Office. The Foreign Office building was designed to impress upon visitors the vast power of the British Empire. In the 1860s, when this Italianate building designed by architect George Gilbert Scott was being built, Canada was still hammering out the articles of Confederation. No wonder then that King, like other state visitors, was expected to feel awed by the power of empire as he was shown up the State Stair to an elaborate hall at the heart of this building. While the *Britannia* mural that currently decorates the space had yet to be painted, King would have passed under the elaborate gold-leaf ceiling and past pieces from the FO's collection of marble sculpture. At the top of the stairs, King was shown into a waiting room by a junior officer, where he waited briefly before being taken into Sir Edward Grey's rooms.

Grey was standing beside a rack of files as King entered the large office. King was favourably impressed by Grey's youthfulness (he was about to turn forty-six) and refinement as he shook the young Canadian's hand, asked him to take off his heavy coat, and offered him a seat in a leather armchair opposite his own place on the office couch. Grey had been a political prodigy. He was elected to Parliament at the age of twenty-three and had risen quickly to the cabinet. He was a moderate Liberal imperialist as he supported policies that led to the consolidation of the Empire as a political strategy rather than as an ideological end. He supported the overseas colonies but insisted on Britain's right to make policy despite the colonies' reservations. He supported the British navy and the Anglo-Japanese Alliance, and yet he also sought improved relations with the United States.[2] He was therefore sympathetic to King's mission, but he was not likely to sacrifice Britain's relationship with Japan because the whites in Canada's west coast communities feared Asian immigrants. After covering the niceties of his trip and delivering Laurier's greetings, King launched into an account of the meetings with Roosevelt. While Grey may have found it unusual that Roosevelt had used King in this way, he was not surprised at the message Roosevelt had wanted to send. This was not the first time Grey had received word from the US president; indeed, he seemed amused and laughed as he mentioned that their mutual friend Arthur Lee had passed on several notes to this effect already.

Arthur Hamilton Lee was a well-travelled Englishman who had served as a military attaché to the British embassy in Washington. He had married a rich American heiress and, according to King, was "an extremely pleasant and agreeable man" who lived in "a very beautiful house."[3] He had been a British military attaché with Roosevelt and the US army in Cuba during the Spanish-American War, and the two were good friends. The president therefore trusted Lee with three long confidential letters that he was to pass on to Grey via King while he was in London, despite the fact that Lee was a Conservative MP and therefore a member of the official opposition. This was highly unusual and distressed King, who was very careful in these matters. As the head of state, Roosevelt should have been dealing with senior members in the Liberal government rather than entrusting sensitive diplomatic information to the opposition. Nevertheless, Roosevelt trusted Lee more than the rather academic and elderly US ambassador, James Bryce. King therefore put him off for a time so that he could avoid breaching protocol or having to explicitly decline the request.

Once King had made his official visits to the high commissioner and the Foreign Office, Lee finally got his chance to speak with King on Monday, March 30. According to Lee, the letters contained a full account of the United States' position on Japanese immigration: that it was necessary to restrict the numbers coming to both the United States and Canada. He assured King that despite German attempts to divide England and the United States, England would never side with Japan over the other English-speaking power. Having learned his lesson in Washington about saying too much, King chose this time to share very little: "In my conversation with Lee I was careful to give him nothing that he could report to the President, other than that there appeared to be but one view as to the rights of the peoples of the North American continent in keeping out Orientals, if they so choose."[4] Presumably King passed on these entreaties to Sir Edward Grey and, in an April 1908 memorandum summarizing King's attempts to communicate the American position to the FO, Grey described Roosevelt's "initiative" on this matter as "so pressing as to be a little embarrassing."[5]

King and Sir Edward had great personal respect for each other, and King felt honoured at this first meeting to have an opportunity to share his thoughts freely with the foreign secretary. The two men sat talking for an hour in Grey's office until a messenger announced that the American ambassador, Whitelaw Reid, was waiting outside. It seems King had arrived on a day designated for Grey's meetings with ambassadors and this amused the foreign secretary. He quipped that it was appropriate since King was acting as the American ambassador on this matter. The earnest King was a bit nervous about the direction the conversation was taking and returned to protocol concerns and the importance he placed on meeting with Lord Elgin before he visited the American embassy. As King was putting on his coat to leave, Grey pointed out the primary difference between the United States and Great Britain on the question of the Japanese in North America: "Where I think the President is mistaken is in believing that the Japanese have any desire to get their peoples on to the American continent, or have any desire to be involved in any struggle with the United States. They are interested in getting their people into Korea and Manchuria."[6] King politely disagreed with the idea that the Japanese were not interested in North America as "both Japan and the United States had visions of empire, that they were each a little jealous of the British empire, had seen the way in which it had grown up, and that in regard to the Pacific they would like to play the roll [sic] that

Great Britain had during the past century on the Atlantic."[7] King tried to make it clear to Grey that Roosevelt (and King) believed strongly "that the Japanese intended to colonize on the Pacific slope of America and Canada" and that "there might be war within a very short time." Grey was of another mind on this. He felt war was unlikely in the near future since naval technology was not yet able to support the movement of a battle fleet the distance required in a way that would allow it to arrive "in fit condition for fighting."[8]

Grey was not alone in this opinion. In another meeting it became clear to King that while Winston Churchill was also no fan of the Japanese, he did not fear an imminent war. He distrusted the Japanese intensely and saw no possibility of Great Britain ever siding with them over the United States. He was equally convinced that war was not possible between the two Pacific powers because Japan was not ready for a battle that would inevitably have to be fought "in the middle of the Pacific" and indeed "did not want war."[9] King took the colonial undersecretary's opinion to heart as he was struck by Churchill's intelligence, "his quickness of perception and his undoubted ability."[10] While Churchill may have been correct in his assessment of the possibility of war, King's primary concern remained what he considered intentional Japanese colonization of Canada's Pacific coast through immigration. He was concerned about the influence of contractors who encouraged emigration from Japan despite the agreements undertaken by the Japanese government. He even went so far as to say that he had come to believe that not only was direct immigration from Japan occurring but that it was doing so "with the knowledge and connivance of the Japanese Government."[11] He may have been mistaken in this assessment, given that Japanese attention was focused on Manchuria and Korea rather than North America. In any case, Lemieux would not have agreed with this as an official position as it flew in the face of the stand taken by the Japanese in negotiating the Gentlemen's Agreement. However, if it turned out to be true, difficulties between Japan and Canada could continue, ultimately leading to Canada's abrogation of the 1894 Commercial Treaty, possible closer connections between BC and the Pacific Northwest states, and any number of diplomatic difficulties between Britain and Japan.

On March 19, after sitting for an official photograph commissioned by the publisher Elliott & Fry and taking breakfast with his secretary and travelling companion, Francis Giddens, at the restaurant attached to their lodgings, King set out on his first call to the Colonial Office. There, before his meeting with Permanent Undersecretary Sir Francis Hopwood on the question of Indian migration, he briefly met with Sir Charles Lucas, an assistant undersecretary and head of the Dominion Department while his superior was engaged. The two men had met previously and had an easy rapport. King found Sir Charles to be, as before, "genial, affable and courteous,"[12] perhaps in part because he had been very complimentary (flattery was very effective with King) and felt Canada was "fortunate" to have King working on its behalf at the Colonial Office. Lucas was encouraged that Laurier had decided that Canada would pay the Chinese for their losses and was very supportive of King's decision to call on the Chinese ambassador while he was in London.[13] In the short gap between King's arrival and his meeting with Hopwood, the two men began a discussion of King's American mission to London. Lucas had obviously read the confidential correspondence describing King's conversations with Roosevelt and appeared sympathetic to the president's fears about both the implications of the Anglo-Japanese treaty for relations with Canada's west in the event of conflict between Japan and the United States and the difficulties of diplomacy with the Japanese in general.

After his meeting with Hopwood on the Indian matter, which we will examine in more detail below, King accepted a lunch invitation from Alfred Lyttelton, the former secretary of state for the colonies, along with a number of other parties interested in dominion affairs. King also accepted a last-minute invitation from the American ambassador, Whitelaw Reid, who was heading to France the next day for a few weeks and did not wish to miss King's visit. King called at Reid's palatial rented home in Park Lane, Dorchester House, at about five o'clock and was greeted warmly by the ambassador. As Reid pointed out to his Canadian visitor, the house had a Canadian connection: Lady Grey (the former Alice Holford), wife of the governor general, had been born there in 1877. Since 1905 Reid had made it his London home. Guests would have been in no doubt as to the nationality of their host as they were greeted coming and going by busts of Benjamin Franklin and George Washington on either side of the door. During their one-hour meeting, the two men discussed a variety of topics but concentrated on the "oriental question." Reid had received word from Washington about the subject of King's visit but seemed to be less concerned than his president about Japan's "political designs" in North America.[14] King wondered if adopting this attitude was some sort of ploy on Reid's part to draw him into unknown waters on the question. Reid had taken a relatively conciliatory stand and, unlike Root and Roosevelt, had adopted the British position that Japanese emigration was a private affair and the country's lack of funds would prevent them from seeking war with the United States.

Revelling in the attention and respect granted to him as a representative of Canada, King was excited when he arrived at the Foreign Office on March 26 for his scheduled meeting with Sir Edward. Grey ordered tea and the two men sat together at a round table, their tea and their documents spread out before them. They began with the Japanese question. Grey had been mulling over King's previous comments about Japanese colonial designs on the west coast, and he wanted to make sure Canada understood what good allies the Japanese had been during the recent hostilities with Russia. From his perspective, they had removed the Russian threat to British possessions in India and, further, they had not pressed their Anglo allies to act against European powers such as France, which had broken the rules of neutrality, when action would have proved to be embarrassing for Great Britain. This calm in the face of American fears of war with Japan made an impression on King. He had a great deal of respect for the foreign secretary and confided in his diary that night that he saw him "more than ever as a man of very sane and calm judgment, of great reserve power and very alert."[15] Perhaps the Americans had been overstating the danger posed by the Japanese after all.

During their meeting, Grey had told King about a reception being held at the Hyde Park Hotel by the Japanese ambassador. Grey seemed amused by the idea and King made a point of dropping by at 11 P.M. He arrived as a Japanese play was ending and as the refreshments were being served. Among the guests, who were largely officials of one kind or another, was His Excellency, Lord Li, the Chinese ambassador to Britain. King noted that he arrived "in Chinese garb," that he "seemed a very happy and agreeable sort of person," and that his father (or perhaps actually his grandfather), Li Hung Chang (Li Hongzhang, d. 1901), was "reputed to be the wealthiest man in the world" during his lifetime.[16] Not only had Li Hung Chang been wealthy, he had been China's leading statesman in the 1890s and had gained extensive experience negotiating with the British. All of London society with any interest in Canada had been alerted to King's visit, and as a result King had a number of such opportunities to socialize with Japanese and Chinese diplomats. After luncheon with the Mintos on March 24, King called at the Japanese embassy. Count Jutarō Komura, the highly regarded Japanese ambassador, politely sat with King on a sofa and listened to his account of the purpose of his mission to London, his hopes for finding a diplomatic solution to the rising levels of Indian immigration to Canada, and his apology for the "unfortunate disturbances" in Vancouver during the summer. Komura felt that the Canadian government had acted "in a splendid manner" in response to the riots, and he and the other Japanese diplomats had been very impressed with Mr. Lemieux during his time in Tokyo. Indeed, he found Lemieux to be "a fine gentleman."[17] The two men exchanged pleasantries about their mutual friend Nossé and then Komura personally walked King to the embassy door and thanked him for his call.

The Japan desk at the Foreign Office was overflowing with materials on Japanese immigration to North America in March 1908. The combination of the departure of the American Great White Fleet, rumours of coming war between the United States and Japan, Roosevelt's immigration initiatives, and King's visits to Washington and London meant that there was much to discuss in London. Canada's relationship to the United States, Great Britain, and Japan was challenged by Roosevelt's decision to send his fleet across the Pacific and around the world between December 1907 and February 1909. This rather provocative move was a response to Roosevelt's fear of war with Japan. He wanted the Japanese government to understand that although he would be fair and just in his dealings with the country and its citizens, he and the US navy were prepared for war in the Pacific should it come. Canada's response to the possibility of the fleet scheduling a visit in Canadian waters was very much defined by the clash between local political demands and Empire interests. While its relationship with Great Britain and the 1902 Anglo-Japanese alliance suggested that the US fleet should not be welcomed in Vancouver, local supporters of close ties with the United States and of its policy in the Pacific demanded an official invitation.

In March 1908 the minister of the interior's agent in Vancouver, T.R.E. McInnes, cautioned strongly against inviting the American fleet to Vancouver because of the fear that it would encourage British Columbians to look to the US navy for their defence and because of the influence such an action would have on the legitimacy of the Vancouver Asiatic Exclusion League.[18] These fears were reflected in Mackenzie King's diary entry at the same time, about the potential for shifting loyalties if the people of British Columbia began to look to the American fleet for protection rather than the British Royal Navy: "It would be most unfortunate if the people of Br. Columbia began to feel any sort of dependence on the American fleet ... I saw real danger ahead if any troubles were to break out in B.C, or any trouble between Japan & U.S."[19] In this connection, the governor general suggested that he might make a point of being in BC when the US navy reached the west coast to reinforce BC's links with the Empire.

London and Ottawa were therefore keeping a close watch on the local activities of the AEL and its possible ties with the activities of exclusionists in San Francisco and elsewhere. Eventually an invitation to the fleet was issued on behalf of the Canadian government. After speaking with Laurier about his change of heart, King concluded that, "Sir W. said that the Br. Gov't had been considering the matter since & had changed their mind. What happened is, I imagine that the B.C. pressure has become stronger, and our Gov't. have yielded to the extent of extending an invitation, the invitation of other countries having changed the situation."[20] In the end, the problem was moot since the American fleet never entered Canadian waters. Having put in at Bellingham and a few other Washington ports for inspection in May, it turned, returned to San Francisco, and sailed on to Honolulu and around the globe. Canada could therefore put off making any official declaration of the shift quietly occurring in its national defence strategy away from the British and toward the American navy—a declaration that King would eventually have to make with Franklin Delano Roosevelt, Theodore Roosevelt's cousin, in 1940.

The second policy matter King was engaged in revolved around the question of limiting the movement of Indian-born subjects of the Crown. Canada had just passed the continuous journey regulation in January and aimed to use it to deport many of the nine hundred immigrants who had just arrived on the *Monteagle*. This was Sir Francis Hopwood's priority when the two men met on March 19 in preparation for King's first meeting at the India Office. After the usual pleasantries, Hopwood mentioned that he planned to attend Quebec's tercentenary celebration with the Prince of Wales in July. King was quick to point out how important the British fleet's visit to Canada would be in light of the pending arrival of the American navy at Pacific ports. Hopwood deflected this concern and expressed his more serious worries about the treatment under Canadian immigration law of British subjects travelling from India. King had his response ready. First, Canada understood that Indians were different from other Asian migrants—that they were subjects of the king. However, he argued, the Canadian government's decision to deport the migrants on the *Monteagle* was based on a "humanitarian" principle. They had been returned to India for their own good since, according to King, "Canada was wholly unsuited to the East Indians, that they were only subjected to unnecessary privation or suffering in going there." Although the patronizing tone and racial biases this reasoning reveals make us wince today, Hopwood felt this was a defensible argument and that it was "the line for [King] to take in talking with the Indian Office." He drove the point home: "Impress that on them very strongly."[21]

King had an appointment scheduled at the India Office the next day. There, while he waited for Morley, King examined the portraits of former "important men" and governors of India. He was excited to find the likeness of Colin Mackenzie, who had served as an officer in India at the turn of the nineteenth century. King felt there was an "ancestral connection" there since he had a memory of Colin Mackenzie "being a relation" of his grandfather, the rebel William Lyon Mackenzie.[22] Morley called King in, examined his letters of recommendation from the governor general and Laurier, and was particularly pleased to see a letter from journalist Goldwin Smith, who had sent a personal note of introduction on King's behalf. The two spoke warmly of visits with their mutual friend and then got down to business. Morley thought that the problem of managing Indian immigration to Canada was one that would take more than King's short visit to solve. He was unconvinced by the argument that the continuous journey regulation was aimed at the Japanese coming from Hawaii. Rather, he thought that Canada had been unfair to British Indian subjects since it was not possible to sail directly from India to Canada. He protested to King, "But you have been much more generous with the Japanese than you have with our own people, the Indians."[23] From the perspective of the India Office, the Indian question needed to be separated from the larger question of managing Asian immigration to Canada. He explained the current situation from the India Office's perspective, saying that "while there was not any open sedition [in India], still matters were very serious and on one or two occasions it had been necessary to take pretty stern measures."[24] He was concerned that trouble was arising and that the problems with managing that part of the Empire were only just beginning. He and his government could therefore not afford to have British subjects from India being treated more harshly than the Japanese in Canada. It was then that King chimed in with the argument he and Laurier had devised and that had been endorsed by the Colonial Office: British Indians were not suited to Canada. It was an act of kindness to send them home, rather than have them suffer in the northern climate. According to this argument, the Indian migrants had been brought to Canada by greedy steamship companies and a handful of unscrupulous Indian businessmen already in British Columbia, most notably a mill owner and Brahmin named Davichand. The idea that Indian immigrants might choose to come to Canada for their own reasons was wholly discounted. Even so, the Canadian government was attempting to slow down immigration from India by negotiating with the Canadian Pacific Railway (CPR)—owner of the Canadian Pacific Line—hoping that its ships would cease providing direct passage from Calcutta to Vancouver. This would not prevent individuals from chartering ships independently of the Canadian Pacific, as the Japanese had from Hawaii, but it pleased Laurier to make some progress, and King considered it a first step.

The question was of Empire interest, argued King, as he and Morley stood over a map of North America, because of the close ties between the US Pacific Northwest and the west coast of Canada. If the president and other Americans encouraged the idea of common interest between the two regions and went so far as to foster the idea that the US navy offered a better defence of the region against Japan than the Royal Navy did, then Canada's links with Britain would be seriously strained, even broken, in the event of war. Vancouver, as King pointed out, was three thousand miles from Ottawa. It was then Morley's turn to use a map to make a point. After King had argued that Indian migrants were unsuited to the cold, Morley pointed to a map of India and showed King that parts of the Punjab district were cold and immigrants from these areas would have been used to a cold climate. Morley was entirely correct about the climate and, unbeknownst to the two men, correct about the origins of most of the Indian migrants to Canada. That King did not know this and chose rather to argue that he "did not think those who had come to our country had had much experience with cold before" shows that his impressions were guided by widely held prejudices rather than study. King hedged on this question of climate, adding that "at any rate if they had they were not used to the class of rough work or labour to which alone they could help to gain remunerative employment in British Columbia."[25] Whether he was taking this position out of ignorance or expedience is unclear since he did not reflect on this aspect of his approach in his diary. King did make it clear that Canada did not want to enact any legislation that would make the control over the movement of British subjects explicit and recommended instead that permits be required for travel and that they be issued by the Indian government. King then re-emphasized Laurier's desire to avoid embarrassing the Empire in this regard, as well as the importance of the question of Asian immigration for Laurier's political prospects in a coming election. King, being the political animal that he was, explained that

> [Laurier] had taken his political life in his hands in dealing with this problem ... it was very questionable if Sir Wilfrid would be able, should he go to the country this fall, to get any support out of the Province of British Columbia. That this had become the one question west of the mountains, and that it was being played upon in other parts of the

Dominion ... that the problem was now assuming such proportions
that it was getting quite beyond Sir Wilfrid's control.[26]

Whether Morley understood the domestic political details or not, King
was charmed by him and Morley now had a sense of the importance of
the question for the dominion government. Morley agreed to communicate with the Indian government within days and to begin to devise
a set of Indian-managed controls that would reduce the flow of Indian
workers to BC without forcing the Canadians to legislate against them
directly.

Over the weekend, King was swept up in a whirlwind of driving in
the country, discussing politics late into the night, attending the theatre,
dropping by "at homes," and dining with London society, but King was
quick to respond to Morley's request for another meeting on Monday
and returned to the India Office just after noon. He found Morley at his
desk in the midst of drafting a lengthy cable to the viceroy of India, Lord
Minto, on the question of Indian immigration to Canada, on which he
wanted King's input. The two men read through the lengthy memo
line by line, and King clarified Canada's position on each point. They
had spent quite a bit of time working through the document when a
junior staff member rushed in with a cable that had just been received
from Vancouver, noting, "a mass meeting of Indians had been held to
protest against the general deportation of their numbers, that they were
all subjects of the King, and that their brother subjects in India would
resent the indifference of the British authorities were they to fail in giving
protection to them ..."[27] King diminished the importance of the meeting
by guessing at the numbers, minimizing them, and suggesting—without
any real knowledge of the situation—that the meeting would have been
attended merely by those facing deportation because they had entered
the country illegally. Once the tension over the cable from Vancouver
had been put aside in this way, the two men finished editing the cable to
Lord Minto.

The Mintos were very much on King's mind after his Monday visit with Morley. He had known the family personally while they were in Canada during Lord Minto's time as governor general, from 1898 to 1904. After dictating an account of his meeting at the India Office to Giddens, King made his way to the Mintos' London home at Great Cumberland Place. King was struck by the look of strain on the faces of Lady Minto and her eldest daughter, noting, "All the Mintos have changed a little since they were in Canada. Lady Minto shows a little the effect of the strain of life in India, and Lady Ruby has lost some of her colour and vivacity." In contrast to her sister, the younger daughter seemed to be better suited to life in India, as King, who often noted the presence of pretty, eligible young women in his diary, remarked, "Lady Violet has grown, and is, I think, the prettiest girl I have seen in England."[28] Over lunch with the family, Lady Minto confirmed King's suspicions about the difficulties of life as the viceregal family in India, and spoke rather wistfully of the joys and friendships that were part of their former life in Canada. These are the kinds of links that the realities of empire administration created at this level of society. Individuals were moved between the dominions, India, and home, building personal and political connections in each of these places and spreading first-hand knowledge (from a particular standpoint) of local conditions and the challenges faced across the globe wherever the British flag flew.

Although King had come to London prepared with a humanitarian argument against Indian migration to Canada, the possible mechanisms by which workers could be prevented from leaving India in the first place were unclear to both the Canadians and the Colonial Office. The answer to this part of the equation was provided at a chance luncheon on March 26 with Richard Jebb, a journalist whose book *Studies in Colonial Nationalism* (1905) King greatly admired. Jebb's paper on Asian immigration provided King with the legal solution the Canadians had been looking for. Jebb pointed out that the 1883 Indian Emigration Act made it "illegal for Indian labour to leave the country without the consent of the Government" and further included "schedules naming the countries to which such labour would be allowed to go." By insisting that it stay off such a list, the Government of Canada could ensure that Indian workers were prohibited from leaving India to immigrate to Canadian ports.[29] This is an excellent example of the kind of exchange of empire knowledge that was passed to King during this visit, even in the informal setting of a lunch with friends.

Eventually Lord Elgin, the colonial secretary himself, was available to meet with King. On Friday, April 3, King met with both Elgin and Morley at the Colonial Office building. It was King's impression when he arrived that the British were intending to allow Canada to legislate as it saw fit, as long as Britain could avoid passing any new legislation in India. It had been King's hope that the Indian law that Jebb had brought to his attention earlier might be used, but at least one lawyer in the CO suggested that it applied only to indentured workers and would require new legislation to make it applicable to regular contract workers. In fact, the 1883 law was intended to mitigate the terrible conditions in which Indian workers had been living in the Natal province of South Africa. Since 1860 large numbers of Indians had been brought to Natal as indentured workers in the sugar industry. Around the turn of the century, a sizable community of Indian workers was living in the province and requests were made to allow for the free entry of Indian traders (the passenger Indians) to serve it. They quickly became a source of unwelcome competition to the white business community, and grumbling turned to legislation limiting where Indians could live and work in the province. The South African approach to Indian migration was therefore a great source of tension in India, and the Indian government was not interested in fanning the flames with new legislation controlling emigration to another part of the Empire. However, the British administration was sympathetic to the Canadian goals.

This complex response was confirmed when King met Morley in Lord Elgin's office. The three men shook hands and Elgin offered his visitors chairs, Morley on the right and King in front of Elgin's desk. Morley then handed King a cable from India in response to the memorandum that the two had worked on together, saying, "You have read the cable which I sent to India, and I think you should also see the reply. Perhaps you would like to read it. You might read it aloud."[30] The cable and the meeting confirmed that for domestic political reasons India could not pass new legislation restricting emigration; that there were no objections to Canada passing legislation to restrict Indian immigration; that official India did not resent the continuous journey regulation; that the Indian government had been informed by Morley that "it was not to the interests of the Indians themselves to come to Canada"; that Canada should, if possible, avoid legislating against British subjects; that negotiations with India were impossible; that the preference was for Laurier to negotiate with the Canadian Pacific Line; and that he had complete freedom within the negotiations to act as he saw fit.[31] King asked for and received permission to discuss the cable with Laurier. He also received permission to announce in the House that he had received word from the viceroy of India that India had issued warnings to potential migrants about the difficulties and dangers associated with emigration to Canada. King then pressed Morley further on the Indian Emigration Act and its applicability to Canada. The three men agreed that it was originally written to control the movement of indentured labourers and that Canada had never been involved in this kind of labour market. However, King asked Morley to reconsider the definition, and he promised to have his legal advisor look at the legislation to see if it could be extended to include contract labour and therefore apply to the Canadian case. By five o'clock King had his answer. Morley's secretary sent a note to his rooms expressing the legal opinion obtained from the India Office "that emigration in the sense of a native of India leaving the country under an agreement of hire to work in Canada was unlawful, and could not be made lawful without the Canadian Government first passing laws for the protection of Indians in Canada which would be subsequently approved by the Indian Government."[32] It was now clear. Canada could use the existing legislation as one of the elements of its strategy.

This was good news for Laurier and King since it solved the contract labour side of the equation. The combination of negotiating with the Canadian Pacific Line and relying on Indian legislation allowed the government to avoid the appearance of having solved the immigration question through an arrangement with a private corporation, or the complications that would arise if one part of the Empire legislated against the movement of another part's citizens. Laurier and King wanted to avoid giving Indian nationalist critics "real grievance against the Empire in not being free to pass to and fro."[33] Even so, the problem of migration by private charter remained a concern for Laurier, and therefore for King. Elgin and Morley dismissed the idea that a private concern would be able to "get Indians" on such a ship, but King pressed the point: "... one could not say whether it might not suit the purpose of the United States to have a shipload of Indians dumped down in Vancouver at the time the American fleet reached San Francisco, with a view to creating a disturbance at Vancouver."[34] King was therefore more concerned with possible American actions than the organized resistance that Indian nationalists might present.

When King was at liberty in London, he accepted invitations from the list of his impressive social connections. Recommended as an honorary member to the National Liberal Club and supported in membership to the Reform Club by Sir Francis Hopwood, most of his time was spent in a whirl of private dinners, lunches, theatre performances, and visits to country estates. Among his patronesses was Lady Aberdeen.[35] As the wife of the former governor general to Canada, she had involved herself in good works, and King was pleased to have been invited to spend time with such a serious and high-minded lady. She, in turn, was delighted to receive King in London and bantered freely with him about mutual friends, the Quebec tercentenary, and the copy of

Top: A view of untroubled Chinatown in Vancouver on a regular workday. (LAC/Department of Mines and Resources/PA-009561)

Above: In the wake of the riots, King was suspicious of boarding-house keepers, thinking that they were implicated in the increase of Japanese immigrants to BC. This is the Yogora Sekine Boarding House, Powell Street, Vancouver. (LAC/W.L. Mackenzie King Fonds/PA-027582)

This is the barbershop of Gentaro Nakagawa on Powell Street, which seems to have escaped damage during the violence. There was significantly more damage in the adjacent Chinese neighbourhood. (LAC/W.L. Mackenzie King Fonds/PA-093268)

King was deeply involved in the investigation into Japanese riot damage. He made several tours of the Japanese quarter and collected photos documenting the losses, such as the damage to this store, V. Kawasaki & Bros., at 202 Westminster Avenue, Vancouver. (LAC/W.L. Mackenzie King Fonds/C-023556)

Left: Rodolphe Lemieux, MP (Gaspé, PQ) and postmaster general, was King's boss at the Department of Labour in 1907. He was tapped by Laurier to conduct delicate negotiations in Tokyo over Japanese immigration to Canada. The result was the Canadian Gentlemen's Agreement of 1907. This is an official portrait taken in 1909. (LAC/Topley Series E/PA-027986)

Below: Because of the letters Lemieux wrote home to his father-in-law, the lieutenant-governor of Quebec, Sir Louis-Amable Jetté, we know that Lemieux and his wife, Berthe Jetté, took advantage of their time in Japan and enjoyed visits to a number of picturesque sites. Here we see them travelling in a group. (LAC/Photographies et album de photographies/e010965384)

Top: As King relied on Sir John Jordan in China he also relied heavily on the influ-ence of Great Britain's minister in Tokyo Sir Claude Maxwell MacDonald. Here we see MacDonald in an unofficial portrait taken in Tokyo by Gertrude Bell in 1903. (The Gertrude Bell Archive, Newcastle University, RTW_vol_5_064, 1903)

Above: King is wearing his brand-new pith helmet taking in some of the sights of India. He preferred the landscapes to the poverty. Here he turns away from the fig-ure seated in the garden behind him to look out over a vista. (LAC/W.L. Mackenzie King Fonds/C-071511)

Top: No expense was spared in entertaining King and the other guests of the maharaja of Benares in January 1909. King and Giddens were taken on a boat trip down the Ganges and treated to a ride on an elephant. Here we see King preparing for his ride. (LAC/W.L. Mackenzie King Fonds/C-055527)

Above: King (and possibly Giddens) during his elephant ride near Benares. (LAC/W.L. Mackenzie King Fonds/C-055517)

Top: During his travels, King remarked often about the ways that work was organized. This was not surprising since, as a long-standing member of the Department of Labour, he was genuinely fascinated by differences in labour practices. In India, he noted the ways women participated in the workforce. Here he is with a group of Indian women. One can only imagine what the bachelor King thought about this encounter. (LAC/W.L. Mackenzie King Fonds/C-071510)

Above: King was unimpressed by Hindu sacred spaces. He much preferred Japanese temple architecture to the chaos of roaming animals and sensual sculptures that were prominent in India. Nevertheless, he took a moment to feed some monkeys during one of his visits. (LAC/W.L. Mackenzie King Fonds/C-055522)

Top: Canada was part of the British Empire in 1909, and King relied heavily on the influence of British officials in Asia, particularly Sir John Jordan, envoy extraordinary and minister plenipotentiary to China for the United Kingdom. This photo shows Jordan and a number of other notables (including King standing beside Jordan, fourth from the left) during a visit to the Forbidden City, where Jordan presented letters of credence to the new prince regent. (LAC/W.L. Mackenzie King Fonds/C-055525)

Above: The initial purpose of King's trip around the world in 1908–9 was to attend the meetings of the International Opium Commission in Shanghai in February 1909. Here we see a group photo documenting that leg of his journey. (LAC/W.L. Mackenzie King Fonds/C-055526)

Right: An early official portrait of the young, ambitious W.L. Mackenzie King, as the deputy minister of Labour in 1905. (LAC/Topley Studio Fonds/ PA-027975)

Left: All of King's hard work paid off. Soon after his return to Canada, he not only sat for the first time as an elected member of Parliament, but he was given the job he had sought for so long—minister of Labour. Here is the official portrait taken of King as a member of the cabinet in 1910. (LAC/Topley Series C/PA-025971)

his department's publication, the *Labour Gazette*, which she received monthly. On March 18 King was invited by Lady Pauncefote, the widow of Lord Julian Pauncefote, the former British ambassador to the United States, for an afternoon political event at her home at Chesham Place. There King attended a lecture and debate on tariff reform by political activist Violet Brooke-Hunt. It was a complicated question for Canadians since their agricultural and manufacturing industries had varied needs, and support for Britain or the United States on tariff questions was often accompanied by a strong ideological preference. In Britain, Joseph Chamberlain had resigned from his position as colonial secretary in 1903 over the question, and it remained of interest to those supporting the idea of imperial preference as a way to protect British manufactured goods from foreign imports by creating an Empire-wide trading bloc that could compete with rising industrial powers such as the United States and Germany.

Brooke-Hunt made a strong impression on King. She was an impressive public speaker, author, and social worker. When King met her, she was an acknowledged force in the education of working men and boys and in the tariff reform movement. Having served as a nurse in South Africa during the Boer War, she had returned to London to continue her work and would die prematurely two years later: thirty-nine years old, exhausted and suffering from infective enteritis.[36] In King's reaction to his encounter with Brooke-Hunt, we see that his confidence in himself, his political skills, and his country's place in the world was growing. King found that he needed to become a defender of the dominions and their perspective. On this occasion, King gave Brooke-Hunt his respectful attention, agreed with her on several points, and disagreed on others. The rather prudish King did, however, feel uncomfortable about women debating emotional political questions. He also felt compelled to mention to her later "that imperialists could do a certain service by using some other word than colonies and suggested the use of the words Dominions or Possessions-beyond-the-Seas."[37]

King was careful about the way he spoke in public about Canadian policy while abroad. One of his informal meetings was with journalist and future Conservative colonial secretary Leo Amery. Amery was born in India to an English father and a mother who was a Hungarian Jew. He was educated at Harrow and Oxford and had reported from South Africa for the *Times* during the Boer War. Amery expressed interest in acquiring written memoranda on Canada's position on immigration in order to pass them on to "prime movers in other parts of the Empire," including Smuts and Jamieson in South Africa.[38] King balked at the request, citing the need to consult with Laurier, who might not wish to make policy for other parts of the Empire. According to King, Amery strongly disagreed and argued "that Canada should help to lead the way in these things; that as an imperial citizen everyone should be prepared to speak out and let the other parts of the Empire know their views."[39] King was not convinced. He was suspicious of men using back channels to accomplish policy goals when their party was not in power, and he was nervous about overstepping his authority: "I would regard it as quite wrong for me to come out with any opinion in a matter of policy affecting the Dominion. The Prime Minister and the Cabinet are the ones who should do this, and they should do it through the recognized channels of the Colonial and Foreign Office, etc." Furthermore, he recognized fully that these Empire-affecting questions were firmly rooted in local conditions, "that nothing in the long run could more easily defeat any kind of cohesion than for one part of the Empire to be dictating or advocating in the land of another a policy on matters which were a party issue."[40]

On April 3 King attended a dinner at the Compatriots Club that left a lasting mark on his feelings about the Empire, dominion government, self-rule, and the British. The Compatriots was a dinner club established by Leo Amery in support of Joseph Chamberlain's tariff reform agenda, aimed at protecting British industry in 1903. The group met monthly and discussed politics in a congenial atmosphere. A series of papers given by Amery; Lord Alfred Milner, the highly influential British colonial administrator in South Africa (and a noted Conservative); and other socially prominent figures had a powerful effect on King's Canadian sensibilities. He was left with no doubt about the existence of a British ruling class that felt it had not only the right, but the obligation, to rule abroad. King could see evidence in the words and actions of the evening's speakers that years of public service in India, Egypt, and South Africa had left the British with the unshakable conviction that they could rule better than those they ruled. In fact, Milner represented the epitome of this kind of thinking, having been a mentor to many successful British administrators in what came to be known as "Milner's Kindergarten."[41] King noted he was left with the impression that "England is divided into two classes—those who believe that men are born to rule, others who believe that people can govern themselves."[42] On the one hand, he was impressed by the power of the Empire and the ability of these men to run it; on the other, he could see that Canada's interests might get lost in a system run by men from the Empire's political centre.

If Lord Milner had not risen to comment at just the moment King was most inclined to speak on the question of Canada loosening her ties to Empire, he thought he might have leapt to his feet despite any reticence toward putting himself forward on policy. Instead, he confided to his journal both his deep concerns about the state of imperialism and the benefits of empire membership:

> I would have pointed out, looking at Canada's action simply in the light of empire building, had Canada negotiated her own treaties a larger portion of the North American continent would probably have been British territory today; that Mr. Lemieux in returning from Japan, had told the Canadian people that it was the assistance of the British Ambassador and the British connection which had enabled [us] to negotiate terms with that country, which had helped to solve the Japanese immigration problem so far as Canada was concerned. That he had pointed out that while the United States, a larger country, was still waiting for this situation, we, because of the British connection, had been able to begin later in the day and end more quickly ...[43]

Further, he felt he might have defended Laurier's stand on imperial preference at the last colonial conference, the importance of recognizing each dominion's right to self-governance, and his hope that he might have an opportunity to clarify Canada's policy and attitude in the councils of empire. Most significantly perhaps, King would take these impressions home and use them to frame his own political life. "Tonight's gathering has impressed me more than any event in connection with this present trip. I feel that it has added a permanent something to such political capital as I may possess."[44]

His strong belief in the importance of self-government within the Empire led King to distinguish between the interests of the governments of India and Britain in his report to Laurier on the Indian Emigration Act. However, when the two met on Saturday to go over the draft, Morley was dissatisfied by this characterization, saying, "But I should not say the Governments of India and England, there is no Government in India ... India is a Crown Colony; she is not in the same position as Canada."[45] After making this change to the text, double-checking that King had understood the India Office's legal opinion on the Indian Emigration Act, and ensuring the letter to Laurier would be "strictly confidential," Morley warmly sent him on his way with the sentiments "It has given me such pleasure to meet you. When you return please give my warm personal regards to Sir Wilfrid, whom I know and had the pleasure of meeting at Montreal, and also my kindest regards to Mr. Goldwin Smith ... Especially to Mr. Smith."[46] King in a moment of flattery thanked Morley for his biography of Liberal British prime minister William Gladstone, saying that it "had influenced [him] more than any book." And when, in turn, Morley wished that King "might have known" Gladstone, King heaped more praise on the senior statesman, enthusing, "I feel it a great privilege and honour to have met and known you, sir."[47]

This fawning over Gladstone and his biographer was probably to be expected since King's visit was occurring in the shadow of a series of heart attacks that had struck the current Liberal British prime minister,

Sir Henry Campbell-Bannerman. The Liberals were feeling vulner-
able and King wanted to convey his personal and party sympathies.
Campbell-Bannerman resigned while King was in London, on April 3.
His decision was announced in the press on April 7, and on April 12
British newspapers carried an announcement of the new cabinet formed
by Herbert Henry Asquith. King noted that there had been a shift toward
youth and "the progressive element" in the party. Reformer David Lloyd
George was chancellor of the exchequer; thirty-four-year-old Winston
Churchill was president of the board of trade; Robert Crewe-Milnes, the
Earl of Crewe, replaced Elgin as the secretary of state for the colonies;
and thirty-three-year-old A.T. Herbert, Lord Lucas, with whom King
had been discussing the United States and Japan, and whom he found so
genial, was the new parliamentary undersecretary of war.[48]

On April 13 King prepared to leave London. He paid his bills, sent
off a last-minute note to Morley, and gave some thought to all that he
had accomplished. While he had yet to visit the Chinese ambassador and
inform him of the Canadian government's decision to pay the Chinese for
damages caused during the Vancouver riots, he was otherwise pleased
with all he had done:

> With this except[ion], which is a mater [*sic*] of course which has come
> up only incidentally, I have been able to carry out, so far as I can see
> at present, the purpose of this mission, as satisfactory, perhaps, as
> the nature and circumstances of the case will permit. It is true that
> I have spent much more time in social engagements than might have
> appeared desirable, but after all they have been something more than
> merely social. The main consideration is that no part of the mission
> has suffered in consequence, unless it be perhaps that the report may
> be a little later in being prepared—that can be done elsewhere, while
> the other cannot.[49]

King had reason to be proud. He had not only impressed the most senior
officials in all three of the departments with whom he had dealings but
had used his social connections to gather information about India that

led directly to his discovery that the Indian Emigration Act could be used to solve Laurier's primary problem concerning Indian immigration without creating diplomatic waves. Finally, he had passed on Roosevelt's concerns about Japan and Japanese immigration to the United States to London without causing any obvious embarrassment for any of the parties involved. The young statesman had proven to be competent and trustworthy and could rest easy on the night train to Edinburgh. He spent a day visiting friends there and then headed back south to Liverpool.

During his trip home, King had time to consider what he had learned in London. First, he felt encouraged to continue working on ways to limit Asian immigration to Canada. He found London sympathetic to Canada's desire to limit the movement of Indians from Asia—so much so that he felt secure in making two important conclusions: "[t]hat Canada should desire to restrict immigration from the Orient is regarded as natural, that Canada should remain a white man's country is believed to be not only desirable for economic and social reasons, but highly necessary on political and national grounds."[50] Canada was a self-governing dominion, and as such was entitled to make its own immigration policy according to the desires of its residents, assuming of course that it did so within the framework set by Empire alliances and treaty agreements. King was convinced that his being sent by Canada to confer was seen in London as a great sign of Canada's willingness to participate in the broader Empire project and the greater "good of the whole."[51] King was sure that, as a result of these discussions, Canada's situation had been clarified and the strategy that had been devised would "serve to prevent such immigration from India as may not be desirable in the interests either of the natives of that country or of the people of this country."[52] He could report with confidence to Laurier that Canada's position on Indian immigration and the particular methods chosen to restrict it, including the continuous journey regulation, were acceptable to the British government and its administration in India. The Canadian government planned to use a combination of negative publicity in India, pressure on the steamship lines, existing

Indian legislation, and the continuous journey regulation to restrict the number of Indian immigrants without openly, officially excluding fellow subjects of the Empire.

In the area of publicity, the plan was to

> offset by warnings which the Government of India has issued, whereby the natives have become informed of the risks involved in emigration to Canada, and of the actual conditions in so far as it is desirable that such should be known to persons about to sever their connection with one country for the purpose of taking up residence in another.[53]

Migrants were to be told that unemployment was much higher than they imagined and that the harsh climate of Canada made life on society's margins even more difficult. The Canadian Pacific Line and any other shipping lines engaging Indian passengers for travel to Canada were to "have been given to understand that the Governments of Great Britain and Canada, and the authorities in India do not view with favour any action on their part calculated to foster further emigration from India to Canada,"[54] and further, that

> The power of the steamship companies to ignore the wishes of the Governments has been rendered largely inoperative by the application to emigration from India of the regulation of the Dominion Government, prohibiting the landing in Canada of immigrants who come to this country otherwise than by a continuous journey from the country of which they are natives or citizens, and upon through tickets purchased in that country.[55]

In addition, Canada sought to use the Indian Emigration Act of 1883, designed to protect workers from indentured servitude, to prevent the movement of workers to British Columbia. Under this legislation, no worker could be "induced to leave India" under a contract without official notification from the authorities of the receiving nation including certification that "provisions as the Governor-General in Council thinks sufficient for the protection of emigrants to that country during their residence therein."[56] Canada could therefore claim that the importation of contract labour from India to Canada was "not lawful" unless the Canadian government passed a law explicitly allowing for it. In order to control the other classes of Indian migrants—those not wishing to come under labour contracts—Canada added the continuous journey regulation and maintained the requirement that each immigrant carry $25.00 at landing. This combination of formal and informal controls was, according to King, "a dovetailing ... of Great Britain's well-known policy in the protection of the native races of India, and Canada's policy in the matter of immigration." It maintained the fig leaf of an idea that it was a humanitarian act, protecting migrants, and as King noted, most important, "The liberty of British subjects in India [was] safeguarded rather than curtailed ... the necessity of enacting legislation either in India or in Canada which might appear to reflect on fellow British subjects in another part of the Empire has been wholly avoided."[57]

King also left Britain with a strong sense of himself as an American within the powerful British system. After all, Roosevelt had seen him this way. Roosevelt had tried to use him to manage the United States' relationship with Great Britain and to foster Anglo-American under-standing. The Canadian could represent distinctly North American interests from within the British Empire administration, and he could get time to sit down with the major players in British international affairs by virtue of Canada's position within the system. The fact that the dominion's interests might be significantly different from those in the Empire's political centre was also reinforced by his time spent in the salons of London society. This in no way took away from the enjoy-ment King felt at being part of that society. His final report on this trip to London glowed with regard for these men and their willingness to listen to the Canadian case in a "sympathetic matter" and to discuss the question with great "frankness and fullness."[58] King's admiration only grew during his subsequent visits.

SIX

The Indispensable Man

By the end of April 1908 King was home in Ottawa. There he returned to his routine of serious reading, walks with friends and political acquaintances, personal and political correspondence, and any social engagements that might bring him into contact with the interesting and the powerful—dinner at his club, dinner parties hosted by Ottawa's establishment, and the bustle of life in the corridors of the House of Commons. He was gratified that people seemed happy to see him home and that he had been missed. His secretary, Giddens, had even named the son that his wife bore while he and King were away Rodolphe Mackenzie in honour of Lemieux and his patron. King was not one to remain idle for long, so he wasted no time getting back to work. There was much that needed to be reported to Lemieux and Laurier. He had personal greetings to pass on to Laurier from Lady Aberdeen and the Mintos, and reports to write up from the commissions regarding Japanese and Chinese damages. Further, a new area of interest had come to his attention during the investigation into the Chinese community in Vancouver: the opium trade. Canadians had long feared gambling and opium use—the vices of Chinatown. However, as long as they stayed within the Chinese community, they remained a problem that could be attributed to the weaknesses of the Chinese rather than a larger social ill. This perspective changed when King went to Vancouver.

On March 25, 1908, while King was in London, the Canadian government officially established a Royal Commission to assess Chinese damages, a step that King had recommended to the prime minister from the beginning. Having been appointed commissioner, King travelled west as soon as he returned home and arrived in Vancouver on May 24, where he met Tung Cheng-Ling, the Chinese imperial attaché, who had been sent from London to observe the proceedings along with the Chinese consuls at San Francisco and Portland, Owyang King and Moy Bok Hin. Tung found that 122 Chinese shops had been damaged in the disturbances. In light of the huge number of claims that would be going before King as the Royal Commissioner, the Chinese community had hired a Vancouver lawyer by the name of Arthur McEvoy to represent them in official matters relating to the damages.[1]

The commission was carried out in much the same way as the investigation into Japanese damages. King had advertised the commission and solicited the help of Chinese community representatives, the Chinese Board of Trade, and their lawyers to put together a list of affected individuals and their claims, which were then forwarded to the Chinese ambassador in London, to the Colonial Office, and back to the Canadian government. He sat daily (except on Sunday, May 31) at Pender Hall from May 26 to June 5, listening to the cases of 227 claimants, using an interpreter when necessary. In total, once some additional, last-minute claims had been added to the list, the Chinese claims amounted to approximately twenty-six thousand dollars, including those losses incurred from loss of business—a total that King considered "moderate" and "fair."[2] The Chinese also generally felt that

King had been just in his dealings, and there was a considerable amount of good feeling when the commission ended its business. In 1909, when the acting Chinese foreign minister, Liang Tun Yen, expressed an interest in visiting Canada, King spoke to him in some detail about his experience in Vancouver that May:

> I told him about the dinner we had had in Vancouver after settling the claims of the Chinese and of the British flag being crossed at the end of the room with that of China, of the forty members of the Chinese Board of Trade, having speeches on the British Empire and the Chinese Empire, and said that I wished very much he might have been present on that occasion. I told him of the wealth of Sam Kee and some of the Chinese residents there and mentioned that there were two Chinese daily newspapers in Vancouver. Mr. Liang seemed much surprised at this statement. He said he thought one paper ought to be enough, but I told him they had their parties there as well as elsewhere, at which he laughed.[3]

The opium question was brought to King's attention by Peter Hing, a member of the Anti-Opium League, an organization based in the Vancouver Chinese community that contacted King while he was on the west coast with a view to gaining his support for their work toward the elimination of the opium trade. While King had no official authority to look into this problem, as a private citizen and an ardent social reformer he felt it was his duty to examine the situation while he was on site. He was helped to see the international importance of the problem by the intervention of Chinese imperial attaché Tung Cheng-Ling, who spoke to him directly about opium and its misuse. Previously King had not been aware of the extent of the problem in Canada, but during the investigation of the Chinese claims he discovered requests by two opium factories for damages incurred during the riots. Each had submitted claims for six hundred dollars to cover losses sustained when their businesses were unable to operate for six days. King was "somewhat surprised at the presentation of claims for losses in such a business," but noted,

There does not appear, however, to be any existing legislation prohibiting the importation of crude opium, or its manufacture in Canada,
and the only restraint upon the manufacture of that article in the City
of Vancouver is the municipal regulation requiring the taking out of a
license and the payment therefor [*sic*] of a fee of $500 before the manu-
facture can be carried on within the city limits.[4]

After a tour of seven factories and a number of opium dens, he came to
see that it was a problem that had begun to involve the white population
(including women) of British Columbia's cities, and that the Canadian
government had been complicit in the trade through its collection of fees
and taxes from opium businesses and the lack of federal legislation to
control the sale of the substance.

King did not wish Canada to fall behind the United States or Great
Britain in this area and made some recommendations in his July 3 report
"[o]n the need for the suppression of the opium traffic in Canada." Most
important among these was the call to ban the importation, manufacture, and sale of opium, "except for medicinal purposes."[5] One week
later, Lemieux proposed exactly this action in the House, resolving
"that it is expedient to prohibit the importation, manufacture and sale
of opium for other than medicinal purposes."[6] Lemieux barely had time
to name the bill before it carried unanimously in the House. There was
no debate and really no presentation of the details at all. It was simply
agreed that Canada should act immediately to pass its first federal act
limiting narcotics. The Opium Act (1908), "An Act to prohibit the
importation, manufacture and sale of Opium for other than medicinal purposes" received assent on July 20, less than three weeks after
King submitted his report. Thus King was now known in international
circles as Canada's expert on opium, as well as Asian immigration. This
new expertise had arisen directly from his role as commissioner in the
various investigations into damages caused by the Vancouver riots and
into Asian immigration. The question of Asian immigration had given
him an unusually high profile for such a young civil servant, and now

Americans seeking to further the cause of opium control also had him to consult.

Periodically that spring King checked in with the prime minister and informed him of the conclusions of his various commission reports. On the morning of May 4, the subject was Indian immigration. This conversation reveals how important King's mission was to the formulation of the government approach that was adopted. When Laurier asked him what his most important conclusions were, King pointed to the "section on Canada's autonomy in matters of legis'n & line taken in regard to basis of arrangements." King wanted to emphasize Canada's right to control immigration, but to do so in the context of Empire. Laurier found the report "moderate and dignified" and asked King to have the minister of the interior craft an order-in-council based on the use of the existing Indian legislation "rendering liable to deportation persons coming without agreements to hire."[7]

Also up for discussion was the matter of King's own agenda: his transition into politics, his selection as a Liberal candidate, his election—taken for granted—in the general election assumed to be around the corner in the fall of 1908, and his emergence as a minister soon after. "Minister of labour" had a nice ring to it, and naturally King rehearsed it in his diary. Of course, Labour would have to become a free-standing department, separated from the postmaster general's department, and that would take some legislative fiddling. But the grand design of these events was now plain to King, and it was now his task to make sure Laurier shared his vision. When King brought the matter up with Laurier on August 29, the prime minister was hesitant because a dedicated Department of Labour would seem to require a "labour man" at its head. King, however, did not see his lack of experience in the area as an obstacle to his advancement and was convinced that he would appeal to the labour unions and their leaders. He confided this ambition quite directly in his diary, writing, "The industrial question is the one I have identified myself with, it is a world question & and increasingly important one, and as either member, deputy or Minister I will hold by it."[8]

By September 9 the prime minister had promised that the postmaster general's department would be separated and reorganized and that the announcement of a new Department of Labour would be made during the coming election. All this was in place even before King had officially begun his run for a seat in Parliament. While he was working on an inquiry on the labour conditions in cotton mills in Quebec, and before he had even officially announced his run for office, King received a letter from Robert Bacon, the US assistant secretary of state, inviting him to consider participating as a member of the British delegation at the International Opium Commission in Shanghai. This was part of the US strategy for managing Great Britain at the opium commission. King would be the "American" voice on the British delegation. He shared both the moral reform perspective and the west coast interests of the Americans, but he would occupy a privileged place within the powerful British delegation and would therefore have access to and influence over key decision makers. King was already considering the impact he could make during his 1909 trip to China in the fall of 1908, before it had been arranged officially. As he noted in his diary, he discussed his potential role with the governor general in September:

> He ... spoke to me of the anti-Opium business in B.C. wh. he said was a good piece of work, & sd. the revelations were most surprising. Spoke of the harm to young girls, etc. He told me he had been speaking to Sir W[ilfrid] about my being sent to China & had strongly urged it saying that it was in the interests of Canada as a nation to take part in international gatherings when the occasion came & that no one could be a better representative than myself. That I had come to be indispensable.[9]

Whether he had truly become indispensable or not, King had put himself at the centre of Canada's relationships with India, China, Great Britain, and the United States. The aftermath of the riots had been the making of King's political reputation and perhaps his career. It was a good time to run for office. To King's delight, after the Liberal Party smoothed the way for his candidacy, there was room for him to run near his childhood home in the riding of North Waterloo. King embraced the local campaign, the necessary stump speeches, patronage, and all that went with the task of seeking election. After five weeks on the hustings, King was elected MP for North Waterloo, Ontario, on October 26, 1908. The election went relatively smoothly for the Liberals, who won 133 of the 221 available seats. The party won a clear and convincing majority despite the anticipated setbacks in BC. King thus became a part of a new Liberal majority government—Laurier's last.

The process of appointing King as a delegate to the Shanghai opium commission was fairly cumbersome—as most international dealings were for Canada while it was still a British dominion. A series of communications were required between the United States State Department, the British embassy in Washington, the Foreign Office in London, the governor general, and the Canadian government. Eventually Laurier's cabinet passed an order-in-council agreeing to King's appointment by the British government to attend as Canada's representative. Even after all this transatlantic traffic had been completed, it was still not clear to King whether he would be able to go at all, having just been elected to Parliament. King expected that his brand new constituents and Laurier would insist on his remaining in Ottawa, where his political skills would benefit the party—and thus cost him "an exceptional opportunity."[10] The senior member of cabinet, Sir Richard Cartwright, seeing the humour in a time when the grandson of the rebel Mackenzie might represent Canada in London, quipped, "Better send Mackenzie and keep the King."[11] However, to King's surprise, the prime minister and his constituents were supportive of the idea. After a few second thoughts about what it might do to his chances in Parliament and his shot at a cabinet post, King agreed and prepared for an extraordinary trip. This mission would take him around the world via London, Port Said in

Egypt, and various points along the length of India, Ceylon (present-day Sri Lanka), China, and Japan. He would consult with dignitaries, intellectuals, activists, and politicians in each of these states, and he would represent his country as an officially elected representative for the first time. He had less than two weeks to get everything in order for his departure on December 14, 1908.

In King's mind, there were four important reasons for Canada to attend the commission in Shanghai, beyond his own professional interest. First, he felt that the social benefit in the control of opium was, in itself, worthwhile and that it "was well for Canada to identify herself with such a movement." Second, there was the benefit of Canada's being seen by other nations as having and defending its own interests. The commission would give Canada "an opportunity of being represented on an equal footing with other nations of the world. This would increase the status of Canada ... and would help to form precedents for like occasions of possibly more serious import." Third, there was the possibility of increasing trade with the Chinese market. This was what King called "the commercial reason." Such a trip "would afford an opportunity of seeing what could be done in the way of commerce between Canada and China; whether there were openings for our trading there ..."[12] Finally, King was most concerned, as always, with taking advantage of the opportunity to learn more about China, with a view to finding solutions to Canada's Asian immigration question. King called this the "international" argument for Canada's participation in the commission:

> The time had come when we must recognize that this continent was face to face with a serious problem, growing out of the relations with the Orient and the Pacific slope and the probable movement of Asiatic peoples; that in some form or another we would, sooner or later, have to face the question of how these peoples could be restricted from coming to this side; that some first-hand knowledge of conditions in the Orient was essential if we were not to be completely in the dark.[13]

While King felt an open discussion regarding Chinese immigration, like the one occurring on the suppression of the opium trade, was not advisable, he was convinced that his trip to attend the opium commission would provide exactly the kind of opportunity he needed "to quietly discuss the situation with the Chinese authorities and find out their feeling in the matter."[14] If, in the end, an agreement like the one Lemieux negotiated in Tokyo could be reached, then it could be announced to the Canadian people as an accomplished fact. The governor general was supportive of the government's decision to send King to China, and it was he who insisted (along with his military secretary, Sir John Hanbury-Williams, who had served in India and elsewhere in Asia) that King prepare for the discussions on opium with a trip to London and stops in India, where he would be introduced to the Empire perspective on the opium trade.[15]

King was sure a trip to India would be exciting and tried to enlist Earl Grey's support in his cause, though publicly he kept up the position that he would only serve at the prime minister's desire and would not press for it. King was encouraged when the governor general supported the idea of an official trip to both India and China, promising to press Laurier for a trip supported by an official secretary (Giddens, of course) and "money for entertaining." He also committed to arrange introductions to "the official people & leading native Indians" in order that King would be properly informed of the conditions in that part of the Empire. Grey and King shared an interest in these matters, as both were concerned "that troublous times [were] ahead in India and that we in Canada would do well to understand the whole Oriental situation. We can thank God we are part of an Empire or we would cease to be a country."[16] Such comments convey King's feelings about Great Britain, Canada, and Empire clearly. He believed most strongly that Canada owed its existence to its position as a British dominion and trusted that Canada could play a role in the management of the Empire. Individuals like him were important because Canada was important to Britain, and as such, these individuals needed to be fully aware of the larger context in which Canada was acting. And so eventually, despite Laurier's misgivings about sending away such a useful party man, the indispensable King was scheduled to go abroad and play his role in the councils of empire. In the privacy of his diary, he allowed himself to express his frustration with the prime minister and his limited view of the foreign policy implications of Asian immigration:

> For a great man he often seems to me to take a very narrow view, especially on matters of foreign policy & relations. He is surrounded by narrow men, which is perhaps a reason, but I really feel that he fears little from the Orient, & recognizes little or nothing in the way of Imperial obligation. This I think we must educate Canadians to realize. If we are to have the protection of the British flag, we must share in the obligations its protection affords.[17]

King left for London carrying letters from Laurier and the governor general for Prime Minister Asquith; the colonial secretary, Lord Crewe; the foreign secretary, Sir Edward Grey; the newly minted peer Lord Morley; the viceroy of India, Lord Minto; and the British minister at Peking, Sir John Jordan, to help him in his official capacity. There were some who had other ideas about what a trip like this could mean for the new member for Waterloo North. As Lady Laurier was seeing King off after a visit at the prime minister's residence, she told him that he "ought to get a wife on a trip like that." Sir Wilfrid even went so far as to suggest that "perhaps [King] might bring back some young lady from China."[18] As was now his habit when going abroad, King would have just his secretary, Francis Giddens, along for the voyage. Whether a young lady would accompany them on their return was for the future to tell. The two men left Ottawa on a snowy Monday, December 14, on the afternoon train for New York, where they spent two days in the usual whirl of social engagements before meeting the brand new *Lusitania* for the transatlantic crossing. The travellers woke late and, despite skipping breakfast, arrived just minutes before the ship's scheduled departure from the Cunard wharf. King's luck must have been good, as the ship happened to be delayed by an hour, and he and Giddens did not have to rush quite as much as they would have had to otherwise.

The *Lusitania* was a floating palace for first-class passengers such as King and Giddens. It had only recently come into service, in August 1907, and represented the state of the art in comfort and speed. As a member of Parliament, as well as an official delegate, King paid $150 for first-class passage in a Promenade Deck stateroom that included an outside view, hot and cold running water, a telephone, and electric light. While he did not have access to a private bathroom like those in the ensuite staterooms on the Boat Deck or in the Regal Suite down the corridor, he could hardly have complained about the conditions in which he was travelling. Passage in first class also afforded him the opportunity to socialize with members of British and American society. King noted particularly his chance to spend time with the new owner of the *Times*, Alfred Harmsworth, recently made Lord Northcliffe, who rose from obscurity to command a prominent and powerful publishing concern.

> Among the first persons whom I met on board were Lord and Lady Northcliffe. Lord Northcliffe invited me to share his table across the Atlantic. I had lunch with Lady Northcliffe and himself at the table in the upper dining saloon and dinner with them this evening in their suite. Among those at dinner tonight were Mr. Kennedy, editor of the weekly edition of the Times, Fred Cook, Canada Times correspondent, L.W. Crippen, Times correspondent, and Mr. Alfred Butes, Lord Northcliffe's secretary.[19]

This unexpected connection made onboard the *Lusitania* afforded King an opportunity in Britain that he had not anticipated. Northcliffe offered his home and the services of his secretary to King for his use while in London. King was grateful but knew he could never accept the invitation as Northcliffe was a supporter of the British Conservative Party and was therefore necessarily opposed to the current British government on whose behalf King was acting. He would, however, be a useful man to know. In the meantime, he and his entourage were very diverting company during the voyage. December 17, day two of the crossing, was King's thirty-fourth birthday. He had stayed up late into the night with Northcliffe and his party and was feeling the effects in the morning. He had a saltwater bath to soothe his aching head and afterward, since he was feeling sentimental about his dear mother, read a book she had sent with him, paying particular attention to the sections she had marked. He then dressed and went for breakfast and a walk on deck with Giddens and Fred Cook. Cook had given King a radiogram form that entitled the sender to an unlimited number of words, so King used it to send "Marconigrams" home to his mother and to Giddens's wife. He spent the evening taking a long walk on deck and having dinner with Northcliffe, discussing where they stood on the Anglo-Japanese Alliance and Japanese settlement in North America. Transatlantic travel seemed to suit King.

The *Lusitania* docked at Liverpool around eleven o'clock on the morning of December 22. Two messages from the Colonial Office were waiting for King at the dock, setting an appointment with Lord Morley for the twenty-third and another with Francis Hopwood, the permanent undersecretary of foreign affairs, for the twenty-fourth. In the meantime, Giddens and King boarded a train for London and travelled to their now-familiar home-away-from-home, the Queen Anne's Mansions near St. James's Park. When King had last visited London, he had been a civil servant acting at the request of his government. He had been well connected, well treated, scrupulously honourable, and successful in his mission. This time, he was a seasoned traveller, an experienced diplomat, and a member of Parliament carrying letters from the prime minister of Canada to his counterpart in London, the secretary of state for the colonies, and to Sir Edward Grey at the Foreign Office. He therefore had a much stronger sense of self-importance and of his mission as official business. When notice arrived that King was expected to meet first with Hopwood's junior officer at noon and then with Hopwood at twelve-thirty, he took it as a personal slight and as evidence of a wider disdain held by the British toward the dominions. Rather than agreeing to meet with the junior, King acknowledged receipt of the note and planned to arrive in time to meet with Hopwood directly at twelve-thirty. He sent Giddens to the Colonial Office at noon to inform the clerk of King's intentions. To be fair, it is not clear that this arrangement was intended as a slight toward the Canadians. The junior officer, Johnson, had wanted to discuss two subjects with King while Sir Francis was occupied in another meeting: King's upcoming negotiations with the Chinese regarding immigration controls and the debates around sending Indian workers to British Honduras rather than allowing them to remain in Canada. Johnson did get his meeting with King, all but cornering him in the waiting room at the Colonial Office, where King remained truculent: "I did not offer to discuss matters, but made it a point of only answering such questions as Mr. Johnson made, letting him see by the replies that I did not intend to discuss the situation with him, though I was very careful not to be impolite in any way."[20] Later when he discussed Johnson's actions with Lord Hopwood, King tried to maintain his status (as he imagined it) by emphasizing the importance of protocol in maintaining policy clarity. Canada, he asserted, wished to ensure that the Colonial Office was fully informed of the government's activities. However, to do this it was important, he argued, that Canadians understand what was official policy and what was the opinion of British individuals. Thus, it was crucial, King insisted, that private citizens (like Johnson) observe the proper forms, and

> if, after becoming acquainted with my mission there were any particular officers of any of the Departments with whom it was desired that I should speak, that I would feel only too glad to have the opportunity, but that I would wish to have the direction of the responsible head before undertaking an interview of the kind. I asked, for example,

what I was expected to know about Mr. Johnson's right to discuss the question of relations between China and Canada without having been so informed by a responsible head.[21]

Since Hopwood's meeting continued to run overtime, King was forced to go on to the India Office for his scheduled meeting with Morley. He would have to speak with Hopwood later in the day. King found a much more satisfactory situation waiting for him at the India Office. Morley shook his hand and expressed his pleasure at King's return to London. In December 1908 Morley was just turning seventy-one years old and King thought him well preserved: "He looks much younger, though his forehead is somewhat deeply furrowed when he raises his brows, and his eyes are set back deep in his head. His face is very thin, and being clean-shaven the features are sharply marked. He is not unlike Emerson in cast of countenance."[22] King was impressed by Morley's vitality and his idealism—his commitment to liberalism. As King put it, "He impresses me as one who is a great lover of liberty, a great believer in the rights of the people and in the people."[23] The two men shared a mutual love of liberalism and a desire to serve. Morley must have been charmed as well since he invited King to spend Christmas with him and his family at Flowermead at Wimbledon. A mollified King took his seat and explained that he was taking the opportunity afforded by his trip to China to stop in London and in India at the governor general's request and to communicate Laurier's desire "to show his sympathy and appreciation of the situation in India and secure an understanding between India and Canada which would be helpful to both."[24] From Morley's perspective at the India Office, the subject of controlling opium was much more complicated than it appeared to Canada since some of the larger semi-independent princely states in India relied on the income from the traffic of opium and would demand compensation if Britain cut off the trade. As he said to King, "It is well enough for people to say to help the Chinese, to do a particular thing, but we must see what this involves."[25]

It was Christmastime and Sir Edward Grey and the British prime minister were out of the city, so King dropped off Laurier's letters with his own calling card at Downing Street, paid a short call on Lord Strathcona, and then went to consult with Sir Francis Campbell, the Foreign Office's China expert. Campbell restated Britain's hope that Canada would help to promote good feelings and increased trade between China and the British Empire. To this end, he promised King the help of the British ambassador in Peking. Campbell recommended that King slip away from the commission in Shanghai to meet with Sir John Jordan in the capital. King also met with the principal clerk of the Colonial Office, George V. Fiddes. Linked with South Africa by having worked there under Lord Milner, in December 1908 Fiddes was also the Colonial Office's expert on the opium commission. Again, King was reminded about the potential loss of British income that would result from opium controls. Fiddes cited opium profits that amounted to "one-half the revenue of the Straits Settlement and one-quarter of the revenue of Hong Kong,"[26] and expressed concern that other states would try to score points against Great Britain by pushing for the regulation of opium markets when it was clear that Britain could not afford to take the same position.

As a representative of one of the dominions and therefore of direct interest to the British government, King was provided with a set of confidential documents to read on the long sea voyage ahead. Sir Edward Grey even took the time to explain the procedures followed in the Foreign Office so that King would fully understand the dispatches he was given to read. When the FO received letters, they were sent to each of the branch officers responsible for the item, and the branch officers' responses were collated into a response memorandum that was attached to the original letter. The package was then sent to the head of the branch, who noted on the memorandum if he agreed to the proposal and if he had any changes to suggest. It was then forwarded to the permanent undersecretary, who gave his opinion on the proposed action and on whether the minister should be consulted. At each level of consultation, the notes and draft responses were attached to the original, so that when Sir Edward received it he would have everything he needed to make a final decision. He could then sign the letter of response without having to take the time to draft it himself. This left him more time to do the important work of meeting with foreign dignitaries, ambassadors, and his counterparts from around the world. Having privileged access to this correspondence and the opportunity to study it at his leisure, King was convinced that despite the great cost and American fears, Britain would take the high road and would be willing to help China reduce the trade in opium:

> The correspondence leaves no room for doubt that the express intention of the British Government is to assist China in suppressing the opium evil, even at very great sacrifice to Britain. The point that it seems desirable to keep in the forefront is that if the opium traffic is really to be suppressed it will not be necessarily by the mere stopping of the export of opium from India, but by making such a stoppage contingent on a corresponding diminution in the area of poppy cultivation in China. To have it otherwise would be to give the Chinese opium producers a greater monopoly of the trade, which would inevitably lead to its increase within the borders of China, rather than its decrease. Here is an instance of [when] what may seem a selfish economic policy may serve to affect an ethical and humanitarian end.[27]

At the moment, however, it was Christmas and all but the most urgent work of the FO could wait. King had Christmas dinner at Flowermead, the home of Lord Morley. After being transported from Southfields station by Morley's carriage, King was met at the front door by a maid and taken to the drawing room, where Lady Morley graciously met him and escorted him down the hall to the family's impressive library where Lord Morley was waiting. Morley's writing table was near the fireplace and surrounded on three sides by floor-to-ceiling shelves of books. A photograph of Lord Rosebery, the former prime minister, sat as a Liberal icon on the library piano. Morley shook

King's hand and introduced him to the rest of the party: his nephew, his sister-in-law, and her husband. King's impression of Lady Morley was of a kind, sincere woman who truly loved her husband and kept a simple home without "ostentatious display." There had been rumours of "some romance" in their story, as when they met she had been married to a man who had gone insane years previously and been institutionalized. Given King's prudish outlook on life it is surprising that he was greatly impressed by this romantic aspect of Lord Morley's life. He had great respect for Morley's choice to live unmarried with his beloved for years, defying social convention, until her husband died and they were able to marry.[28]

The Morley dining room was overseen by other Liberal heroes. The images of John Stuart Mill and William Ewart Gladstone—the latter the subject of Morley's well-known biography—hung beside the mantel. Over dinner the group discussed topics such as the weather in Canada, Roosevelt's latest letter to the British and his hunting plans in Africa, the Russians' recent experiment in constitutional government, the Duma, "Canadian rivers, fruits, etc., railways in the United States, Christmas customs in England and elsewhere."[29] However, "after the ladies had withdrawn"[30] the men turned to the important questions of Empire politics: China and Japan. Eventually, Morley returned to his primary intention: to discuss the challenges facing Lord Minto in India and King's preparation for the opium commission. To this end, he laid out an itinerary for King's travels in India and a list of men with whom he wished King to meet in order for him to fully understand the role opium played in both Indian finances and culture. These included governor of Bombay Sir Sydenham Clarke and Lord Minto in Calcutta. Further, King noted,

> he would give me the names of one or two gentlemen to whom I could speak freely as to conditions in India; they would give me a true statement of conditions, not to be given, for example, to the people of North Waterloo, but which I might impart privately to Sir Wilfrid. I would

be informed on the real conditions, so that the Government of Canada might be made fully aware of them.[31]

These conditions, according to Morley, included the usual arguments about Indian finances, as well as the claim being made by some that opium was eaten by Sikhs and others the same way the English smoked tobacco, without falling into the extremes one had come to expect from those addicted to smoking opium. Lord Morley was happy to help King and was pleased at his appointment to the commission, appreciating his position as neither British, American, nor Indian in his connection to the question. When King asked for recommendations of books on the topic, Morley readily agreed, and as the two left the dining room Morley took King by the arm and told him personally how pleased he was to have King take the task on. At 3 A.M., the always-diligent King finished dictating his impressions of the evening to Giddens. When summing up these views in his diary, he noted,

> What impressed me most in the views expressed tonight, and in the manner of their expression, was the admission of a very critical and dangerous state of affairs in India—the immensity of the problem; his feeling that there was no certainty or safety about the situation no matter what was done; that the numbers of educated native people were much greater than we are accustomed to think, but that differences between them make it impossible for them to be united in a common patriotism. I believe Lord Morley shares the view commonly attributed to Goldwin Smith,—that the ultimate destiny of the American continent is one and united, not divided as at present, and that the yellow peril is the greatest of all questions. Lord Morley applied to it the term "terrible."[32]

The next day, on Boxing Day, King travelled to Sutton Place, Lord Northcliffe's country home, where he spent the evening with several of his fellow passengers from the transatlantic crossing on the *Lusitania*. After most of the other guests had left, King and Giddens stayed on, enjoying a late-night talk with the newspaper baron and two of his *Times* correspondents. King enjoyed the visit immensely and left Sutton Place the next day armed with more letters of introduction, including one referring him to the well-connected *Times* correspondent in China, George Ernest Morrison. The Christmas holidays provided King with another eagerly awaited opportunity. He was keen to accept Sir Edward Grey's invitation to spend time at Fallodon, the eighteenth-century family seat in Northumberland. Despite his anticipation of the day, King almost missed his ten o'clock train from London to York on Monday morning, December 28. It was a rush, but he made it and settled in with the day's newspapers for the ride north. Since King was never one to waste time, he spent his few hours on a stopover in York admiring Yorkminster Cathedral.

The snow had been falling heavily at Fallodon, so Grey had a path from his house to the station shovelled. He arrived in person at the station on foot wearing a peaked cap and dressed in a golfing suit and gaiters. He walked King home through the snowy woods, leading the way like Good King Wenceslas for his page. Grey's first wife, Dorothy, had died in 1906, so Fallodon was a quiet, slightly melancholy widower's home. Once the two men had made their way from the station and settled themselves in the library, King explained the purpose of his mission to China—that in addition to participating in the opium commission, he sought on behalf of the Canadian government to investigate the possibility of a settlement regarding immigration like the one achieved by Lemieux in Japan. This would allow Canada to eliminate the head tax and have a more consistent immigration policy. Grey was supportive and thought the Chinese would be willing to discuss any proposal that allowed for "saving their face."[33] Sir Edward reminded King that Sir John Jordan was at his disposal and stressed how able and modest a man he was: "He has come to know the Chinese very well and he understands them and they have great confidence in him."[34] Grey encouraged King to take Jordan's advice as to whether the Chinese would be either willing to consider such a proposal or carry it out. If he should think it would be impossible, King was instructed to do nothing rather than press the idea. Britain's trade with China was extensive and if China should boycott trade with England, the cost would be unsustainable. When King raised Roosevelt's idea of racial zones and a conference to divide the world along racial lines, Sir Edward was unenthusiastic. Rather he asked King to limit his activity to a Chinese agreement to curb immigration levels. If that became possible, then he would consider including Japan in some sort of larger plan.

When King inquired whether the constitutional limits on Canada's foreign policy could include a treaty arrangement between China and Canada, Grey was supportive.

> Sir Edward replied that we could have a treaty if we wished, he saw no reason why should we desire a treaty, a Canadian might not be appointed to negotiate the treaty; that the correct point of view was to come back always to the King as the one by whom the appointment was made. If it were a Canadian the King would appoint him as a British subject, and there was no reason why it should be an Englishman.[35]

Sir Edward was also open to King's musings about having permanent Canadian representation at Britain's embassies in the United States, India, China, and Japan.

> I pointed out, for example, that had we had an attaché to the embassy in Japan, we might have taken up all the Japanese difficulty at the time it commenced, and possibly have stopped the whole question before it assumed the alarming proportions it did; that there was a possibility of a repetition of the kind in China; if we had a representative there we would be in a position to have the Chinese government notified in a minute through the ambassador by our representative there on conditions affecting Canada.[36]

While Grey was supportive of the idea in principle, he feared that other dominions might also desire this kind of representation in Britain's embassies and that it "might develop a cumbersome machinery."[37] He was willing to consider Canada differently as "Canada was really a nation." "Besides," said Sir Edward, "having a man like Sir Wilfrid Laurier at the head of your country makes many of these things possible which would otherwise be difficult. Sir Wilfrid has an understanding of large questions and an appreciation of responsibilities, and is not likely to become involved in any way in anything which would be complicated."[38]

Grey's confidence in Canada also extended to the country's relationship with the United States. Grey saw no reason why Canada should not establish a representative in Washington since most of the dealings involving the two countries were already being done directly. He differed, however, from Roosevelt on the question of Japanese intentions toward the continent. Grey mentioned yet again that China and Japan were not a military threat to North America. While Australia was isolated in the Pacific, Canada and the United States were just too far from Japan to be threatened by invasion. The real danger, according to Grey, was in the industrial growth of China. From his perspective,

> It was hard to say what might happen once China commenced adopting on a large scale, the industrial system which we have today. With labour so cheap, it would be possible for her to compete with all parts of the world to the detriment of the other parts. It was hard to say, even, if the whole centre of commercial greatness in the world might not shift to the Orient in consequence of this ...[39]

Grey could see that British advantages in trade due to the Industrial Revolution and the country's strong navy were in relative decline and that once China turned its attention to industrialization it would quickly rise to prominence.

King was struck by Grey's intelligence, modesty, and "the simplicity and beauty of his nature."[40] The foreign secretary was keen to be outdoors, and when King awoke in the morning, he found Grey feeding the birds outside his door.

He had cleared away a little path and was putting out some porridge which he said was for the robins and some of the other birds, but which most of the starlings stole. He then showed me the red squirrels which were outside of his library window. He had a bowl of nuts for them inside, but as it had been snowing hard all night and was too cold to leave the window open, he had put some on the outside shelf, so that they could feed there.[41]

He also took King to see his duck pond, where he had collected more than twenty species of ducks from around the world; his greenhouses; and the trees he had planted throughout the forested sections of his property. These walks outside provided an opportunity for the two men to explore a wide range of topics, from women's suffrage to general advice the older man had for a young civil servant to the beauty of poetry. Grey encouraged King to read the works of great scholars such as Gibbon, and noted that he had chosen *The Decline and Fall of the Roman Empire* as his holiday reading in order to put his own work in a larger perspective and to remind himself of the sweep of world history. As the two men took long walks in the snowy woods, they recited their favourite verses to each other. For King, a young public servant on the verge of great responsibilities, Sir Edward's guidance for success in public life was welcome and deeply moving. King carefully noted the wisdom Grey had shared on the importance of character and compromise:

There is nothing truer in public life than this, that a man who would save himself will lose himself, and one who is willing to lose himself will be honoured by the people. The other point is how far to go in the matter of compromise. Compromise is necessary if one is to achieve anything in public life. Of course one can get out and spend one's life writing pamphlets against this or that, but to do the work in a cabinet and a government which is really going to tell in the long run, one must compromise, and one has to be continually guarded as to the extent, to be sure of the line on which compromise is made, no one can have his own way in all things. Circumstances, after all, will determine most things for us in life. We do well not to plan too far ahead. The plan will work itself in the light of circumstances.[42]

It is tempting to think about this advice in the context of what King would eventually become—a deft politician, a master of compromise, and a successful and long-serving prime minister. As he left King at the train station, Sir Edward recited Robert Browning's verse, a touchstone for Grey's own time in office:

All I could never be,
All, men ignored in me,
This, I was worth to God, whose wheel the pitcher shaped.[43]

King was personally overwhelmed by his experience with Grey, particularly by the older man's generosity and the poetic ideas he shared during the walk back to the train station. Of course it was his diary to whom he confided, "Everything considered, it was, perhaps, the most remarkable conversation I shall ever have with any man."[44] But King's encounters in London are politically significant as well. He had met with the heads of the departments most central to the administration of the government of India and Britain's foreign policy, and had done so as a representative of Canada, Canada's interests, and the wider interests of Great Britain and her empire. He had managed to win the confidence of the senior British Liberal statesmen through a combination of competence, enthusiasm, and position and had been privy to the most confidential debates on questions relating to India, China, and the opium trade. And, at last, he was ready to travel east for the first time—into Britain's eastern possessions and beyond.

SEVEN

The Journey to India

For the first time, King was truly going abroad. Although he had spent time years ago studying in Berlin and many recent days in the social whirl of London, he was about to leave the comfortable drawing rooms where his Edwardian liberalism was of the same variety as his hosts and head out into less familiar territory. While his travel diary cannot always be relied on in its interpretation of the less familiar societies in which he moved, it does provide us with a way of reading King and his developing world view. We see his faith in the power of the Empire to protect Canadian interests abroad and his increasing awareness that Canadians needed to contribute to support both their own interests and a project bigger than themselves. We observe that he was able to connect with the gentlemen across Asia who shared his experience of an American education, diplomacy, anglophilia, or a love for liberal ideals. In some ways, he may have had more in common with the English diplomats, American preachers, Indian nationalists, Chinese mandarins, and Japanese officials with whom he met than he did with the average Canadian. They too sought to make the world a better place through their service in government. Of course, they often had a different sense than King of what that future might look like, and the Canadian would find diplomacy a tricky game at this level.

On December 31 Giddens and King settled their bill at the Mansions. After breakfast they left for Victoria Station, where they caught the boat train for Dover and Calais and from there, a "train de luxe" to Marseilles.[1] King enjoyed a fine dinner served by an eccentric French waiter who reminded him of Napoleon, and King turned in before midnight. He was asleep in his first-class car somewhere just beyond Paris when the new year, 1909, arrived. Before retiring, he took a moment to reflect on the events of 1908. The year had indeed been altogether "remarkable,"

opening with trips to Washington to discuss the Japanese situation with the President; then a special mission to England in that connection and in connection with the immigration of Hindus to Canada; a journey later to the Pacific Coast to settle the Chinese claims, which, by the way, was in large measure due to my own pressure in the matter. Growing out of the Chinese settlement was an investigation into the opium question and the special reports on these matters; then an enquiry under Royal Commission into conditions in the cotton industry and the severance of connection with the Civil Service to enter the political arena. On top of this, a general election, being returned member of parliament for North Waterloo, the county of my birth; and later, appointed special commissioner to an international congress at Shanghai, China, with extra missions to India and China growing out of the same. Another trip to England in the same year, and interviews with the Minister of Foreign Affairs and the Minister for India.[2]

With the exception of the cotton industry investigation, each of these events and accomplishments was linked directly with the Vancouver riots and their effects. King had done his duty and taken advantage of his opportunities. He was now a young man with real prospects for a bright future in the dominion government. But while King's personal prospects seemed boundless on that winter morning, his train had ground to a halt. A few kilometres from Dijon, there had been an accident in a tunnel and the track was blocked. The passengers had to detrain at a small station, take a local train to Dijon, and continue their trip to Marseilles in far less comfortable quarters. The cold, snowy weather continued all day, almost as far as the coast, and the coaches that had been pressed into service were without adequate heat or a warm meal. King was relieved when he and Giddens finally reached their stateroom on board ship at Marseilles and had "the first warm meal of the day."[3] The two could settle in for a while as this ship would carry them across the Mediterranean, through the Suez Canal, and on to India.

King's peace was marred by the knowledge that on December 28, 1908, at 5:20 A.M., a devastating earthquake and subsequent tsunami had struck near Messina on the island of Sicily. Buildings along the coast were washed away and even navigation through the straits had been affected. He became aware of the disaster when his liner was diverted south of Sicily to avoid waters that had become treacherous due to rock falls and shifts in the seabed. King was moved by the effects of the disaster and the enormous loss of life it caused. He reflected on the fragility of life but then turned his attention quickly back to his mission to understand the opium trade and the situation in India. He spent his time on board reading some of the books Lord Morley had recommended. He also had a copy of *India and Its Problems* (1902), by William Samuel Lilly. Lilly was a barrister and former member of the Indian civil service who had been forced by ill health to return to Britain, where he took up a new career as secretary to the Catholic Union of Great Britain and as an essayist. His work on India had particular currency because of his hands-on experience as secretary to the Government of Madras. *India and Its Problems* outlined the variety of landscapes, religions, and interests of India's regions and hypothesized that this diversity posed a challenge for Indian self-rule:

The population of India consists of a vast and most mixed multitude in various stages of civilisation, of whom not one man in ten and one woman in one hundred and sixty is able to read: a multitude belonging to at least fourteen distinct races, speaking some seventy-eight different languages, and divided from each other by customs and creeds, as much as by huge mountain ranges, vast forests, trackless deserts, and great rivers.[4]

It is no wonder, then, that as he read, King's attitude toward Indian self-rule became less certain than it had been at his desk back in Canada:

I have started out with a feeling of strong sympathy for the self-government of India. Little by little I am coming to see wherein self-government, like everything else, is a matter of education, capacity and training. While doubtless there are a few who could govern, to grant self-government to these people would be to construct an oligarchy, selfish and self-centred, who would become more tyrannical than any English government is ever likely to become, simply because they would not be prepared to hold the scales evenly between all classes of population.[5]

But while Lilly was informative, King never discarded his instinct that Canada and India had the right to self-government in common. Later, in Calcutta, he would voice this feeling, although he tied it conditionally to India's willingness to control the movement of its people to Canada because he considered Indian workers racially "unfit" for settlement in the north. The contradictions revealed in his diary demonstrate that in his dealings with Asia he struggled to find a balance between his own competing beliefs. His liberal ideology upheld the right to self-government and his respect for education brought him close to gentlemen of a kind from all parts of the globe. And yet his acceptance of the idea of a hierarchy of races suited to particular regions made it difficult for him to support immediate Indian independence outright.

King was happy to spend a lot of time alone during this part of his voyage, contemplating the view from the ship and catching up on his research about India, since he was far less impressed by his fellow passengers than he had been on the *Lusitania*. He was generally unimpressed by the British returning to their posts in India and by the average American tourist:

> On the whole the passengers on board have been agreeable enough, but for the most part uninteresting. With the exception of Mr. Gladstone [one of W.E. Gladstone's sons] there has been little to gain in conversation with many of them, but perhaps in this particular the fault has been mine, not theirs. I find on the whole that the Americans are a pleasanter people to travel with than the English provided one escapes the noisy and talkative Yankee. The reserve of the English and their precision of manner in many particulars is not calculated to further intimacy or friendship. The best type of Englishman is all for minding his own business, the worst type of American of looking after everybody's business but his own. The best companion on the voyage is the one of either race who approaches the mean between these two extremes.[6]

Again King found himself comfortable somewhere in between the British and the American social styles, even at the dining table. Of course he was about to experience something altogether new, and the familiar irritations of American gregariousness and English reserve fell away as the sun was setting on January 6, and King saw the Egyptian coast for the first time. By ten o'clock his ship had anchored at Port Said, launching King's first experience in the east. As he looked over the coast he imagined Jerusalem, the Holy Land, and its sites lying just beyond the horizon and he was overwhelmed by the sense of really being abroad. The port itself was busy with visiting American ships and the coal barges that had pulled up alongside. Shouting porters hurried aboard carrying fuel for the steam-powered ships. King hired a barge to take him ashore with Giddens and then paid two shillings to engage a local guide who showed them the town, its shops, mosques, churches, hotels, and cafés. While the two men relaxed at a restaurant, they watched a contortionist perform and the peddlers ply their trade. Later the guide hired a carriage for another two shillings and took them on a tour of the Arab quarter. King bought bread and meat from a street vendor and, to his surprise, noted that "the bread we had bought tasted remarkably well. It seemed clean and wholesome."[7]

In addition to this introduction to street food, King received from the guide a lesson in the fundamentals of Muslim prayer. He was conscious of the power of Islam and the implications it had for India:

> I was particularly struck by the fact that the Mahommadan should have so strong a hold at a spot in the immediate vicinity of the Holy Land. I was no less struck by a remark in Lilly's *India and her* [*sic*] *Problems* to the effect that the Hindus would probably be converted to the Moslem religion and hold to it before they would take to the Christian. Both seem to me explained because of the Moslem religion emphasizing what must be apparent to every mind, that some divinity *is*, that there is an all pervading presence in the universe, best described as God.[8]

In his ignorance of the variety of practices within Islam, King was impressed that all Muslims could worship at the Mosque at Port Said and he was therefore convinced that there was a clarity within the Muslim faith that gave it an advantage over the various sects of Christianity and their conflicting approaches to worship. As a Presbyterian with an appreciation for Anglican services, he was of course much more familiar with the tensions within the Protestant churches and between Protestant and Catholic groups.

King had seen the Empire in action in Canada. He had watched the pageantry of Parliament, was on intimate terms with the governor general, and had even seen the inner workings of government in London. However, the mighty reach of the Empire abroad was given form for King in the architecture of the governor's residence at Port Said. The building was divided in two and occupied by both the English governor and his Egyptian counterpart. To King, this British presence at the head of the Suez Canal seemed evidence of the Empire's power and of "how the British flag controls the strategic points on the earth's surface."[9] He made the observation again many times during his travels, including this diary entry while he was in Aden:

> On a voyage like this, one begins to realise how far-sighted England's policy has been, and how carefully her statesmen have guarded the interests of the future generations. Gibraltar, Malta, Port Said, the Suez, Aden, are so many will-nigh [*sic*] invincible and impregnable strong-holds, securing for English trade an unmolested highway to the East.[10]

His musing was correct. In the nineteenth century Britain had, in a variety of ways, used its naval power and expanded its political control into the parts of the world where its industrial and commercial interests had previously drawn them. The Suez Canal was the fastest route to India, and so Egypt became important in British foreign policy. In a similar way, South Africa became a British colony in order to protect the longer sea route to Britain's Asian interests around the Cape of Good Hope. The British flag therefore flew all over the world at strategic naval locations. King had always felt that it was a great privilege to belong to the Empire and be protected by the flag, but the power of this flag was presented to him in a new way and with new possibilities: "if the British and American nations could agree on an alliance against injustice they would be all powerful in controlling the peace of the world."[11] He may have overestimated the power of an Anglo-American partnership, but the observation is important: King was a believer in cooperation between the British and the Americans. One is struck by King's youth, his innocence, and his naive impressions of this day in Port Said. He himself described the visit romantically as

> like a dream, going about in the mild, liquid atmosphere, with the moonlight shining brightly as at early dawn ... The whole sight was so strange—our guide with a long cloak and fez, our driver with his black face and white cloth about his head. It was after two when we

returned to the ship, having had by far the most interesting evening on the whole trip.[12]

King's ship spent all of January 7 travelling through the Suez Canal. In addition to being impressed by the American ships that he saw again as they passed his liner in the canal, King was awed by the desert and the "biblical" landscapes that he saw from the rail:

> The scenes are those which are familiar to one from the pictures descriptive of biblical stories, the Arabs with their bright costumes and flowing robes, the camels tracking across the desert or crouching on all fours by the shore, occasional oases of palms or railway or signal station. One sees only small huts and mud houses, with occasional residences which look like so much stage scenery at different points along the way.[13]

While he noted the impact of "civilization," such as the trains, the canal, and the steamer, he largely viewed the sights of the region as being "much as they were thousands of years ago."[14] King's imagined Egypt was firmly rooted in his knowledge of the Bible, the romantic orientalism character-istic of the time,[15] and his understanding of British power. Everything he saw en route to India reinforced these preconceptions.

King's ship arrived in Bombay on the morning of January 16, just over two weeks after he had left London and over a month since leaving snowy Ottawa. He took a tender from the ship to shore, cleared the customs area, and then he and Giddens checked themselves into their double room at the very prestigious Taj Mahal Hotel, "having experi-enced the novel sensation of a stranger in an Oriental city for the first time, the natives half-clad, the women the bearers of burdens, oxen instead of horses for hauling loads, tropical vegetation, bright coloured flowing garments and peoples of all nationalities."[16] Despite the exotic-ness of the surroundings and being thousands of miles from home, King was still giving serious thought to his professional future. While he had dismissed the idea of an academic career, he was still interested in receiving his PhD. He had fulfilled all of the requirements for a Harvard degree, with one exception—he had not completed a thesis. And so while en route to India, King penned a request to Harvard's president, Charles Eliot, asking if he could submit a number of his official reports on Asian immigration in lieu of a thesis. When he arrived in Bombay, he sent off a package of documents to Cambridge, which comprised a variety of reports including those on his 1908 mission to England; the 1906 coal strike in Lethbridge, Alberta; the opium trade; telephone operators' working hours; and the Quebec cotton industry. After some consideration, it was his work on "oriental immigration to Canada" that was eventually accepted by the faculty. King subsequently defended and earned his Harvard PhD in June 1909.

In the meantime, there were practical matters to take care of. After confirming their travel arrangements, King and Giddens hired a middle-aged, impressively mustachioed local servant named Luchman, who had come with strong letters of reference and had been recommended by Cook's, King's travel agency in London. King agreed to pay Luchman "the maximum rate," forty rupees a month; to fund his third-class train travel; and to give him an advance of fifteen rupees "for clothes." King sent a cable to Ottawa announcing his and Giddens's safe arrival in India and the two men outfitted themselves for the 2400-kilometre train trip to Calcutta. Although King and Giddens had paid $196.13 for a two-person first-class sleeper, they also needed to pick up "the necessary travelling outfit, pith helmet, blankets, bedding, pillows, twoels [sic], etc."[17]

The train platform in Bombay that night was quite a different experience than King was used to in Ottawa. The three men passed up and down the platform, looking for their carriage and struggling to keep up in the throng of people boarding the same train, while a band of porters followed, carrying all their luggage. Their compartment included a small adjoining area for Luchman, who retired to it immediately after making up his new employers' beds for the night. He slept far more soundly than his novice travelling companions, who were grateful for the tea he brought to their beds the next morning. The villages, towns, and fields through which the train travelled were fascinating and King spent the next day and a half watching India as it passed by his window. He made notes inspired by what he saw, about the organization of labour, the use of women and children in various occupations, the health of the fields, and the effects of British influence on the country. On the whole, his observations reinforced his faith in the good intentions and effective governance of the British Empire in India since his measure was primarily the spread of railway transportation and irrigation across the subcontinent.

King, Giddens, and Luchman arrived at Calcutta on January 18. Calcutta's crowds impressed King far less favourably than the equally crowded but more picturesque port of Bombay. While Luchman was arranging for the baggage to be brought from the station, King made a visit to the residence of the viceroy, former governor general of Canada Lord Minto. It turned out to be too late for calls by the time he got there, so he began his drive back to the Grand Hotel. By extraordinary coincidence, King ran into Lord Minto's daughter, Lady Eileen Minto, on the way and she brought him straight home to her father's personal aide-de-camp, Colonel J.R. Dunlop Smith. Smith reviewed Lord Morley's instructions and arranged for King to meet the next day with J.S. Meston, the secretary of the Finance Department, and W.L. Harvey, a member of the Viceroy's Council and minister of industry and commerce. In Smith's opinion, Meston was "the right person to see in regard to opium" and Harvey, "to discuss immigration matters."[18] Eventually Minto emerged from his rooms and greeted King warmly. As King noted in his diary, during their short conversation, Minto assured him that "In regard to the immigration question ... we [the Government of Canada] had caused him no trouble whatever; that our action had been much appreciated here; that of the many bodies which he had received as viceroy, he did not recall a single objection in regard to the emigration to Canada." He put the blame squarely on the CPR and its private advertising campaigns.[19] Harvey took the same position as Minto on Canadian attitudes to Indian immigration—blaming the CPR and the terrible treatment of Indian workers in South Africa for causing ill feeling between India and other parts of the Empire. King also repeated his request for information regarding the role of opium in Indian society and an update for Laurier on India's current political situation.

Since a number of the men whom Minto wished King to speak with were expected to attend a formal dinner that evening in honour of Lady Violet Minto's wedding, an invitation was arranged for King. He also had formal interviews at the government buildings with Sir Harold Stewart, secretary of the Home Department (formerly the Central Criminal Intelligence Department), and Meston. The offices were ranged along wide corridors and positioned so that a breeze could blow freely through. Perhaps it was because of these breezes that the Indian clerks' tables along the walls of these large rooms were covered in bundles of documents that had been carefully tied with string and set in rows. King was particularly struck by the racial divide between the army of Indian clerks working in the civil service and their English managers. Despite Lilly's warnings that self-government would be difficult if not impossible, it still seemed to King an untenable proposition for this divide in government and elsewhere in Indian society to continue without further reform: "The history of the United States and of Canada, the history of South Africa, all present strong parallels, and India will not escape its place in the group in the matter of relation[s] to the Mother Country."[20] He was sure that someday, when the people of India recognized that their foreign interests were not identical to those of Britain (a difference evident, for example, in the British desire to reduce the amount of Indian opium sold in China), there would be a strong movement to establish the nation as an independent actor either within the Empire, as Canada had, or without.

Signs of this desire for self-rule were becoming more obvious and Minto had a tough few months dealing with the impact of Curzon's plan to partition Bengal, even confronting an attempt on his own life. Lord Minto looked tired and worried, and King noted Meston's explanation for this:

> He said the Viceroy had no doubt had a very anxious time of it during the past few months, that there were many who would seek to take his life simply because he was Viceroy, and that he knew this, but that he had never lost his head at any time ... The attitude of the peoples toward each other would have to completely change. The days of the patriarchal attitude [as represented by Curzon] had past.[21]

Lady Minto gave King her own explanation for her husband's worn look during a dinner party at Government House, observing that

> the last six months in particular had been very trying months for Lord Minto, that the work altogether was extremely heavy, as he was expected to be familiar with European politics, to know of the correspondence that was taking place with the Home Government, to be familiar with the administration in India, to entertain the native princes and to share in the life of the country.[22]

Lord Minto was indeed weighed down by the serious problems of the Indian administration, but it was also a time of change for his family. He was "losing" Lady Violet, the pretty young woman King had noticed in London in 1908.[23] Wednesday, January 20, was her wedding day to Major Lord Charles Petty-FitzMaurice, the youngest son of Lord Lansdowne, the former British foreign secretary responsible for signing the Anglo-Japanese Alliance. The couple planned to move to his home in Scotland, causing some pain to her father, who would miss her terribly. King had been in London at the time of Violet's sister, Ruby's, wedding in 1908 and here he was again, in the presence of another Minto family wedding, completely by chance.

> I waited to see the different carriages drive from Government House to the church, and they certainly made a very fine appearance. Lady Violet

Elliot looked very beautiful sitting by her father with a veil over her face. She looked such a child. Lady Violet and His Excellency were in a covered carriage, but the windows at the side being drawn, one could readily get a glimpse. The Viceroy's native bodyguard of lancers riding before and after the Viceregal coach made a splendid appearance. The course from Government House to the church was lined with people, dressed in a great variety of colours and presenting a fine appearance. Troops were lined up along the whole route of the procession.[24]

Having no official invitation to the wedding itself, King spent his afternoon stopping in on a number of newspapermen to whom he had been recommended, but with whom he was not interested in speaking at any length, thus fulfilling his social responsibilities with a minimum of fuss.

He was more concerned with the details of the formal meeting scheduled for the next day with W.L. Harvey and B. Robertson, the secretary of the Department of Commerce and Industry. The two men assured King that the Indian government would not be inclined to pass any legislation restricting Indian emigration. But King needed something to take back to Laurier that could be used to assure anti-immigration-minded Canadians that the government had been acting to manage the flow of Asian migrants, so he took action:

> I asked if the government would be prepared to give a written expression of opinion which might be of service to our government in meeting any agitation for legislation aimed against all Asiatics. It was clear that the present arrangement was working well, and present indications were that it would continue so. A written statement to this effect from the Government of India would place our government in the position of being able to continue its policy of being able to deal with individual countries.[25]

In this way, Laurier would have a defence against local criticism in Vancouver and elsewhere that claimed—or might claim—that he was not going far enough to control Indian migration to Canada. While reticent, Harvey agreed to allow King to submit a draft of such a letter to the viceroy.

King also met with the eminent Bengali politician Surendranath Banerjea. Born in 1848 into a Brahmin family, Banerjea was an influential moderate-liberal politician with an anti-British bent. He was one of the first Indian members of the nation's civil service in 1871 (although dismissed on dubious grounds), one of the founders of the Indian National Association, and the founder and editor of the *Bengalee* newspaper. An American working for the YMCA, E.C. Carter, had informed King ahead of his meeting about the rumours surrounding Banerjea's dismissal from the civil service. While Carter suggested that it was due to "supposed dishonesty," other accounts, including Banerjea's autobiography, attribute his 1873 dismissal to jealousy, an error in paperwork, and systemic racism.[26] Though they disagreed about the basis for dismissal and aspects of the subsequent legal case, Banerjea's critics and his supporters agreed that he had a powerful mind, extraordinary charisma, and a strong desire to see the end of British rule in India.

King's first impression was of a scholar with impeccable English and a wide base of historical knowledge. Banerjea attributed the current independence movement to the partition of Bengal—the result of the policies of Lord Curzon. Though Lord Morley had acknowledged the error of this measure, Banerjea could not support him because "he was not strong enough to remove that injustice, though admitting it."[27] Banerjea supported self-government, pointing to Canada as a positive example, and assured King that enfranchisement would be successful since the people of India "did more thinking on these questions than commonly believed."[28] On the question of opium, he was enthusiastic about controls and the reduction of trade. King did not miss the opportunity to share Canada's current immigration policies with Banerjea in the hope that he would revise his thinking on how Indians were being treated in Canada. Banerjea had heard about the earlier deportations, but King noted that after he had explained Canada's position, Banerjea "expressed himself as entirely satisfied with our attitude, which he thought was fair."[29] As we saw earlier, King had remained optimistic about the effect that the support of the self-governing dominions might have on the Indian independence movement, but in his conversation with Banerjea, he linked this support to Indian willingness to restrict the migration of workers to Canada.

> I pointed out that I thought it was fortunate for the movement for self-government in India to know that she was a part of the Empire, inasmuch as Canada, South Africa and Australia all being self-governing, their sympathies would naturally be on the side of the movement, but to hold the sympathy of Canada it would not do to start any movement from India which would antagonize the working classes of Canada, as would be the case if large numbers emigrated.[30]

This comment is a striking example of the fact that, in 1909, there was no getting around public fears of the mass migration of South Asian workers to Canada. King understood this situation clearly, and while he was sympathetic to the Indian independence movement, he could not be seen to endorse it if India was unwilling to effectively restrict the movement of its citizens. In fact, such a public statement supporting Indian independence in 1909 would likely have ended his political career in Canada.

On January 23, after an afternoon betting at the horse races—which seemed a poor British import to King, who viewed gambling as a vice—Giddens and King ran for the train to Benares. King did not make the long train trip merely to see the holy Hindu and Buddhist sites. Rather, this item in his itinerary had been added in order that he might see one of the historical centres of the British–Indian opium trade and discuss the matter with some of the men who profited most from it. When their train arrived just before noon the next day, King, his travelling companions, and the viceroy's brother were met at the station by the chief secretary of the maharaja of Benares. A powerful force in the region, the maharaja, Sir Prabhu Narayan Singh, was on good terms with the British, had been knighted in 1891, and had married the daughter of the first Nepalese prime minister. His chief secretary took the group of guests to the maharaja's official guest residence, Nandesar House.

Once King was settled in a beautiful large room with a door to a wide veranda, he was taken on a tour of one of the most sacred Hindu sites, the Golden Temple, which did not impress:

> The Golden Temple was most disappointing. Instead of being a large building as one might expect from the name, it was little more than a series of courts, very narrow passage ways, more or less filthy, because of the freedom with which animals were permitted to walk about, and because of the race, garlands of flowers and other stuff which devotees are in the habit of strewing before their favourite gods. We were not permitted to enter the temple, but had a glimpse of part of the worship through a small aperture in one of the walls.[31]

The ecstatic worship of the Hindu gods was beyond King's ability to understand. To him and many other British officials in India, it was mere idolatry and absurdity and made the idea of Indian self-government seem only that much farther away. King was much more interested in the view from the Ganges. While none of the house guests of the maharaja had yet to meet their host, he had arranged for a crew of ten rowers to take King, the viceroy's brother and nephew, and Giddens for a day-long ride along the holy river. In contrast to his peevishness at the sights and sounds at the Golden Temple, King found the view

> one of the most wonderful, if not the most extraordinary, in the whole world. The left bank of the river is crowned with rows of palaces or temples, from the base of which, to the water's edge there are huge flights of steps. These are covered from dawn till noon with thousands and thousands of bathers who come from all parts of India to bathe in the sacred water of the Ganges. Were it not for the idolatry and super-stition which lies back of it all, there could be no more pleasant or beau-tiful sight than these terraces, with persons bathing in bright coloured

garments, and gracefully ascending and descending, or gathered in groups about some priest, fakir or before some shrine, while dogs and cows walk peacefully about as though, as in fact they believe to be the case, they were all one and the same community.[32]

That the scene he described would be impossible without the religious life associated with the river makes King's observations seem extremely limited by his own experience and beliefs. He continued in this vein: "To one accustomed to the western world, Benares is like a beautiful city, inhabited by a bewildered race. One feels the ignorance the the [sic] superstition and the viciousness like a great nightmare; so much outward beauty, so infinite the darkness beneath."[33] It was all just too much for King's Presbyterian sensibilities. He, like many Western visitors on their first visit to India, was overwhelmed, but rather than acknowledge this fact, he relied on the language of Edwardian racism to explain his feelings.

After the trip down the Ganges, the maharaja had arranged to join his guests for dinner at the guest house. While King and the others waited for his arrival at noon, a magician did tricks on the veranda. Eventually, the maharaja arrived with his heir, Aditya Narayan Singh, and greeted his guests warmly. King was glad of the chance to speak with the maharaja's son about the role of the British in India and the possibility of self-government. His opinions strengthened King in his feeling that the British were a force for good, that self-government would come, but that it would take time to overcome the country's divisions. After lunch Sir Prabhu Narayan treated King and the others to an elephant ride, followed by a tour of the temple at Durga and the British excavations of the Buddhist sites at Sarnath, the birthplace of the Buddha. King was far more comfortable with the "chaste" Buddhist sculptures than he had been at the Hindu temple:

I was much struck by some carvings which looked as though they might have been stone representations of Boticelli's [sic] paintings. There was the same sweep and grace about the lines of the figures. There was a huge figure of the Buddha, and a great many small imag[es] of him. There was nothing, however, which approached idolatry and there was no indication of the sort of suggestive figures which we saw in the Neepal Temple and which is apparent in so many of the Hindu gods. I found it most impressive moving about these ruins of antiquity, and on the spot with which is associated the name of a founder of a religion which today has more followers in the world than any other existing religion.[34]

After a final dinner at the maharaja's guest house, complete with dancing girls, musicians, and singers, Giddens and King caught the midnight train back to Calcutta. The two men had very little turnaround time in Calcutta on January 26 to prepare for the trip to Colombo, the departure point for their ocean voyage to China. As pressed as he was for time, King still managed to catch up on the reports from home and was pleased to read about Sir Wilfrid's speech on Asian immigration in the House:

It has been a pleasure to read in the papers that Sir Wilfrid has spoken of the Asiatic question in the debate on the speech from the throne. His statement that the problem of Asiatic immigration should be dealt with by negotiation and diplomacy, rather than by the methods adopted from time to time in British Columbia, has been most favourably commented on in the press here. Canada's attitude is in fine contrast to that of other countries, and is being specially contrasted in India today with the attitude of South Africa. It is interesting to note, too, that at the moment the President is having difficulty with California to prevent that State from passing legislation prohibiting Asiatics from holding land, and in maintaining the peaceful arrangement which he has with Japan, while the Premier of Australia, in making known new areas open for colonization, declared emphatically against the admission of Chinese.[35]

South African discrimination had become well known in India after 1893, when Mohandas K. Gandhi began to defend Indians in South

Africa against racist policies there and Indians returning after the Boer War publicized the extent of the problem. Having been compared favourably to South Africa in this area was not a great feat for Canada, but maintaining this status was often a consideration when formulating policy in Ottawa. The links, then, between Canada's policy and the dilemmas of her partners and allies were often on King's mind, no more so than while on his travels through the more distant parts of Britain's empire.

On January 29, after reaching the coast at Tuticorin (also known as Thootukhudi), King settled up with his hired servant, Luchman, and boarded a steamer, the *Pundua*, which would take King and Giddens to Colombo, the capital of the island of Ceylon. King was enchanted by his short stay on the island, noting the general happiness of the people and his fascination with the tropical plants and animals, particularly the beautiful botanical gardens at Kandy. He even managed to find an evening of theatre in Colombo, but was more interested in observing the theatregoers than the performers. At Colombo, King and his secretary boarded a German liner named the *Princess Alice*, which was scheduled to carry them to Shanghai. The distances King had covered and the number of sights he had travelled to see were beginning to wear on him, and he was relieved to be back on board a ship, where he could escape the mass of people, foreign cultures, and the tropical heat. King was grateful to have some time to himself on the German ship to read and write and, by interacting with passengers and crew, to remind himself of his German constituents in Waterloo North and his time as a student in Germany. The contrast, evident in his diary entries, between King's level of comfort with the other white travellers on the European liner and with the Indians he had recently left behind is stark. It is hard, for example, to ignore the racism in his February 2 entry. After his first night on board the *Alice*, he wrote, "It is impossible to describe how refreshing it is to be again with people of one's own colour. One becomes very tired of the black races after living among them. It is clear that the two were never meant to intermix freely. I find it very pleasant to be on a German ship."[36] While he had come to greatly admire the educated Indian gentlemen he met, clearly the visit to this outpost of Empire left intact his discomfort in the face of difference and poverty. He remained quite convinced of the enormous cultural differences between South Asian cultures and his own, and therefore of the general necessity for continuing British influence in the region.

EIGHT

Diplomacy in China

The United States was at the forefront of the international movement to control the traffic in opium. The US government lacked Britain's financial interests in the trade, had encountered the vice in the Philippines, and perceived opium use to be a growing concern on its own west coast. The moral reform movement of the time had identified the vice of opium smoking as particularly pernicious, tied as it was to fears of the "yellow peril" and Asian influence on the Pacific Rim. At the time, Anglo-Saxons across the globe were anxious about the future of their race and often felt most imperilled by an ambiguous Asian threat that seemed both contemptible and highly dangerous. These fears were directed at Asian communities up and down the west coast, and focused on reforming the hygiene and moral underpinning of Chinese, Japanese, and Indian neighbourhoods. On the initiative of the US government, the Anglo-Oriental Society for the Suppression of the Opium Trade (a British organization) and Bishop Charles H. Brent, formerly of Boston and currently the episcopal missionary bishop of the Philippines, organized the International Opium Commission in Shanghai, which included representatives from the United States and the countries with the strongest ties to the opium trade: Great Britain, Germany, China, France, Japan, the Netherlands, Portugal, Russia, Turkey, Persia, and Siam (present-day Thailand). Brent sat as the commission president, presiding over the group of delegates and managing the meeting's agenda. Although functioning at the commission as an American representative, Brent was originally a Canadian. He was the son of the canon of Toronto's St. James Cathedral, had studied at Trinity College School in Port Hope, Ontario, and had graduated from Trinity College at the University of Toronto—all pillars of the Canadian Anglican establishment. And he had encountered the problem of opium smoking during his pastoral work in Manila in the years after the US takeover of the Philippines in 1901. From the beginning, then, the Shanghai commission had the character of a moral crusade. *The Lancet*, Britain's premier medical journal, was critical of the fact that only four of the thirty-two representatives were trained doctors.[1] The work of the commission clearly emphasized the diplomatic, social, and moral aspects of the trade in opium.

Whereas the United States was most concerned with the moral question and wanted the trade in opium stopped completely, Great Britain had the diplomatic complexities of the matter in view. King was fully briefed as to the relationship between Great Britain, the Indian growers and manufacturers of opium, the English middlemen in Britain's Asian outposts, and the Chinese trade. He had been shown the bilateral agreements whereby China and Britain planned to reduce opium use in China incrementally. In fact, Britain had already agreed to send fewer chests of Indian opium to China every year for the next ten years. The British government was not interested in an immediate stop to the flow of opium, as that would have serious consequences for British finances and relationships with local governments in India and elsewhere. A significant gap was therefore evident between the interests of Great Britain and the United States going into the discussions at Shanghai. King was the man in the middle, comfortable with the moral approach and fully briefed on the British diplomatic side. King, as we know, was officially in the British delegation despite having received his invitation from the Americans and being very much a Canadian. Brent and the commission began work at the Palace Hotel in Shanghai on February 1, 1909. King would not arrive in the city until February 16. While little was achieved in the end by the commission in 1909, the work it did eventually led to other international discussions, including the 1912 Hague International Opium Convention.

Unlike Bishop Brent, who had been living in and travelling through Asia for the better part of a decade, King was taking it all in for the first time. When the commission opened, King and Giddens were still en route, exploring ports of call in Malaysia and Singapore—seeing the sights, shopping for inexpensive suits, and observing the daily lives of the people they encountered. They happened to be in Penang, Malaysia, on Chinese New Year. This was King's first experience of Chinese life outside the bachelor worker culture of the Chinese community he had investigated in Vancouver. He recorded his first impressions:

> I was much surprised to find so many Chinese. They seemed to be everywhere, although there were a few Malays in evidence. One's first impression of the Chinese is that they are a large [*sic*] finer sort of people than the Indians. They seemed to be very active, industrious and stronger. The build of the average Chinaman we have seen tonight is more solid than the build of those who come to Canada.[2]

King, as usual, had an eye for the ways in which work was organized and the ways in which labourers lived. He was impressed by the workshops he came across in the shopping districts and by the quality of the products they were producing. On February 7 King reached Singapore and his thoughts turned away from his new suits and once again to the opium question since such a great amount of the city's revenue was based on its trade.

The next stop on the journey to Shanghai was Hong Kong. King spent no more than two days in the British colony, but it evoked in him strong feelings about Canada, Empire, and the world. Along with the other impressive sights of Hong Kong harbour, King was excited and pleased to see a Canadian Pacific ship among the docked vessels. This symbolized for King Canada, Canadian trade, and the links between his home and the wider Empire project.

> In view of the C.P.R. one feels Canada's connection with the Empire at this point more than at any other we have reached in our journey round more than half the globe. It is delightful to see the offices of the C.P.R. occupying the best business corner in the city. What this means to Canada may be grasped when one stops to think of the situation as it would be under other circumstances. All that British power stands ... here [for] the defence of Canadian trade between the Orient and Canada ... Viewed in this, which is the true light, it behooves one to recognize obligations as well as the rights of citizenship within the Empire.[3]

As in Port Said, the idea of Empire that King had inherited at home was reinforced by the physical presence of Empire institutions abroad. For King, it seemed as if he was an important part of an international community of British Empire subjects. He recognized the multi-ethnic, multinational nature of this empire connection and took pride in his membership. King's pride in the Empire, the benefits that he felt it provided to the Dominion of Canada, and the obligations that he believed Canada owed in turn are obvious in these reflections on the sights in Hong Kong harbour. The next day, King had a shipboard conversation with Reginald Brabazon, Lord Meath, a conservative politician, enthusiastic imperialist, and the future founder of Empire Day. King had even more detailed ideas about Canada's potential role in the Empire after speaking with Meath:

In these days of organized effort and large consolidations as between individuals and nations it is a fortunate thing for the Dominion that she is the largest part of the largest empire the world has ever seen ... Her geographical position, geography being a determining factor is all in her favour to this end. If it can be done I think we should support a large shipbuilding industry, the more of the carrying trade of the world we can bring to our shores the better it will be for the future greatness of the Dominion.[4]

These musings on empire and greatness also led King to consider the role of government and commercial interests. As a liberal, it is not surprising that he was convinced that it was "one of the first duties of government to control commercial greed and to safeguard the broad political interests by seeing that the commercial motive is kept in its proper place, always to conserve the interests of future years and generations in any action." He took this a step further in his assessment of how he himself should play this role in the coming opium commission negotiations:

I imagine that irreparable harm has been done to the future relations between the Western and the Oriental world by the extent to which negotiations up to the present have been directed by persons whose main concern was commerce and gain. One may, I think, reasonably conclude that the feeling of China at this moment is one of antipathy to foreigners and their interference in the domestic affairs of China is naturally resented. This is something to be kept in mind in dealing with the opium problem. Careful regard for China's own wish in the matter must be had throughout, and action must be along conciliatory and not coercive lines if there is to be any permanent good about it.[5]

King saw himself as both an outsider in the matter and a possible mediator in the process. He was aware that he shared both the American desire for moral reform and the British reluctance to sign on to a multilateral resolution that might interfere with the bilateral agreement they had already negotiated with the Chinese, aimed at reducing the opium trade.

On February 16, 1909,[6] King reached Shanghai and had his chance to act the statesman. When he arrived, King was met with a note from the head of the British delegation, Sir Cecil Clementi Smith, assigning him rooms at the Palace Hotel where the rest of the British commissioners, who had already been meeting for two weeks, were lodged. A very competent and experienced senior civil servant, Smith was fluent in Chinese and had extensive experience in British colonial administration. He had previously served as the colonial treasurer at Hong Kong, colonial secretary and later governor and commander-in-chief of the Straits Settlements, lieutenant-governor and colonial secretary of Ceylon, and high commissioner and consul-general for Borneo and Sarawak. King was very much his junior in every way.

Nevertheless, King immediately occupied a very interesting role in the workings of the commission. He had been invited by the Americans, but he was committed to working with the British delegates as a "cabinet"—to discuss the matter freely until a common strategy had been established and then to adhere to the British position. He also wished to defend the Dominion of Canada's ability to ensure that opium trafficking did not become a larger problem in Canada, where it was a relatively recent phenomenon. (In this regard King was a bit naive, for as he himself had discovered in 1907, opium was already being processed in Vancouver and abused by all kinds of Canadians.) And so King took a position in between the American enthusiasm for the complete suppression of the trade in opium "for other than medical purposes" and the British reluctance to move too quickly to reduce the trade in what had been a highly profitable commodity for British interests since 1773. Despite this desire on the part of the British for evolution rather than revolution, change in the opium trade was already happening in China. Huge shifts had occurred over the past ten years and the Chinese government's desire to reduce its population's consumption of the drug was sincere if not wholly effective. In 1906 China and Britain had come to an agreement to both assess Chinese opium suppression measures and reduce the amount of opium being shipped to China from India by 10 percent per year for three years. If, after three years, it was felt that China's work in controlling opium dens had been effective, Britain would agree to continue to reduce the sale of opium every year until it was cut to zero.[7] Thus, China and Britain arrived at the conference with an agreement in hand and with no interest in reframing it. China's primary goal at the Shanghai meetings was to raise the international profile of its own attempts to change the culture of opium use within its empire. King characterized the Chinese position:

> I learned that the Germans and Japanese appear to be falling in with the American point of view on any matters of difference, and that the Chinese and English are holding together. The attitude of the Chinese Government as explained by Sir Cecil Smith, is that they wish the matter gone into as little as possible. They look upon it in part as outside interference. This, I think, is most important to ascertain absolutely; because the success of the whole object depends largely on how the Chinese may view this inroad of foreigners to deal with a question which concerns primarily themselves.[8]

King was committed to raising the discussion above purely commercial concerns, but also to doing so in the spirit of compromise. King remembered Sir Edward Grey's advice on the importance of compromise for a public servant and kept it in mind as the commission moved forward in its work.

> It is quite clear that the whole issue is going to ultimately turn on the interests of trade and commerce versus the desire of philanthropists and moral reformers. Here one is brought face to face with a question of compromise, which is a necessary part of all such proceedings. My intention is to do all in my power as a member of the Commission to aid in the suppression of the opium traffic, to watch carefully for the right moment for effective action, but to attempt nothing which is certain in the end to prove inoperative or which considering the question from the other side, is not likely in the long run to effect the object desired.[9]

Thus King found himself in a position he would take often during the rest of his career in Canadian public life: as a conciliator in the midst of strongly divided groups, namely, the British and the Americans, trying to manage a challenging policy question. The British and the Americans were not the only delegations with strong and complicated positions on opium. The Persian delegate was reputed to be an opium merchant and the Portuguese had, until the recently announced US legislation, been the largest exporter of opium to the United States.

The US opium commissioner was Dr. Hamilton Wright, who, King was pleased to note, was a graduate of McGill University in Montreal. He had an ongoing research interest in tropical diseases and had lived and worked extensively in Asia. King and Wright spent some time socializing in Shanghai and when, on February 18, Wright proposed that the commission expand its investigation "into the medical aspect of the opium question," King agreed. He felt that medical research into possible "cures" for opium addiction were an important facet of the reform movement. This notion was a non-starter for the British delegation, none of whom had medical training. They were planning to vote to reject the motion when King intervened: "I suggested substituting an alternative along the lines of what the British delegation were prepared to suggest [supporting scientific exploration], as it seemed to me [that] to simply negative [*sic*] the motion to investigate anti-opium remedies might give rise to the impression that the British delegates were opposing the reform movement."[10] King's idea was accepted by the group. Sir Cecil prepared a resolution creating a medical subcommittee, which squeaked through the next day in a close vote of seven to six.

More antagonism between the American and British delegations was to come. Dr. Wright had written a series of resolutions that seemed to be intended to undermine British relations with China and had been lobbying the other delegations behind the scenes without informing the British. One of the resolutions implied that Britain was not moving quickly or resolutely enough to finalize an arrangement between India and China. King disagreed strongly with this position. He felt the American resolution was poorly written, that it should not attack existing treaty obligations between states, and that in any case the size of the task was so enormous that realistic expectations were critical. "Ten years is a miraculously short time to attempt to substitute an alternative industry for what in some respects is the largest existing industry in two empires."[11] King managed to mediate between the sides on several of the resolutions. First, he saw the reality behind the gap between the Americans' position and that of James B. Brunyate, the acting financial secretary to the Government of India. Brunyate was standing firm behind Britain's intention not to condemn the use of opium in India outright. From his meetings with Lord Morley, King was aware that Sikhs in India often ate opium in tablet form and that it was rarely smoked. He was therefore in a position to convince Brunyate to agree to an amended resolution that declared the *smoking* of opium "an evil."[12] Similarly, he convinced the British to agree to the resolution against smuggling by eliminating the clause that condemned countries who manufactured opium, and including only those who exported it to states in which it was illegal.

King's experience at the commission confirmed Sir Edward Grey's warning about the ineffectiveness of international conferences and changed his mind about the possibility of a similar conference on emigration. He saw clearly now that too many elements behind the logic of bilateral agreements could not be discussed in an open forum:

> There was a point during the discussion when Sir Cecil Smith wished to withdraw altogether, and asked the other members of the delegation whether the delegation should or not. I strongly urged not withdrawing, as I felt any such action would have afforded grounds for misunderstandings which it would have been difficult to explain away. I am beginning to see the significance of Sir Edward Grey's objection to an international conference on the question of emigration, and of

course it is applicable to international conferences on any question, namely, that questions might be asked which could not be answered, and concerning which it is embarrassing, if not impossible, to explain why no answer could be given.[13]

The International Opium Commission thus completed its sessions on February 26, 1909, with some minor recommendations in principle that allowed the participants to leave without embarrassment but without any tangible results beyond an official report that would be published later. King had demonstrated his intelligence and political acumen internationally and had added to his impressive social circle, having made close contacts among the American, Chinese, and British commissioners. Once the commission had closed its doors, he could turn his attention to the quiet discussions he planned to have with the Chinese government. Since he had concluded that bilateral and direct negotiations between states was most effective, he was reinvigorated in this second mission: to investigate the possibility of negotiating with the Chinese government for emigration restrictions.

He began the process by meeting with a number of the Chinese delegates while he was still in Shanghai, among them Loo Yuck Lin, a former consul in South Africa, and T'ang Quo An, a member of the Chinese Foreign Office (the Wai Wu Pu) and a fellow Harvard graduate.

I took occasion to speak to them about the restriction of Chinese labour, and they were of the opinion that China could regulate the emigration from her own country. They saw the reasonableness of restricting competition along labour lines. They referred to the settlement of the Chinese claims in most appreciative terms. They also told me that a Chinese Consul-General had been appointed at Vancouver, and that Mr. O[w]yang King was the person, or at least had been offered the appointment. I spoke of knowing him personally and mentioned that he would be a thoroughly acceptable person; that I hoped his appointment might lead to the development of friendly relations and commerce between Canada and China.[14]

King's support for Owyang King stemmed from his interactions with the highly respected Chinese diplomat during his time as commissioner in Vancouver after the riots. Owyang King had arrived in North America as a student in 1872 and graduated from Yale University. After being stationed in San Francisco for fourteen years, where he served both as vice-consul and as consul general, he was sent to Vancouver by the Chinese consul general in Washington to observe the claims process in 1907, and it was there that he and Mackenzie King had become acquainted.

The new Chinese consul in Vancouver, the riots, and immigration matters were all mentioned again when King met with Tsai Nan Huang, a Shanghai customs official. King's name was well known to Huang because of his role in the Chinese claims process in Vancouver, and Huang took the opportunity to tell King how pleased he was at the way the Chinese had been treated in the wake of the riots and to ask King about Canada. Once again, King conveyed Canada's regret about the violence in Vancouver and explained that it could be attributed to the divisions that characterized the BC labour market. He also expressed his "hope that some day China might find it possible to restrict her own immigration so that this side of the problem would be solved and the way cleared for her scholars and students to visit our institutions."[15] King did not record any response from Huang to this suggestion beyond his arrangement to speak about it further with Jui Ching, the provincial treasurer of Kiangsu.

King also spoke privately and more extensively on many topics with T'ang Quo An. The two men enjoyed each other's company and near the end of their conversation King expressed the hope that T'ang would visit Canada someday. King obviously had a great deal of respect for T'ang, who was well educated and a gentleman. And yet King's struggle with his own and his society's prejudices against Asian cultures lingered in his approach to immigration.

> During the course of conversation I happened to mention to Mr. T'ang that I hoped he might some day see Canada, when I recalled the fact

that he could not do so without paying the $500 tax. I mentioned this to him, and explained how the law had originated, expressing the hope that some day we would see a change in this particular, that I thought at any rate in the case of scholars and officials entry to the country could be obtained by passport, etc., in his own case even now. The last words he said when he left the room were that he hoped he would get a chance to visit Canada one day, and in that event he would seek to get a passport from me. In conversation I found him an exceptionally interesting and entertaining man to talk with, a mind active and discerning, and a sympathetic, congenial and warm nature. To treat such men as being inferior to ourselves is to my mind the self-pride which goes before a fall. As a people we will do well not to let our ignorance betray us into false attitudes.[16]

King may have still struggled with the racial frameworks of his time, but he was developing a sincere, international perspective on events. He was surprised by the shift in his thinking about Canadian news when he had an opportunity to read a paper from home and discovered that the events reported in Canada's *Globe* had ceased to seem quite as significant to him. However, one news item was of real interest: on February 22 the paper announced the establishment of the new Department of External Affairs for Canada. He was pleased when Giddens pointed it out to him, and wrote prophetically, "This, I think, is an excellent and very necessary step. I would rather have charge of such a Department than any other of the Government, and believe it would be made of infinite service to the country. Perhaps some day the opportunity will come."[17] That day would eventually arrive in 1921, when, as the incoming prime minister, he was also entitled to take on the role of secretary of state for external affairs.

King's trip to Peking to investigate the possibility of offering the Chinese an arrangement similar to the Gentlemen's Agreement that Lemieux had negotiated with Japan is a relatively little-known episode in both King's life and Canada's immigration history. This obscurity is perhaps not surprising since no official treaty or letter of understanding was ever signed as a result of his meetings. However, during this quiet mission King demonstrated remarkable skill. Through his exceptional debating prowess and thorough knowledge of the labour situation in British Columbia, he managed to persuade Liang Tun Yen, the acting head of the Department of the Wai Wu Pu, of the merits of a bilateral agreement that would eliminate the head tax and would rely on a Chinese passport system to control the exit of workers from China rather than their entry into Canada. Liang's weakness in the Grand Council, which was struggling with the far bigger problems associated with the growing unrest that would eventually bring down the already weak imperial regime, meant that he could not push the legislation through. But this failure does not diminish the value of the fascinating diplomatic work of the young British statesman from Canada.

On February 28 King and Giddens said their goodbyes to Shanghai and, after boarding a special train on the brand new Shanghai and Nanking Railway along with the rest of the British delegation, the railway manager, and two of its Chinese directors, left for Nanking. When they arrived, the governor of Nanking, Tuan Fang, sent a train to take them into the old city, where they were met by the governor's carriages. The entire delegation was treated to an excursion to view the Ming Tombs. Though this sight did not impress King, he was very enchanted by the governor's personal collection of silk paintings: "The detail, as well as the tone and perspective of one of these paintings[,] was quite exceptional."[18] King and the others were then officially received by the governor and his officials, photographs were taken, and gifts were presented. The party then shared an elaborate meal at a table sporting both British and Chinese flags. In his dinner speech, the governor thanked the British delegation and expressed his hope that they would continue to assist China in the elimination of the opium trade, to which Sir Cecil responded with support and assurances that Britain would meet its obligations.

After side trips to visit a new ironworks and an American school near Hankow (which both impressed King immensely), the delegates continued their journey to Peking by train, arriving on the afternoon of March 6. As promised, the British ambassador, Sir John Jordan, met the group at the station and arranged for them all to dine together at the embassy later that evening. Jordan had informed the Wai Wu Pu of King's visit, but no one had expected the British commissioners to have finished their work in Shanghai as quickly as they did. The guest rooms at the embassy were full, and though he had hoped to have King stay with him, Sir John arranged rooms for King at a hotel until his visitors had gone. Sir John was eager to speak with King at dinner. And, as usual, King made careful notes about his conversation that evening with both Sir John and the secretary of the legation, C.W. Campbell, who had been assigned to help King during his mission in the capital.[19]

King was told that the Wai Wu Pu had been thrown into disarray in recent weeks due to a series of unforeseen personnel changes at the highest levels. The formerly powerful general and government advisor as head of the Wai Wu Pu, Yuan Shih Kai, who was a modernizer and in conflict with the emperor, had been dismissed in January 1909, soon after the death of both the emperor and the dowager empress in November 1908. After his dismissal, Yuan retreated to his home in Hunan, and rumours swirled about why this might be necessary.[20] So, when King arrived in Peking, the Chinese had little time to spare from the crisis to meet with him. In response to the changes, Liang Tun Yen had become acting president of the Wai Wu Pu. He was an able civil servant who had been educated in the United States and spoke English fluently, but he had an overwhelming amount of work to do in fraught circumstances. Jordan had been in touch with him about King's visit, and his initial reaction to the Canadian's mission to discuss emigration seemed positive, but Liang was anxious to avoid the kinds of friction that had been caused by American immigration controls, such as local boycotts of American goods and protests against the interrogation of Chinese students from wealthy families who had tried to enter the United States. Jordan did not know, and was not authorized to share, the details of Canada's arrangement with Japan, so Liang was interested in learning about the agreement directly from King, to whom he was predisposed on account of King's involvement in the settlement of the Chinese claims in Vancouver.

Before King's first meeting with Liang, he, Jordan, and Campbell seriously discussed the possibility of suggesting to Liang that Canada could remove the head tax on the entry of Chinese workers in return for China's commitment to control the emigration of its subjects. King was aware that it was not the kind of change that would pass easily through Parliament—and without implications for future elections—so he felt that if it was to be done, it should be done quickly and effectively, with as little debate as possible, "so that the time between now and another election would give the country sufficient evidence of the effectiveness of the arrangement."[21] If no bilateral arrangement was possible and the number of Chinese migrants continued to rise, King was sure that in the future the Canadian government would be forced into raising the amount of the head tax or passing exclusionary legislation. (He was correct about this. By 1923 Canada had passed the Chinese Immigration Act, which provided the regulations necessary to completely exclude Chinese immigrants.) He asked that Jordan pass this message on to Liang so that he would have a full understanding of the Canadian position in advance of their meeting. As an aside, Jordan also mentioned that Sir Edward Grey had passed along to him King's suggestion about the institution of a Canadian position at the embassy in Peking, and Sir John was enthusiastic, noting that "Canada was missing her opportunity in not furthering trade" in China. Such was the effectiveness of Canada's "trade commissioner" in Shanghai at the time that the British ambassador did not even know he existed.[22]

King had learned a lesson from Lemieux's error during his visit to Tokyo and made a point of dropping in to see the American minister to China, William Woodville Rockhill. While he kept his purpose quiet, he did discuss the general conditions in China and Japan with the minister so that there could be no complaint from the United States that Canada had made a diplomatic misstep by failing to make a visit. Then, after a day spent seeing the grounds of the emperor's Summer Palace with the son of the governor of Nanking, King returned to Peking for meetings with Jordan, to work through the memorandum on Chinese immigration that King had drafted for his meeting with Liang. King and Sir John spent quite a bit of time discussing the details of the memorandum. The two went through each paragraph so that Sir John understood Canadian intentions and he gave advice on potential Chinese reactions. Through it all, King emphasized the importance of restricting Asian immigration generally in British Columbia: "I then spoke of the last general election, of the loss of no less than five seats by the Government over the Asiatic question; also mentioned Templeman's defeat and Ralph Smith's inability to contest a by-election for fear of defeat. This would show the strength of public feeling in the West."[23] The power of public opinion and its impact on electoral politics was inescapable where immigration from China was concerned.

Sir John's help in preparing for King's talks with Liang was critical. As Lemieux had learned when he took on the Japanese in Tokyo, Canada's grasp of the ebb and flow of Britain's long diplomatic relationships was lacking. Canadians did not generally have access to the kind of documents Grey had given to Lemieux on the negotiations connected with the Anglo-Japanese Commercial Treaty, or to King on the opium question. This kind of diplomatic record keeping was still in Canada's future, as the nation had only just created its Department of External Affairs and a professional diplomatic corps, and Britain still had the final word on foreign affairs. King's knowledge of the diplomatic background between Britain and China was therefore relatively limited. By his own account, he was even surprised to learn from Jordan that the Chinese were likely to argue that Canada's Chinese head tax conflicted with the terms of an existing treaty with Great Britain that had been negotiated before Canadian Confederation. As King noted, according to the Peking Convention of 1860,

Chinese in choosing to take service in British colonies or other parts beyond sea are at liberty to enter into engagements with British subjects for that purpose, and to ship themselves and their families on board any British Vessel at the open ports of China; also that the high authorities aforesaid shall in concert with Her Britannic Majesty's representative in China, frame such regulations for the protection of Chinese emigrating as above as the circumstances of the different open parts may demand.[24]

King was unlikely to be convinced of the Chinese case, but this did raise the larger question of Canada's interests under the treaty obligations of the British Empire. As King put it,

The question of the right of the mother country to barter away the privileges of the Dominion through past, present or future treaties was one of supreme importance, more important even than this particular question that we were discussing. The reading of the clauses ... [in the treaty] showed me clearly that no thought had been given to colonial interests as distinguished from subjects of the United Kingdom at the time the treaty was drawn, and it seems to me that we cannot do better at the moment than have this question raised and settled one way or other in connection with this very matter.[25]

This situation would have reminded King of British actions in the negotiations connected with the 1871 Treaty of Washington, which gave Canada no compensation for Fenian raids and rented to American fishermen the right to fish in Canadian waters. And it certainly would have brought to mind the more recent, and perhaps more irritating, decision made by the British to side with the United States in the Alaska boundary dispute. King was ready to defend Canada's sovereign rights, as he would do to the end of his career. In this case, at stake was the right to control the flow of people across the nation's borders and a stronger voice in the way the Empire was run more generally. As Sir Robert Borden would do again ten years later at the Paris Peace Conference, King pointed out to the British representative that the time had come when we had either to consciously keep before us the idea of an empire, and have this in mind in shaping policies, or decide that we were to be separate countries and shape our policies in that direction; that the old relation of mother country and colony had passed, so far as the Dominion was concerned; that we regarded ourselves as a nation; that nothing was stronger than the national feeling in the Dominion.[26]

Despite King's commitment to Empire, immigration was, for him, still a matter of growth and self-government. On March 4, after visiting an American school in China, he wrote,

I am beginning to see the essential need of Canada shaping her policy from a national view-point. Let her remain a part of the empire for the good of our own people; let her demand a position of equality with that of every other unit. Let her cease to think in colonial terms and to act in any way as with a colonial status. Let her become a nation or other nations will rob her of this right.[27]

Jordan had been to Canada. He had spent some time with Canadians and experienced this national feeling himself and so he understood the kind of feeling King was referring to when King made the suggestion that Canada needed to be treated as a nation in this case. Having fully briefed Sir John on the Canadian position, King agreed to meet with him again in the afternoon and to go with him to see Liang Tun Yen at the Wai Wu Pu. Jordan introduced King, and Liang graciously greeted his Canadian visitor. Liang asked him if it was his first visit to China and King mentioned how impressed he was by the number of Chinese men he had met who, like Liang, had graduated from American universities. As the two men sat themselves at a long table with their secretaries, Liang explained that during his time at Yale he had travelled only briefly to Canada on a day trip to Niagara Falls. And yet his time in the United States was enough to provide the two men with some common ground.

King made his case as he had outlined it that morning to Sir John. When Liang asked directly about whether the head tax conflicted with existing British treaties, King—thanks to Sir John—was ready with a reply:

> I thought this point was questionable; that every treaty had to be read in the light of the conditions under which it was entered into and conditions existing at the time it was framed; that Great Britain could never have intended by treaty to bargain away the rights of British subjects in a colony to the extent that their very existence as a people would be imperiled, which was what an interpretation such as he had given to the treaty would mean in the light of conditions as they are at the present time. I said it was quite true that we had the power to exclude Chinese altogether, and that I hoped he would recognize in the purpose of my coming here, wherein we were desirous of doing what was fair in that we were willing to refrain from exercising this power should China be willing to undertake to restrict her own labour emigration.[28]

Liang's schedule was exceedingly full, so when it became clear that some items needed clarification, such as Canada's definition of "labour" and the terms of the agreements with Japan and India, King agreed to write a short memo for Liang's consideration and to meet again the following day. Far from being convinced by King's arguments, Liang still believed that Canada's position conflicted with agreements made in British treaties and that the best way to solve the question of gaps in the standards of living between states was to allow the free movement of labour. The negotiations were going to take time, and that was something that King did not have. If his dream of a place in the cabinet was to come true, King was going to have to be back in Ottawa before the end of the shortened parliamentary session. He had roughly until Easter to complete his mission and Liang was looking tired. Sir John attributed this perceived exhaustion to Liang's hectic schedule, to his struggle with unexpected diplomatic problems, and, ironically, to his rumoured continued use of opium.[29]

On March 10 King moved from his rooms at the Wagon-Lits Hotel into the British embassy compound. He was situated much more comfortably than he might have been nine years previously, as this was the site of the fifty-five-day siege of the legations during the Boxer Rebellion. King had a quiet room at the end of a hall with ensuite bathroom, sitting room, and two fireplaces, where he and Jordan could confer conveniently and discreetly on the negotiations. Sir John had already spoken with Liang that morning, and while the Chinese official had been convinced of the dangers of Canada's political difficulties, this did not sway him toward supporting restriction. Rather, he was as convinced as ever of the importance of the free flow of people.

Sir John and King went alone, without secretaries, for a more informal and confidential discussion at Liang's home that afternoon. Liang's argument was straightforward and correct:

> It seems to me that if we are to restrict our labour, it is simply that we are to undergo the odium of doing an unpleasant thing, so that you may escape the odium. If labourers are to be kept out why should we keep them out instead of you? I do not think there is a politician who could recommend such a thing to his government, and I do not think the Government would be willing to attempt any such task.[30]

King tried to explain that while he personally did not favour exclusion, the Canadian government might be forced into such a position by the feelings of the man on Main Street: "What I had intended to convey was that the Canadian people would create the trouble and unrest, the occasion being the alarm created by numbers of Asiatics coming to the country." In response, Liang reminded him that it was the Canadian government's responsibility "to restrain its own people,"[31] not the Chinese workers. It was during this private meeting, however, that King was able to create some movement on the question. Liang seemed to warm to the idea of China restricting the emigration of its own people when King showed him the details of the confidential agreement with Japan. It was then that

Liang mentioned that a graduated system of control might be acceptable to the Chinese—that a number of Chinese labourers could be agreed on, such as ten thousand per year, and any seeking entry after that might be refused by the Canadians. While ten thousand was far above a number that would be acceptable to the Canadian government, Liang had significantly opened himself to the possibility that his government might be willing to use a passport system to control the emigration of its subjects in return for the elimination of the head tax.

While King waited for Liang to discuss the Canadian demands with his council, he and Brunyate made a trip to see the great imperial temple at the heart of the Chinese capital, the Temple of Heaven. King had been unimpressed by much that he saw at the Hindu temples in India, but he seemed to have developed an appreciation for the simplicity of Buddhist and Taoist architecture, and was particularly taken with this temple complex in Peking.

> When one reflects on what the Temple of Heaven really signifies one cannot but feel that there is a greatness of conception about it which far exceeds the temples filled with fanciful images or even the innumerable signs, paintings, crucifixes and the like. It stands there as a simple expression of belief in a Supreme Being which pervades the universe. The absence of symbols denotes the true relation between man and his creator. It is curious that in this so-called pagan country one should find the most sublime expression of the underlying belief of all religions worthy of the name.[32]

Perhaps his deep respect for the Temple of Heaven endeared King to the Chinese ancestors, for on March 17 he made a second formal visit to the Wai Wu Pu, during which the negotiations shifted. King took advantage of a point of agreement on the mutual desire to end the explicit rules aimed at Chinese immigrants, and he and Liang made significant strides toward an agreement restricting Chinese workers and possibly eliminating the head tax.[33] Liang and King were able to negotiate the possibility of control through the issuance of official passports, but the form that the agreement would take remained an obstacle. King was even more committed to the idea of a written treaty than Lemieux had been in Tokyo in 1907, and the Chinese declared that a letter of assurance was as far as they would go. Not only did the Chinese wish to avoid signing more foreign treaties, but the practical and symbolic details of signing a treaty with Canada, which could not sign for itself, were complicated. In response to these concerns, King noted

> that the necessary formalities in connection with treaties would of course be complied with; that Canada had entered into treaties with France and was negotiating treaties at present with the United States. Mr. Liang said, "But we have a treaty with the British Empire already, and you wish us to enter into a treaty which does away with its provisions," or words to this effect.[34]

King tried to explain that Sir Wilfrid considered a treaty as a contract between individuals, so there would be no confusion over the terms. When this did not seem to convince Liang, the two men decided to concentrate on the terms and to leave the matter of form for later. The terms, as summarized by King and agreed to by Liang, were

> that contract labourers shall be prohibited without the consent of both the Chinese and Canadian Government [sic]; that so far as free labour and labour other than such as comes under contract is concerned, it is to be restricted to such numbers per annum as may be agreed upon, and restriction is to be effected by the issuing of passports by the Waiwupu, not to exceed the number agreed upon; these passports to be vised by a British Consul or our own officer ... that the poll-tax be removed.[35]

King underlined the point that the head tax could only be removed if the passport system was proven effective; otherwise, "a howl will go up all over the country."[36] Of course, the number of passports to be issued had not yet been decided, and this consideration was likely to be an even bigger roadblock to an agreement. King went back to the British embassy and sent off a telegram to Laurier asking for his input on the question of the number of Chinese that Canada could allow. Laurier's response arrived the next day: "Will answer early next week."[37] On March 24 a second telegram from Sir Wilfrid arrived. This time, he set a limit at only one thousand Chinese passports.[38] As time went on, it became clear that the gap between the two countries' desired numbers might become irrelevant since the Grand Council was balking at making an agreement at all. Its members feared that the passport system would be unwieldy, would be corrupt if organized in Peking, and would result in misunderstandings about the Chinese position on emigration restriction, potentially leading other countries, such as Holland—which sought to control the movement of Chinese into its Pacific colonies—to require embarrassing restrictions as well. The Wai Wu Pu therefore expressed its wish to wait, think further, and raise the question again when the new Chinese consul general, Kung Huai Hsi, had arrived in Ottawa—a request that King viewed as a delaying tactic.

Ultimately, no agreement was reached while King was in Peking, and the head tax would remain a reality for Chinese immigrants to Canada until it was abolished in 1923, and the Chinese were excluded altogether. This failure to achieve a formal agreement with the Chinese government made King's success in Peking largely invisible to posterity, but the negotiation process displayed King's growing ability as a negotiator and diplomat. In the end, Liang and King got along very well and had great respect for each other. Before he left China, King wrote a letter to Sir Edward Grey thanking the British for their assistance and for all the work that Sir John had done on Canada's behalf. He was given a chance to read a draft of Jordan's letter to Grey praising King's performance as a diplomat and the good works he had performed on behalf of the Empire, and promising to support the immediate creation of the position of Canadian commercial attaché to the British legation in Peking. On April 1 Sir John Jordan met King at the train station and the two men said their goodbyes.

CONCLUSION

Closing the Circle: Japan and Home Again

It was clear that King was too late to make it home by April 11 for Easter, but he had received word from Ottawa that he had six weeks before the House was likely to adjourn for the summer. So, despite the fact that Laurier had yet to submit to the House the bill creating the new Department of Labour as he had promised he would (it was eventually submitted on April 30), King was pleased to be heading home. The rest of the voyage would take him across the Pacific and home via Vancouver, with stops on the way in Manchuria and in Japan to follow up on Lemieux's visit to Tokyo. Reflecting on his time in Peking and the immense help Sir John had offered, King was very grateful for the ambassador's efforts and his kind words of encouragement. Again Canada felt its hand strengthened through the intervention of Britain's diplomats in the region. The support these men gave and the pressure they put on their counterparts in Tokyo and Peking was a large factor in Lemieux and King accomplishing as much as they did. It was generally recognized that the British were a powerful force in Asia and that they were watching the work of their dominion's representatives abroad in order to ensure that Empire interests were maintained.

King began thinking seriously about Japanese power four days later as he reached the heavily fortified Manchurian harbour of Port Arthur, the site of the first battle in the Russo-Japanese War and, subsequently, of a lengthy siege. King mused on the industry of the Japanese in this conquered land:

> It is a new sensation to be among people in a country that had been recently conquered. It is amazing to see with what faith the Japanese are making of Port Arthur and Dalny [Dalian] cities that will in time compare with any in Europe or America. Six years ago this whole terminus of the Liao-Tung Penninsula [*sic*] was the home of the Russians. Today there is hardly a Russian in the whole place and the Japanese live as though they had owned the country always.[1]

After this impressive day in Port Arthur, King and Giddens took a train to Dalian, where they met the steamer *Yeiko Maru*, which would carry them to Shimonoseki, Japan. In some ways, Japan appealed to King. He found the spring landscapes beautiful, and he even had a friendly face to meet him at the station in Shimonoseki when his old friend, the former Vancouver consul Kishiro Morikawa, joined him for a brief but "pleasant" visit.[2] King's trip up and down the length of Japan was largely unofficial and consisted mostly of visits to various temples, theatrical performances, and gardens. He found the shopping exceptional, the tea ceremony beautiful, and the Japanese geishas of great interest and "nothing in the least vulgar,"[3] further noting how much fun he had had reading the palms of the young geishas and that they too had seemed to enjoy the childish game.

King's first official duty was to meet with Sir Claude MacDonald in Tokyo. MacDonald gave King a copy of Sir John Jordan's concluding report to London on the Canadian immigration negotiations in Peking.

From King's perspective, the report was complimentary and he was pleased, if a bit naive in his understanding of its contents. He summarized the report in his journal:

> Making all allowance for the more than generous tone of the despatches I think no one could read them without feeling that so far as the mission to China was concerned it has been conducted and resulted as satisfactorily as could reasonably be expected. It has removed the blame from the Dominion of any feature which may be odious in existing legislation against China, and has materially improved relations between not only the Dominion but the British Empire and the Chinese Empire. As being the first time that Canada has been brought into official relations with China the event is not without historical significance. From every point of view it was much more important than the Opium Commission, which so far as the public is aware, is the only mission.[4]

King's estimation of the "historic" nature of his work and the extent to which he had shifted China's attitude toward Canadian immigration policy are overstated, and both were quickly forgotten.

While he was in Tokyo, King also stopped in at the Foreign Office to see Japan's former ambassador to Great Britain, the foreign minister Count Jutarō Komura; Kikujirō Ishii, now the vice-minister; Tatsugoro Nossé, the former consul general to Canada; and his replacement, Takashi Nakamura. Nakamura was a strong choice to send to Canada since he had been involved in emigration control in the Foreign Office. Ishii felt that Nakamura and King would be able to work together to quickly solve any difficulties that might arise and that the Canadians "could feel certain that any matters regarding immigration would receive immediate attention."[5] In addition to reassurances from Nossé and Nakamura, Shuichi Hagiwara, the director of Commercial Affairs in the Foreign Office, produced a statement for King outlining the Japanese government's success in limiting the number of its citizens travelling to Canada. King described his discussion with the director:

> He said I would see from the statement that Japan was far within the mark which she had indicated as the one to which her restriction would be confined. That I would see there were very few who had gone, and that a larger number had returned, so that there were actually fewer Japanese than before. He mentioned that this work was all under him, and that the Foreign Office were exercising the greatest care and would continue to do so.[6]

Hagiwara also mentioned that a shift in the procedures surrounding the issuing of passports had been implemented. Rather than allowing all prefectures to issue passports, the government now required people wishing to travel abroad to get a passport through the governors of one of the three prefectures with the major ports—Nagasaki, Yokohama, and Kobe. It appeared as though the Japanese were indeed fulfilling their promises under the Gentlemen's Agreement and would work with the Canadians to ensure that no further trouble arose in BC.

These assurances were reinforced by the strength of the personal ties between King and the gentlemen of the Japanese Foreign Office. King was well cared for by the Japanese officials with connections to Canada while he was in Tokyo. Former Japanese consul Seizaburo Shimizu had left the city in 1901, but his connection to Canada was strong and he and his wife treated King and Giddens to a visit in their family home.

> They received us in their Japanese home in Japanese style. We took off our shoes on entering and sat on the floor, each with a little brazier in front of us, and had some tea and Japanese refreshments. It was very beautiful sitting in this little house, one side of which was completely open. The simplicity of Japanese life is something all nations might do well to imitate.[7]

On another occasion, King attended an outdoor reception hosted by Baron Yanosuke Iwasaki's family[8] in honour of the marriage of one of Iwasaki's sons to one of Nossé's daughters. Nossé was convinced that his daughters' years of schooling in Canada were the reason that they had so many offers of marriage from very desirable suitors. It was a great honour for his daughter to marry the son of one of the country's most wealthy businessmen. Another marriage had brought Colonel John McCook's daughter to Tokyo. King had met her in New York before he sailed for London, and in the meantime she had married Peter Augustus Jay, the first secretary of the American embassy in Tokyo, and was pleased to invite King to her home. There she introduced him to Thomas O'Brien, the American ambassador, and although the conversation remained on a social level, King did appreciate the contact with the American embassy officials. King noted the continued American wariness of the Japanese and their motives and predicted that a future war might well be fought over Manchuria.

On April 16 Komura hosted a dinner in King's honour at the Foreign Office, which gave King a chance to socialize with all of the most prominent officials in the department, including Komura himself. King was seated beside Komura at dinner, so they had plenty of time to talk about Japanese industry, China, the International Opium Commission, and their mutual alma mater, Harvard. Komura took the opportunity to speak frankly with King about Japanese emigration. Since Japan was an island, he argued, expansion was a requirement and their aim was to expand into Korea and Manchuria in order to protect these areas from Russian encroachment. Thus Japanese settlement in North America was of little interest to the government and was even a potential drain on Japanese numbers at a time when those absent citizens would be of more use in defending their home country.

King also had a chance to spend a day in the countryside near Ofuna with Sir Claude MacDonald and Thomas O'Brien. During the Second World War, Ofuna would house a naval prisoner-of-war camp, but in 1909 it was a place where visitors could see a picturesque temple and a great Buddha statue. It is interesting that King was not half as charmed by Sir Claude as Lemieux had been, much preferring the Liberal diplomat Sir John Jordan in Peking to the Tory military man that MacDonald was. It did not help that he felt MacDonald was uncomfortably conde-scending toward the Canadian cause, noting, "Personally, I could not help feeling a little inner resentment at the patronizing manner in which he spoke of the services of the embassy in connection with the arrange-ment effected with Japan. That might better have been left to a Canadian to express."[9] King observed further,

> From the way in which Sir Claude spoke generally I felt that he was inclined to emphasize very much the service which is being rendered to Canada through the British embassy; that he was inclined to emphasize the colonial status; for example, of Lemieux's visit he said quite frankly that of course nothing could have been done had it not been through the British embassy, virtually that Canada had no standing in Japan.[10]

Even if the idea displeased King, MacDonald was correct about this aspect of the relationship. Until Canada opened its first legation in Tokyo in 1929, it had no official presence in Japan. In the meantime, it relied on Great Britain to both provide and pay for consular services—a situation that was becoming a nuisance to the British taxpayer. Canada would be better served, mused King, by establishing its own represen-tatives abroad, who would be carefully chosen for their aptitude and professionalism. This might be contrasted with the practice of selecting for the position of trade commissioner primarily businessmen seeking to make a profit, or appointing as Canada's high commissioners to London mainly independently wealthy gentlemen who had the ability to pay for the expenses of a mission. In short, Canada needed to shake off its colonial relationship with Great Britain and create a partnership, within the Empire structure if possible, that included equal representation for Canada abroad by professional and competent diplomats.

On April 20 King and Giddens boarded a train for Yokohama, where they were scheduled to meet their Canadian Pacific Line ship, the *Empress of Japan*. There had been an accident on the railway during the night and no trains were able to make the complete journey. Fortunately,

King was now a man of influence. By contacting the CPR he was able to delay the departure of their ship and, through the good graces of an interpreter, to arrange for their bags to be carried by hand past the site of the railway accident. Tired and hungry, the two men eventually arrived at the pier and, after ensuring that their luggage had been loaded, took a moment to watch the sun set over Mount Fuji as they sailed out to sea, toward Vancouver and home. King could only revel in the beauty of the moment for a short time before his usual anxieties returned: "While a little longer stay in Japan would have been pleasant, I am glad we are taking the last trip of the home voyage. It has been a long absence from Canada and the anxiety of seeing those one loves and protecting one's own interests grows a little as the days increase in number. All of this helps to make the return voyage as happy as the start."[11]

King was pleased to have a chance to catch up on the news from home. He had been sent copies of the *Globe* and he read them with great interest during his days at sea. His new experience of Empire and the role of shipping seem to have been reflected in his views on the emerging Naval Crisis and the way that it would impact the constitutional relationships between Great Britain and its dominions. Britain was struggling to maintain its advantage in naval power in the face of an enormous shipbuilding initiative in Germany. The imperial centre sought financial support from the dominions to underwrite the huge expense of building state-of-the-art dreadnought-class ships. Some Canadians, mostly Tories, were enthusiastic supporters and believed that the fastest way to support the Royal Navy was by infusing it with a large amount of cash. Others, often Liberals, felt that Canada would be better served by building its own modest navy, which it could use to support Britain in crises, but which would otherwise be under Canadian command. A third group, heard from in Henri Bourassa's newspaper *Le Devoir*, wished for no such thing and pushed for the complete rejection of these requests, as organizing and paying for Canada's land defences was already an enormous undertaking done for the benefit of the British Empire. King reflected on this question as he read the *Globe*, and concluded that

> Canada should do something in the way of naval defence of Canadian shores and that her scheme in this particular might be made to fit in as parcel of a larger scheme of imperial organization. We should sacrifice nothing in the way of our constitutional rights of maintaining control of all expenditures raised by our own taxation, but we should be prepared to remove the possible insinuation that any portion of the expense of the British navy is incurred on account of Canada ... As a corrective to a good deal of the talk of Canada contributing cash and dreadnaughts [*sic*], I think it would be well for someone to ask in the House of Commons how many positions are held in the British navy, army, British consular and diplomatic service and civil service abroad by Canadians. I see no reason why we should not develop the industry of shipbuilding, and also train some of our own people to naval and marine service.[12]

King's views on this subject recall his feelings about the port at Hong Kong, the role of Britain in securing Canada's interests, and the symbolic power of the Canadian Pacific ships anchored in the harbour. His position also seems to be a response to MacDonald's concerns about the cost of maintaining the dominions' diplomatic services and their independent representation abroad. In any case, King remained a progressive-era liberal with an unshaken faith in reason to improve the lot of any government's citizens, declaring, "[H]owever great might be the problems which lie before the world, with organized society as it exists today the human intellect would be equal to the task which lies before."[13]

On a sunny May 1, King caught sight of Victoria and it seemed to him as if he "had seen nothing more beautiful in our whole trip around the world."[14] He was home. Though he had a raft of friends he would have liked to visit in Vancouver, rather than delay he boarded a train heading east the next day so as to catch Parliament while it was still in session. King had received a telegram letting him know that

Laurier had been true to his word and the new Department of Labour was in the works. He may not have known officially that the department was his to lead, but that had always been the plan, and the press was already assuming it was the case. He entered Parliament as an elected representative for the first time on May 10, 1909. Since the other first-time members had taken their oaths of allegiance on January 20, King took his oath alone and tried (unsuccessfully) to slip into his seat in the House unobserved. Despite the false modesty, a number of members of the house on both sides of the aisle took a moment during the day to shake his hand and congratulate him on his membership in Parliament. On June 2 Laurier appointed him minister of labour and his lifelong dream was realized—he was a member of the cabinet. That very day, he received word from the Harvard Graduate School. His report on "oriental immigration to Canada," written in the wake of the riots, had been accepted as a thesis. All that remained was his oral examination, which he passed, and the convocation ceremony on June 30, for which he was invited to give the address on behalf of the graduates. His speech was on the topic of the peaceful resolution of international disputes and was appropriately titled "Reason above Force."

CANADA'S HISTORICAL NARRATIVE has recently placed significant emphasis on the First World War for the creation of a Canadian national identity. We are told that our origins as an international actor are found in the trenches at Vimy or at the conference tables of Paris in 1919. However, we cannot understand Canada's political development during the Great War without understanding the state of affairs before the war began. This volume has looked for adjustments to this view in political and diplomatic sources before 1914 that are critical for expanding our understanding of the development of the Canadian nation. Rather than abandoning political biography as a genre, this present work has aimed to use the details of King's travels between 1907 and 1909 to show how some Canadians were exploring new ways to protect Canadian interests abroad in the first decade of the twentieth century—within the British Empire system, but with a strong sense of Canada as a nation. We cannot properly understand Vimy or the Paris conference without understanding how we arrived at the crises they represented and the range of possible solutions that were at our disposal. King's discussions on immigration, Indian independence, and opium suppression are examples of the important ways Canadian needs were defended in these years, despite their running counter to British policy.

Most important, King saw that Canada's interests were not always represented adequately by the British embassies abroad or by the Colonial and Foreign offices in London, and that a time was coming when Canada would require its own regular representation, even if that representation were located in the British embassy complex. In 1907 King could see that the high commissioner in London and the ad hoc diplomatic "commission" in Paris were inadequate for keeping the Canadian government informed in a changing world, and so in 1927, under King's leadership, Canada opened an embassy in Washington, and in 1929 it established an embassy in Tokyo, King's last diplomatic stop on the 1909 world voyage. The investigation into the riots in Vancouver therefore provides a stunning example of how an examination of local violence can reveal the tensions and changes within much larger international systems. In this case, the riots brought to a critical level the growing difficulty of maintaining a balance between the pressures of local economic development and the movement of labour in an increasingly global market. They made the debate surrounding the development of legal tools to police state boundaries international and public. And they highlighted the growing tension arising within the British Empire when the policies of London conflicted with the goals of the dominions. If the British were going to maintain their relative power in a world increasingly dominated by the United States, Japan, and Germany, the systems and structures that had been built over time to manage the Empire needed revision.

In Gore Vidal's historical novel *Empire,* Roosevelt sneers at the idea of adding the "Canada Claims" on Alaska to his State of the Union Address, declaring, "The subject bores me." Secretary of State John Hay tops this comment with his own experience of Canadians: "Bores you? Think of me, hour after hour, day after day, in close communion with Our Lady of the Snows …"[15] The trouble with Canadian diplomats in the twentieth century, Gore seems to suggest, was that they were not going away. Roosevelt and his successors were going to have more and more contact with them as Britain gradually conceded that Canadian negotiators were better suited to represent themselves on Canadian topics—particularly in Washington—than the Colonial and Foreign offices were. This was going to mean that the United States was increasingly going to have counterparts across the table with far more local knowledge of Canada and who cared deeply about the details and the outcomes of negotiations. A study of the documents surrounding King's work in the years before the First World War is therefore a powerful way to access these shifting relationships. King was a transitional man, who could arguably represent a variety of positions from a rational, reasonable, and liberal perspective. He was therefore a defensible choice when otherwise radical steps were being considered: setting up a commission to compensate victims of the riots seemed fair when King was managing the details. Roosevelt could take advantage of King's social connections in the United States and bring him to Washington as a potential intermediary between the US and British governments. On King's recommendation, the Canadian Parliament found for the first time, and without debate, that banning the production of opium for non-medical uses was not only reasonable but immediately necessary. When the US government sought an end to the trade in opium, civil servants decided that in addition to their own delegation, a Canadian on the British side was an obvious choice. A social visit by King to Sir Edward Grey led to a verbal agreement that Canada could establish its own representation in a number of cities abroad. And finally, no one blinked at King's taking on a secret agenda, backed by the British, to negotiate Chinese immigration controls while he was in Peking.

This work not only raised King's political profile at home and abroad, but it put him in a position to see directly how Canada and its role were changing. Since September 1908 he had seen first-hand how the Americans, the British, the Chinese, and the Indians perceived Canada and Canadian policies. He had borne witness to the extent of the problem of the opium trade in Canadian society, had compiled thousands of hours of commission materials into a number of important government reports on Japanese and Chinese losses and Indian immigration, had been treated with respect in London's halls of power, and had been shown the challenging links between Indian and British interests. He had shown himself to be a fair adjudicator and had therefore made friends in both the Japanese and Chinese civil service, and finally, had been elected to Parliament and was about to serve in the cabinet. Through all this, and even in the face of the fears of those living on Main Street, King retained his faith in the principles of liberal government and his dedication to the improvement of society through the knowledge of experts (like himself) and the rational formulation of public policy. If Main Street feared Asian migration, he believed there must be ways to manage it without threatening Canadian unity, Canada's relationship with the United States, or Empire policy. King chafed at any suggestion that Canada was a colony, and he debated the relative value of Canada's North American and British policy orientations. When he returned to electoral politics in 1919 after a brief turn studying labour relations for the Rockefeller Foundation, he carried this remarkable list of accomplishments, concerns, impressions, and assumptions with him back to Ottawa.

King had come a long way since September 1907. The "trouble" in Vancouver had brought about a series of unplanned opportunities for the Canadian who would one day be prime minister and for the state he would lead. Importantly, it directed King's skills in negotiation and conciliation from labour conflicts into the areas of diplomacy and states-manship. His youthful moral reform instincts remained, but they also brought him into the world of international trade policy. This combination of deep interest in local labour conditions and international diplomacy would become central to the way King understood government and directed policy in the 1920s and from 1935 to 1948. In these later years, he continued to take a close interest in the flashpoints of Canadian labour conditions—particularly the questions of assimilation and immigration—and he sought to maintain close control of Canada's foreign policy through personal links with foreign dignitaries and through official channels as the minister of external affairs. An important example of a policy that balanced local labour and international needs, from the final years of King's career, is the Liberal government's creative policy toward Europe's displaced persons (DPs) between 1947 and 1953. During the post-war refugee crisis, King was wary of how Canadians might react to a mass movement of refugees who were neither British, French, nor American. King and his team were aware that it was important for Canada to make a sufficient contribution to the new international community being built by the brand new United Nations, but King also knew what Canadians who were unhappy with immigration policy were capable of. After all, he had seen what the residents of Vancouver had done to Chinatown in 1907. And so great efforts were made to assure Canadians that DPs were coming to Canada to work on pre-cleared one-year contracts at jobs that no Canadians desired in remote locations, and that they would not cause labour conflicts.[16] This faith in the importance of government in managing both local labour needs and international relations had become a hallmark of King's statecraft, as had his mistrust of "unassimilable" immigrants.

The details of King's life abroad presented here have shown that his racism was complicated, but certainly not negated, from time to time by his belief in reason, education, and expertise—his liberal ideology. He often viewed gentlemen indigenous to the very regions from which he was working to exclude labourers as his social and intellectual peers. They were allies, informants, competitors, and obstacles to his success. They piqued his interest and were therefore described and named and had voices in his diary and formed an important part of his thinking on the regional dilemmas with which he wrestled.

Nevertheless, throughout his career King continued to hold on to his sense of what we have come to call "white (male) privilege." He was comfortable with the idea that the white, European, Christian culture of which he was a part was at the top of the racially based cultural hierarchy. All of the major players in this story—Earl Grey, Laurier, King, and others—largely shared this world view, and expected Britain to play a "civilizing" role in its non-white colonies until the British subjects native to these areas were ready for some form of self-government. King found it natural that it would be Britain that would decide when this would occur. As a white man, he expected to be able to move freely across borders and to have a voice in his government, and he defended the right of his country to control the ethnic balance of its society, even when it meant excluding other British subjects. It was this sense that the socio-cultural order of things was "natural" that afforded King some of his most effective political arguments in favour of controls. He traded on his society's belief that Canada was not a place suited to Indian migrants to sell the idea that laws preventing immigration were humanitarian rather than exclusionary, and he expected that Canadians would agree that Asian immigrants could not "assimilate" the way others could. The fact that racism was widespread and banal made it all the more powerful.

None of this is intended to take away from King's great talent for electoral politics, policy-making, and diplomacy. He had a rare ability to assess the range of possible action and devise a workable strategy that would bring him closest to his chosen policy outcome even when it required compromises. Other people's racism was just one of the factors King was taking into account. His own prejudices remained largely unexamined in the background of his thought and were put aside whenever he had dealings with a gentleman from abroad.

If there remains any doubt about the way King used his experiences in Asia in 1907–1909 throughout his political career, an example from his return to Parliament in 1935 should remove it. In October 1935 Japan had just appointed a new minister to its embassy in Ottawa, and King and the Liberal Party had just been soundly returned to Parliament with a majority after five years in opposition. The Great Depression continued with little room for optimism, Europe was unsettled, and relations between Japan and Canada were tense following the Asian power's invasion of Manchuria and subsequent departure from the League of Nations. Because of the Great Depression, the question of trade remained pressing even in the midst of this military crisis. No responsible prime minister could walk away from potential trade gains during such tough global economic times.

Despite the complexity of the international environment and the growing tension, King was confident in his ability to manage Canada's foreign policy, and he continued to insist on adding the Department of External Affairs to the list of state matters under his personal direction. His long list of friends and contacts abroad at the highest levels created a legitimate foundation for his sense of security in this area, some of whom were made in Vancouver and on the 1908–1909 trip. King masterfully used these personal ties to build a relationship with Japan's new minister, Satumatsu Kato. Consider his notes on their first meeting, where the mention of familiar characters from his travel diary was instrumental.

> I spoke of the many friends I had in Japan; of my visit there in 1909; of cables received since the Liberal victory on October 14th from Prince Tokugawa, Mr. Tamura, Mr. Ohta and others. I spoke of the kindness to me of Baron Ishii and Count Komura, when I visited Japan in 1908 [*sic*]; also of the Liberal Government being the first to send representation from Canada to Japan to the Osaka Fair, and of our Government

having opened the Legation in Japan. I sought to have him realize that I had made acquaintance with his country and had the friendliest of feelings toward it.[17]

With these connections established, the two men spent a moment exchanging greetings from mutual friends in London, after which King, Satumatsu, and the minister's wife shared a champagne toast to their mutual health. And then, ever the statesman, as he was walking out the door of Satumatsu's residence, King made an overture to begin mending fences and restart the difficult trade negotiations.

NOTES

INTRODUCTION

1. W.L. Mackenzie King, *The Mackenzie King Diaries, 1893–1931,* "Private Diary, International Relations, Missions to Great Britain, United States and Japan, 1908, v.1, January–March, 1908," February 18, 1908, p. 110. (Toronto: University of Toronto Press, 1973, microfiche v.95).
2. O.D. Skelton, *Life and Letters of Sir Wilfrid Laurier*, v.2 (Toronto: Oxford University Press, 1921) pp. 354–5.
3. Quoted in J.E. Kendle, *The Colonial and Imperial Conferences, 1887–1911* (London: Longmans, Green and Co. Ltd, 1967) p. 90.

ONE: THE RIOTS

1. See Canada, Dominion Bureau of Statistics, *Fourth Census of Canada, 1901*, v.1 *Population* (Ottawa: S.E. Dawson, Printer to the King's Most Excellent Majesty, 1902) p. 284, and Canada, Dominion Bureau of Statistics, *Fifth Census of Canada, 1911*, v.2 *Religions, Origins, Birthplace, Citizenship, Literacy and Infirmities, by Provinces, Districts and Subdistricts* (Ottawa: C.H. Parmelee, Printer to the King's Most Excellent Majesty, 1913) pp. 170–1.
2. National Archives of Great Britain (hereafter NA), Foreign Office (hereafter FO) 371/274, Foreign Office: Political Departments: General Correspondence from 1906–1966, Japan. Code 23 File 22241-30377, p. 299. Sir Claude MacDonald to Sir Edward Grey, November 16, 1907. Available online at http://discovery.nationalarchives.gov.uk/SearchUI/browse/C2757925?v=h.

3. Patricia Roy, *White Man's Province: British Columbia Politicians and Chinese and Japanese Immigrants, 1858–1914* (Vancouver: University of British Columbia Press, 1989) p. 154.

4. Robert Craig Brown and Ramsay Cook, *Canada, 1896–1921: A Nation Transformed* (Toronto: McClelland & Stewart, 1974) pp. 68–9.

5. W.L. Mackenzie King, C.M.G., Commissioner, *Report of the Royal Commission, Appointed to inquire into the methods by which Oriental labourers have been induced to come to Canada*, 1908, pp. 55–60.

6. Library of Congress (hereafter LOC), Theodore Roosevelt Papers, Series 1, reel 78, October 18, 1907, Translation of cablegram received at 5:15 a.m., Taft to Root and President, p. 5.

7. NA, FO 371/274, Foreign Office: Political Departments: General Correspondence from 1906–1966, Japan. Code 23 File 22241-30377, p. 205.

8. Ibid., Mr. Bryce to Sir Edward Grey, p. 206 (verso).

9. Kornel Chang, "Circulating Race and Empire: Transnational Labor Activism and the Politics of Anti-Asian Agitation," *The Journal of American History* 96(3), December 2009, p. 687.

10. I am indebted to the detailed work of H.H. Sugimoto, who not only compiled the most comprehensive and well-documented account of the events of 1907 but also situated them in a broader history of migration and diplomacy. H.H. Sugimoto, *Japanese Immigration, the Vancouver Riots and Canadian Diplomacy* (New York: Arno Press, 1978).

11. City of Vancouver Archives (hereafter CVA), MCR-1-14, Vancouver Council Minutes, January 15, 1906–30 September, 1907, line 19, p. 690.

12. Quoted by H.H. Sugimoto, *Japanese Immigration, the Vancouver Riots and Canadian Diplomacy* (New York: Arno Press, 1978) p. 117. Originally described in the *News Advertiser*, September 8, 1907.

13. Roy, *White Man's Province*, p. 192.

14. Library and Archives Canada (hereafter LAC), "Fierce Race Riot at Vancouver: Mob of Frenzied Laborites Attempts to Demolish the Oriental Quarter," *Manitoba Free Press*, September 9, 1907, p. 1.

15. Roy, *White Man's Province*, pp. 192–3.

16. NA, FO 371/274, p. 205.

17. Ibid., p. 329.

18. LAC, "Fierce Race Riot at Vancouver: Mob of Frenzied Laborites Attempts to Demolish the Oriental Quarter," *Manitoba Free Press*, September 9, 1907, p. 1.

19. W. Wang, "Perspectives on the 1907 Riots in Selected Asian Languages and International Newspapers." Accessed November 17, 2011, at www.instrcc.ubc.ca/1907_riotwj/index.htm.

20. Quoted in Wang, "Perspectives on the 1907 Riots."

21. H.H. Sugimoto, *Japanese Immigration, the Vancouver Riots and Canadian Diplomacy* (New York: Arno Press, 1978) p. 126, ff. 73.

22. CVA, Vancouver Board of Police Commissioners Fonds, series 180, 75-A-5 file 4, Vancouver Police Department II, June 4, 1907, R.G. Chamberlain report.

23. CVA, Vancouver Council Minutes, MCR-1-14, September 16, 1907, p. 711.

24. Wang, "Perspectives on the 1907 Riots."

25. NA, FO 371/274, p. 233.

26. Ibid., p. 228 (verso).

27. William Hemingway, "A Japanese Hornet's Nest for John Bull," *Harper's Weekly* (New York), October 5, 1907, p. 1448.

28. Sugimoto, *Japanese Immigration,* p. 131 ff. 87.

29. Allan Morley, *Vancouver: From Milltown to Metropolis*, 2nd ed. (Vancouver: Mitchell Press, 1969) p. 123.

30. O.D. Skelton, *Life and Letters of Sir Wilfrid Laurier,* vol. 2 (Toronto: Oxford University Press, 1921) p. 350.

31. NA, FO 371/274, pp. 251–2.

32. *The Vancouver Daily World,* quoted in H.H. Sugimoto, *Japanese Immigration, the Vancouver Riots and Canadian Diplomacy* (New York: Arno Press, 1978) pp. 135–6.

33. CVA, 75-A-5 File 2, Police Court Reports, "Statement of Cases Disposed of in the Police Court during the month of September, 1907."

34. NA, FO 371/274, pp. 208–10.

35. Ibid., p. 210.

36. Ibid., p. 228.

37. Ibid., p. 326 (verso).

38. LAC, William Lyon Mackenzie King Diary, September 7, 1907, c2091. Accessed February 1, 2011, at www.collectionscanada.gc.ca/databases/king/001059-119. 02-e.php?&page_id_nbr=4362&interval=20&&PHPSESSID=c986tc1rtdc4en3jmi 5q9uk443.

TWO: EYES ON VANCOUVER

1. NA, FO 371/274, Foreign Office: Political Departments: General Correspondence from 1906–1966, Japan. Code 23 File 22241-30377, p. 180.

2. Ibid., p. 183.

3. LAC, Grey of Howick Papers, mfm-C-1356, p. 495A.

4. NA, FO 371/274, p. 283.

5. Ibid., p. 251 (and verso).

6. LAC, Grey of Howick Papers, mfm-C-1356, pp. 475–81.

7. LAC, Grey of Howick Papers, mfm-C-1356, pp. 515–6.

8. NA, FO 371/274, p. 198 (verso).

9. Library of Congress (LOC), Theodore Roosevelt Papers, Series 2, v.74 reel 346, pp. 132, 134, and 139. Roosevelt to Melville E. Stone, general manager, Associated

Press, July 26, 1907; Roosevelt to Whitelaw Reid, U.S. ambassador to Great Britain, July 26, 1907; and Roosevelt to Root, July 26, 1907.

10. LOC, Theodore Roosevelt Papers, Series 2, v. 73, reel 346, p. 485. Roosevelt to Root, July 13, 1907.

11. LOC, Theodore Roosevelt Papers, Series 2, v. 75, reel 346, p. 156. Roosevelt to H. Cabot Lodge, September 11, 1907.

12. LOC, Theodore Roosevelt Papers, Series 2, v. 73, reel 346, p. 481. Roosevelt to Root, July 13, 1907.

13. LOC, Theodore Roosevelt Papers, Series 2, v. 74, reel 346, p. 254. Roosevelt to Root, August 8, 1907.

14. LOC, Theodore Roosevelt Papers, Series 2, v. 74, reel 346, p. 12. Roosevelt to Sternburg, July 18, 1907.

15. LAC, Grey of Howick Papers, mfm-C-1356, p. 516.

16. NA, FO 371/274, p. 270.

17. Ibid., pp. 271–2.

18. LAC, Laurier Papers, MG26-G, mfm C-1162, Lord Grey Letters, 1904–1911, p. 204468, September 9, 1907.

19. LAC, Grey of Howick Papers, mfm C-1357, p. 475, September 10, 1907.

20. This kind of reference to "Japs" was undoubtedly racist as it was embedded in the wider Anglo-Saxon racial hierarchy of the time. However, it would not have had the shock value it does today as it was used in common parlance. LAC, Grey of Howick Papers, mfm C-1357, p. 507, September 19, 1907.

21. LAC, Grey of Howick Papers, mfm C-1357, pp. 494–5, September 16, 1907.

22. LAC, Laurier Papers, MG26-G, mfm c1162, Lord Grey Letters, 1904–1911, pp. 204516–21, September 20, 1907.

23. W.L. Mackenzie King was informed that it was during Queen Victoria's Jubilee celebrations in 1897, but Buchignani, Indra, and Srivastava date this trip to the coronation a few years later.

24. Norman Buchignani, Doreen M. Indra, and Ram Srivastava, *Continuous Journey: A Social History of South Asians in Canada* (Toronto: McClelland and Stewart, 1985), p. 11.

25. NA, FO 371/274, p. 328. T.R.E. McInnes confidential report on Asian immigration.

26. LAC, Laurier Papers, MG26-G, mfm C-1162, Lord Grey Letters, 1904–1911, p. 204705, November 14, 1907.

27. LAC, Grey of Howick Papers, mfm C-1357, p. 497, September 11, 1907.

28. In *The Kind of People Canada Wants: Canada and the Displaced Persons, 1943–1953* (Vancouver: University of British Columbia Press, forthcoming), I discuss the ways this concept of "suitability" informed labour decisions in the 1940s.

29. Norman Buchignani, Doreen M. Indra, and Ram Srivastava, *Continuous Journey: A Social History of South Asians in Canada* (Toronto: McClelland & Stewart, 1985) pp. 13–4.

30. NA, FO 371/274, p. 277.

31. LAC, William Lyon Mackenzie King Diary, September 7, 1907, c2096. Accessed February 1, 2011, at www.collectionscanada.gc.ca/databases/king/001059-119. 02-e.php?&page_id_nbr=4372&interval=20&&PHPSESSID=c986tc1rtdc4en 3jmi5q9uk443. The same diary entry suggests that after discussion with some colleagues Mackenzie King suggested Lemieux as the best choice for the mission to Japan.

32. P.C. 1907-2435, October 4, 1907, Appointment W.L. Mackenzie King Commr [Commissioner] to enquire immigration of Oriental labourers—S.S. [Secretary of State], 1907/11/00 [NB. This date is incorrect on the LAC website: accessed June 1, 2011, at www.collectionscanada.gc.ca/databases/orders/001022-119.01-e. php?&sisn_id_nbr=141844&page_sequence_nbr=1&interval=20&&PHPSESSID= jnss9u23dldm7es8bnmb7hqaa4].

33. LAC, William Lyon Mackenzie King Diary, October 11, 1907, p. c2107. Accessed February 1, 2011, at www.collectionscanada.gc.ca/databases/king/001059-119. 02-e.php?&page_id_nbr=4395&interval=20PHPSESSID=rvnfce8q2vr5fhijk36s9 dcpr3.

34. Ibid., October 12, 1907, p. c2108. Accessed February 1, 2011, at www.collections canada.gc.ca/databases/king/001059-119.02-e.php?&page_id_nbr=4396&interval =20PHPSESSID=rvnfce8q2vr5fhijk36s9dcpr3PHPSESSID=n2p2mpaeidq1m2t4v4 et14chb4.

35. The Chinese claims would be added in a second investigation that began in May 1908.

36. LAC, Mackenzie King Diary, October 15, 1907, p. c2111. Accessed February 1, 2011, at www.collectionscanada.gc.ca/databases/king/001059-119.02-e. php?&page_id_nbr=4402&interval=20PHPSESSID=rvnfce8q2vr5fhijk36s9dcpr3P HPSESSID=n2p2mpaeidq1m2t4v4et14chb4.

37. LAC, William Lyon Mackenzie King Diary, October 20, 1907, p. c2112. Accessed February 1, 2011, at www.collectionscanada.gc.ca/databases/king/001059-119. 02-e.php?&page_id_nbr=4403&interval=20PHPSESSID=rvnfce8q2vr5fhijk36s9dc pr3PHPSESSID=n2p2mpaeidq1m2t4v4et14chb4.

38. Ibid.

39. LAC, William Lyon Mackenzie King Diary, October 21, 1907, p. c2113. Accessed February 1, 2011, at www.collectionscanada.gc.ca/databases/king/001059-119. 02-e.php?&page_id_nbr=4408&interval=20PHPSESSID=rvnfce8q2vr5fhijk36s9dc pr3PHPSESSID=n2p2mpaeidq1m2t4v4et14chb4.

40. W.L. Mackenzie King, *The Mackenzie King Diaries, 1893–1931,* "Private Diary, International Relations, Missions to Great Britain, United States and Japan, 1908, v.1, January–March 1908," February 18, 1908, p. 5 (Toronto: University of Toronto Press, 1973, microfiche v.95-G4).

41. W.L. Mackenzie King, *Report by W.L. Mackenzie King, C.M.G., Deputy Minister of Labour, Commissioner, Appointed to investigate into the Losses Sustained by*

the Japanese Population of Vancouver, B.C., on the occasion of the riots in that city in September, 1907, Sessional Paper No. 74g, 1908, pp. 9 and 11.

42. Ibid., p. 12.
43. Ibid., p. 18.
44. LAC, MG27 II D10, v.4, Nossé to Lemieux, November 5, 1907, p. 154.
45. Mackenzie King, *Report into the Losses Sustained*, p. 14.
46. W.L. Mackenzie King, C.M.G., Commissioner, *Report of the Royal Commission, Appointed to inquire into the methods by which Oriental labourers have been induced to come to Canada*, 1908, p. 21.
47. Ibid., p. 22.
48. According to King, 2,779 Japanese moved from Hawaii to BC in the first ten months of 1907.
    Mackenzie King, *Report of Royal Commission*, p. 55.
49. Ibid., p. 51.
50. Ibid., p. 31.
51. Ibid., p. 48.
52. Ibid., p. 45
53. Ibid., p. 66.
54. Ibid., p. 80.
55. Ibid.
56. NA, FO 371/274, p. 368.
57. Ibid., p. 369 (verso).
58. LAC, Earl Grey Correspondence with Sir Wilfrid Laurier, MG27II B2, mfm. 1357, 593. November 16, 1907.
59. NA, FO 371/274, pp. 292–3.
60. Ibid., p. 394.
61. Ibid., p. 394 (verso).
62. Mackenzie King, *Mackenzie King Diaries, 1893–1931*, "Missions to Great Britain, United States and Japan, 1908, v.1, January–March, 1908," February 4, 1908, p. 9 (Toronto: University of Toronto Press, 1973, microfiche v.94).
63. NA, FO 371/274, p. 315.
64. LAC, Laurier Papers, MG26-G, mfm. C-1162, Lord Grey Letters, pp. 204566–7.
65. The Chinese damages would be considerably higher at approximately $26,000. See p. 128.
66. NA, FO 371/274, p. 316.

THREE: LEMIEUX IN TOKYO

1. Patricia Roy, *A White Man's Province: British Columbia, Politicians and Chinese and Japanese Immigrants, 1858–1914* (Vancouver: University of British Columbia Press, 1990) pp. 188–9.

2. Quoted in Melva Jean Dwyer, *Laurier and the British Columbia Liberal Party, 1896–1911: A Study in Federal-Provincial Party Relations*, MA Thesis, University of British Columbia, 1961, p. 84.

3. He presented his credentials in Tokyo on October 15, 1907. For a link to Thomas James O'Brien's appointments with the Department of State, see http://history.state.gov/departmenthistory/people/obrien-thomas-james

4. For more on the life of Rodolphe Lemieux, see René Castonguay, "Lemieux, Rodolphe," in *Dictionary of Canadian Biography*, vol. 16, University of Toronto/Université Laval, 2003–. Accessed June 26, 2013, at www.biographi.ca/en/bio/lemieux_rodolphe_16E.html

5. P.B. Waite, "Pope, Sir Joseph," in *Dictionary of Canadian Biography*, v.15, University of Toronto/Université Laval, 2003–. Accessed June 27, 2013, at www.biographi.ca/en/bio/pope_joseph_15E.html

6. NA, FO 371/274, Foreign Office: Political Departments: General Correspondence from 1906–1966, Japan. Code 23 File 22241-30377, p. 411 (verso). Memorandum presented by the Honourable Mr. Lemieux on behalf of the Canadian Government, setting forth the circumstances of his mission and the proposals of his Government for dealing with the question of Japanese immigration into Canada—proposals which have the support of His Majesty's Government.

7. PC 1907-2256, October 12, 1907, "Mission of the Honourable Rodolphe Lemieux to Japan to arrange means to prevent recurrence of anti-Oriental disturbances in British Columbia." Accessed October 5, 2012, at www.collectionscanada.gc.ca/databases/orders/001022-119.01-e.php?&sisn_id_nbr=136321&page_sequence_nbr=1&interval=20&&PHPSESSID=u8o4a84da0pl2lheo54st8cou6.

8. NA, FO 371/274, p. 224. An October 17 memo explicitly mentions that the Canadian mission was coming "to discuss with the Japanese authorities the question of immigration into Canada."

9. Ibid., p. 226.

10. Ibid., p. 227 (verso). Emphasis in original.

11. Ibid., p. 236.

12. Ibid., p. 238 (and verso).

13. John Price, "'Orienting' the Empire: Mackenzie King and the Aftermath of the 1907 Race Riots," *BC Studies* 156, Winter 2007/8, p. 61. Also LAC, MG27 II D10, v.4, Lemieux fonds, text of an interview, p. 199.

14. LAC, MG27 II D10 v.4, Lemieux fonds, Lemieux to Louis Jetté, his father-in-law, November 16, 1907, p. 171.

15. NA, FO 371/274, MacDonald to Edward Grey, November 16, 1907, p. 299.

16. LAC, MG27 II D10, v.4, Lemieux fonds, Lemieux to Mackenzie King, November 17, 1907, p. 181.

17. LAC, MG27 II D10, v.4, Lemieux fonds, Lemieux to Laurier, November 18, 1907, p. 192.

18. LAC, MG27 II D10, v.4, Lemieux fonds, Lemieux to Jetté, November 25, 1907, p. 284. "L'Ambassadeur Américain voudrait bien me voir. Les E.U. suivent avec

intérêt ma mission. Mais *'timeo Danaos et dona ferentes.'* Donc j'évite avec soin l'Ambassade Americaine."

19. LOC, Theodore Roosevelt Papers, Series 1, reel 78, pp. 2–3. Translation of cable-gram received at 5:15 a.m., Taft to Root and President, October 18, 1907.

20. Ibid., p. 3.

21. Ibid., p. 4.

22. Ibid., p. 5.

23. Ibid., pp. 9–10.

24. Ibid., reel 79. O'Brien to Roosevelt, November 27, 1907.

25. NA, FO 371/274, p. 310.

26. "Treaty of Commerce and Navigation between Great Britain and Japan. Signed at London, July 16, 1894," in Lewis Hertslet, *Hertslet's Commercial Treaties: A Complete Collection of the Treaties and Conventions, and Reciprocal Regulations, at Present Subsisting between Great Britain and Foreign Powers* (Butterworth: London, 1840), pp. 691–2. Accessed June 1, 2011, at www.heinonline.org. myaccess.library.utoronto.ca/HOL/Page?handle=hein.ustreaties/comcoltc0019&col lection=ustreaties&index=ustreaties/comcoltc&id=723.

27. NA, FO 371/274, p. 411 (verso).

28. Ibid., p. 412.

29. Ibid., p. 260.

30. LAC, MG 27 II D10, v. 4, Lemieux fonds, Lemieux to Jetté, November 17, 1907, pp. 182–3. His letter used the following words to describe his feelings about the temple: "... le clou de l'après-midi a été notre visite à l'un des grands temples de Boudha ... mais c'est bien l'un des spectacles vraiment extrordinaires de ma vie."

31. LAC, MG 27 II D10, v.4, Lemieux fonds, A rattled Lemieux to Laurier on November 22, 1907 the day following the 2:17 a.m. earthquake, p. 236.

32. LAC, MG 27 II D10, v.4, Lemieux fonds, Precis of the meeting held at the British embassy on December 4, 1907, p. 406.

33. LAC, MG 27 II D10, v.4, Lemieux fonds, Lemieux to Laurier, December 4, 1907, p. 412,

34. NA, FO 371/274, p. 374 (verso).

35. LAC, Earl Grey Correspondence with Sir Wilfrid Laurier, MG27II B2, mfm. 1357, 631. December 5, 1907.

36. LAC, MG27 II D10, v.5, Lemieux fonds, Lemieux to Jetté, December 9, 1907, p. 448.

37. LAC, Earl Grey Correspondence with Sir Wilfrid Laurier, MG27II B2, mfm. 1357, 628–9. December 5, 1907.

38. LAC, Laurier Papers, MG26-G, mfm. C-1162, Lord Grey Letters, p. 204807.

39. LAC, MG27 II D10, v.5, Lemieux fonds, Lemieux to Jetté, December 10, 1907, p. 457.

40. NA, FO 371/274, p. 283.

41. LAC, MG27 II D10, v.5, Lemieux fonds, Laurier to Lemieux, December 11, 1907, p. 502.

42. LAC, Earl Grey Correspondence with Sir Wilfrid Laurier, MG27II B2, mfm. 1357, 637. December 14, 1907.

43. NA, FO 371/274, p. 411. Contained in a memo describing the negotiations from Sir Claude MacDonald to Sir Edward Grey.

44. Ibid., pp. 409 and 409 (verso).

45. Ibid., p. 382.

46. Ibid., p. 389 (verso). December 18, 1907.

47. LAC, MG27 II D10, v.6, Lemieux fonds, MacDonald to Edward Grey, December 21, 1907, p. 663.

48. NA, FO 371/274, p. 435.

49. Ibid., p. 436.

50. LAC, MG27 II D10, v.6, Lemieux fonds, King to Lemieux, December 30, 1907, p. 768.

51. For details about Lemieux's argument to cabinet, see John Price, "'Orienting' the Empire: Mackenzie King and the Aftermath of the 1907 Race Riots," *BC Studies* 156, Winter 2007/8, pp. 63–6, and LAC, Laurier Papers, nos. 132060–90.

52. R.L. Borden, *The Question of Oriental Immigration, Speeches (in part) Delivered By R.L. Borden, MP in 1907 and 1908*, p. 27. Microform version: catalogue key 1693492. Original publication held at National Library of Canada: ISBN 0665751044.

53. Ibid., p. 26.

FOUR: THE MAN IN THE MIDDLE

1. LAC, Mackenzie King Diary, January 12, 1908, c2173. Accessed February 1, 2011, at www.collectionscanada.gc.ca/databases/king/001059-119.02-e. php?&page_id_nbr=4468&interval=20PHPSESSID=i9gk0dmkaa6vqg0b1ssvclvnl6.

2. For more on Borden's critique of the agreement, see Chapter Three.

3. For more on Lemieux's agreement, see Chapter Three.

4. LAC, P.C. 1908-27. Accessed December 20, 2010, at www.collectionscanada.gc.ca/databases/orders/001022-119.01-e.php?&sisn_id_nbr=142346&page_sequence_nbr=1&interval=20&&page_id_nbr=273553&&&&&PHPSESSID=dck5cv78p37mnhb0kckp6glqi1.

5. W.L. Mackenzie King, *The Mackenzie King Diaries, 1893–1931*, "Private Diary, International Relations, "Missions to Great Britain, United States and Japan, 1908, v.1, January–March, 1908," February 2, 1908, pp. 1–2. (Toronto: University of Toronto Press, 1973, microfiche v.94).

6. Ibid., February 18, 1908, pp. 2–3 (Toronto: University of Toronto Press, 1973, microfiche v.95).

7. LAC, Mackenzie King Diary, January 25, 1908, c2175. Accessed February 1, 2011, at www.collectionscanada.gc.ca/databases/king/001059-119.02-e. php?&page_id_nbr=4475&interval=20PHPSESSID=i9gk0dmkaa6vqg0b1ssvclvnl6.

8. Ibid., c2177.

9. Mackenzie King, *Mackenzie King Diaries, 1893–1931*, "Missions to Great Britain, United States and Japan, 1908, v.1, January–March, 1908," January 28, 1908, p. 3. (Toronto: University of Toronto Press, 1973, microfiche v.92).

10. Patricia Roy, *White Man's Province: British Columbia Politicians and Chinese and Japanese Immigrants, 1858–1914* (Vancouver: University of British Columbia Press, 1989) p. 128.

11. Mackenzie King, *Mackenzie King Diaries, 1893–1931*, "Missions to Great Britain, United States and Japan, 1908, v.1, January–March, 1908," January 28, 1908, p. 1. (Toronto: University of Toronto Press, 1973, microfiche v.92).

12. Ibid., January 29, 1908, pp. 1–2. (Toronto: University of Toronto Press, 1973, microfiche v.92).

13. Carman Miller, "Grey, Albert Henry George, 4th Earl Grey," in *Dictionary of Canadian Biography*, vol. 14, University of Toronto/Université Laval, 2003–. Accessed June 27, 2013, at www.biographi.ca/en/bio/grey_albert_henry_george_14E.html.

14. Mackenzie King, *Mackenzie King Diaries, 1893–1931*, "Missions to Great Britain, United States and Japan, 1908, v.1, January–March, 1908," January 31, 1908, pp. 3–4. (Toronto: University of Toronto Press, 1973, microfiche v.92).

15. Ibid., January 31, 1908, p. 5 (Toronto: University of Toronto Press, 1973, microfiche v.93).

16. Ibid., January 31, 1908, p. 9 (Toronto: University of Toronto Press, 1973, microfiche v.93).

17. Ibid., January 31, 1908, p. 8 (Toronto: University of Toronto Press, 1973, microfiche v.93).

18. NA, FO 371/474, p. 38. Theodore Roosevelt to Sir Wilfrid Laurier, February 1, 1908.

19. Mackenzie King, *Mackenzie King Diaries, 1893–1931*, "Missions to Great Britain, United States and Japan, 1908, v.1, January–March, 1908," February 1, 1908, p. 11. (Toronto: University of Toronto Press, 1973, microfiche v.93).

20. Ibid., February 1, 1908, p. 15 (Toronto: University of Toronto Press, 1973, microfiche v.93).

21. These included former civil lord of the admiralty Arthur Lee, and Liberal MP Sir Edward Strachey.

22. Mackenzie King, *Mackenzie King Diaries, 1893–1931*, "Missions to Great Britain, United States and Japan, 1908, v.1, January–March, 1908," February 1, 1908, p. 7 (Toronto: University of Toronto Press, 1973, microfiche v.93).

23. Ibid., February 1, 1908, p. 5 (Toronto: University of Toronto Press, 1973, microfiche v.94).

24. Ibid., February 4, 1908, p. 39 (Toronto: University of Toronto Press, 1973, microfiche v.94).

25. Ibid., February 3, 1908, p. 8 (Toronto: University of Toronto Press, 1973, microfiche v.94). King was sure that Laurier was going to fill the pause with his name, but he chose to check himself and say "Canada."

26. NA, FO 371/474, p. 38. Sir Wilfrid Laurier to Theodore Roosevelt, 20 February, 1908.

27. Mackenzie King, *Mackenzie King Diaries, 1893–1931*, "Missions to Great Britain, United States and Japan, 1908, v.1, January–March 1908, February 18, 1908, p. 5 (Toronto: University of Toronto Press, 1973, microfiche v.95).

28. NA, FO 371/274, File 22241-30377, p. 326 (verso).

29. Ibid., p. 327 (verso).

30. Ibid.

31. NA, FO 371/474, File 6871-9080, p. 30.

32. NA, FO 371/274, File 22241-30377, p. 328 (verso).

33. Ibid., p. 330 (verso).

34. Ibid., p. 329 (verso).

35. NA, FO 371/474, File 6871-9080, p. 31 (verso).

36. Ibid., pp. 31–2.

37. Ibid., p. 32 (verso).

38. Ibid.

39. Ibid., p. 33.

40. The Natal Act of BC was discussed in the FO on several occasions in February 1908. NA, FO 371/473, File 3178-6840, pp. 25–6.

41. Ibid., p. 26.

42. Ibid., p. 48, February 22, 1908.

43. Ibid., pp. 51–2, March 4, 1908.

44. Hugh Johnston, *The Voyage of the Komagata Maru: The Sikh Challenge to Canada's Colour Bar*, 2nd ed. (Vancouver: UBC Press, 1989) p. 7.

45. NA, FO 371/475, File 9160-16096, p. 487.

46. Ibid., p. 488.

47. LAC, Laurier Papers, MG26-G, Correspondence, mfm C-1162, Lord Grey Letters, 1904–1911, p. 204707.

48. NA, FO 371/274, File 22241-30377, p. 206.

49. Mackenzie King, *Mackenzie King Diaries, 1893–1931*, "Missions to Great Britain, United States and Japan, 1908, v.1, January–March, 1908," February 17, 1908, p. 2 (Toronto: University of Toronto Press, 1973, microfiche v.95).

50. Ibid., February 18, 1908, pp. 2–3 (Toronto: University of Toronto Press, 1973, microfiche v.95).

51. Ibid., February 7, 1908, p. 2 (Toronto: University of Toronto Press, 1973, microfiche v.95).

52. Ibid., February 25, 1908, p. 3 (Toronto: University of Toronto Press, 1973, microfiche v.96).

53. *Report by W.L. Mackenzie King, C.M.G., Deputy Minister of Labour, on his Mission to England to Confer with the British Authorities on the Subject of Immigration to Canada from the Orient, and Immigration from India in Particular, Sessional Papers*, no. 36a, 1908.

54. Mackenzie King, *Mackenzie King Diaries, 1893–1931*, "Missions to Great Britain, United States and Japan, 1908, v.1, January–March, 1908," February 4, 1908, p. 1. (Toronto: University of Toronto Press, 1973, microfiche v.94).

55. NA, FO 371/474 File 6871-9080, p. 11. Copy of Minute in Council, no. 456. March 2, 1908.

56. Ibid., p. 48. April 3, 1908.

57. Mackenzie King, *Mackenzie King Diaries, 1893–1931*, "Missions to Great Britain, United States and Japan, 1908, v.1, January–March, 1908," February 4, 1908, p. 6. (Toronto: University of Toronto Press, 1973, microfiche v.94).

FIVE: THE MISSION TO LONDON

1. W.L. Mackenzie King, *The Mackenzie King Diaries, 1893–1931*, "Private Diary, International Relations, Missions to Great Britain, United States and Japan, 1908, v.2, March–April, 1908," March 16, 1908, p. 3 (Toronto: University of Toronto Press, 1973, microfiche v.97).

2. For more on the complexities of Grey's foreign policy position, see Keith Robbins, "Sir Edward Grey and the British Empire," *The Journal of Imperial and Commonwealth History* 1 (2), 1973, pp. 213–21.

3. Mackenzie King, *Mackenzie King Diaries, 1893–1931*, "Missions to Great Britain, United States and Japan, 1908, v.2, March–April, 1908," March 30, 1908, p. 5 (Toronto: University of Toronto Press, 1973, microfiche v.100).

4. Ibid., March 30, 1908, p. 7 (Toronto: University of Toronto Press, 1973, microfiche v.100).

5. NA, FO 371/475, Foreign Office: Political Departments: General Correspondence from 1906–1966. Japan. Code 23 File 9160-16096, p. 181.

6. Mackenzie King, *Mackenzie King Diaries, 1893–1931*, "Missions to Great Britain, United States and Japan, 1908, v.2, March–April, 1908," March 18, 1908, p. 6 (Toronto: University of Toronto Press, 1973, microfiche v.98).

7. Ibid., p. 7 (Toronto: University of Toronto Press, 1973, microfiche v.98).

8. NA, FO 371/475, File 9160-16096, p. 181.

9. Mackenzie King, *Mackenzie King Diaries, 1893–1931*, March 28, 1908, p. 2 (Toronto: University of Toronto Press, 1973, microfiche v.100).

10. Ibid., p. 6 (Toronto: University of Toronto Press, 1973, microfiche v.100).

11. NA, FO 371/475, File 9160-16096, p. 181.

12. Mackenzie King, *Mackenzie King Diaries, 1893–1931*, "Missions to Great Britain, United States and Japan, 1908, v.2, March–April, 1908," March 19, 1908, p. 1 (Toronto: University of Toronto Press, 1973, microfiche v.98).

13. Ibid., April 1, 1908, p. 6 (Toronto: University of Toronto Press, 1973, microfiche v.101).

14. Ibid., March 19, 1908, p. 9 (Toronto: University of Toronto Press, 1973, microfiche v.98).

15. Ibid., March 26, 1908, p. 7 (Toronto: University of Toronto Press, 1973, microfiche v.99).

16. Ibid., March 27, 1908, p. 8 (Toronto: University of Toronto Press, 1973, microfiche v.99).

17. Ibid., March 24, 1908, p. 2 (Toronto: University of Toronto Press, 1973, microfiche v.99).

18. NA, FO 371/474, File 6871-9080, p. 28.

19. LAC, Mackenzie King Diary, March 3, 1908. Accessed June 1, 2011, at www.collectionscanada.gc.ca/databases/king/001059-119.02-e.php?&page_id_nbr=4484&interval=20PHPSESSID=2opg654d9bs4k3rjhnjeau88a1.

20. LAC, Mackenzie King Diary, c2192, April 28, 1908. Accessed June 1, 2011, at www.collectionscanada.gc.ca/databases/king/001059-119.02-e.php?&page_id_nbr=4490&interval=20PHPSESSID=i9gk0dmkaa6vqg0b1ssvclvnl6.

21. Mackenzie King, *Mackenzie King Diaries, 1893–1931*, "Missions to Great Britain, United States and Japan, 1908, v.2, March–April, 1908," March 19, 1908, p. 4. (Toronto: University of Toronto Press, 1973, microfiche v.98).

22. Ibid., March 20, 1908, p. 1 (Toronto: University of Toronto Press, 1973, microfiche v.98).

23. Ibid., March 20, 1908, p. 3 (Toronto: University of Toronto Press, 1973, microfiche v.98).

24. Ibid., March 20, 1908, p. 2 (Toronto: University of Toronto Press, 1973, microfiche v.98).

25. Ibid., March 20, 1908, p. 10 (Toronto: University of Toronto Press, 1973, microfiche v.98).

26. Ibid., March 20, 1908, pp. 13–4 (Toronto: University of Toronto Press, 1973, microfiche v.98).

27. Ibid., March 23, 1908, p. 7 (Toronto: University of Toronto Press, 1973, microfiche v.99).

28. Ibid., March 24, 1908, p. 1 (Toronto: University of Toronto Press, 1973, microfiche v.99).

29. Ibid., March 26, 1908, p. 1 (Toronto: University of Toronto Press, 1973, microfiche v.99).

30. Ibid., April 3, 1908, p. 1 (Toronto: University of Toronto Press, 1973, microfiche v.101).

31. Ibid., April 3, 1908, pp. 10–1 (Toronto: University of Toronto Press, 1973, microfiche v.101).

32. Ibid., April 3, 1908, p. 14 (Toronto: University of Toronto Press, 1973, microfiche v.101).

33. Ibid., April 3, 1908, p. 7 (Toronto: University of Toronto Press, 1973, microfiche v.101).

34. Ibid., April 3, 1908, p. 9 (Toronto: University of Toronto Press, 1973, microfiche v.101).

35. Ishbel Hamilton Gordon (née Majoribanks) was a philanthropist and an advocate for women. During her time in Ottawa, between 1893 and 1898, she involved herself in a variety of projects including the National Council of Women of Canada and the Victorian Order of Nurses.

36. Andrew S. Thompson, *Oxford Dictionary of National Biography*, "Hunt, Violet Edith Gwynllyn Brooke (1870–1910)," first published 2004; online edn, October 2006, http://dx.doi.org/10.1093/ref:odnb/50755.

37. Mackenzie King, *Mackenzie King Diaries, 1893–1931*, "Missions to Great Britain, United States and Japan, 1908, v.2, March–April, 1908," March 18, 1908, p. 9 (Toronto: University of Toronto Press, 1973, microfiche v.98).

38. Ibid., April 1, 1908, p. 1 (Toronto: University of Toronto Press, 1973, microfiche v.100).

39. Ibid.

40. Ibid., April 1, 1908, p. 3 (Toronto: University of Toronto Press, 1973, microfiche v.100).

41. Walter Nimocks, *Milner's Young Men: The Kindergarten in Edwardian Imperial Affairs* (Durham, N.C.: Duke University Press, 1968).

42. Mackenzie King, *Mackenzie King Diaries, 1893–1931*, "Missions to Great Britain, United States and Japan, 1908, v.2, March–April, 1908," April 3, 1908, p. 24 (Toronto: University of Toronto Press, 1973, microfiche v.101).

43. Ibid., April 3, 1908, p. 20 (Toronto: University of Toronto Press, 1973, microfiche v.101).

44. Ibid., April 3, 1908, p. 26 (Toronto: University of Toronto Press, 1973, microfiche v.101).

45. Ibid., April 4, 1908, p. 1 (Toronto: University of Toronto Press, 1973, microfiche v.101).

46. Ibid., April 4, 1908, p. 3 (Toronto: University of Toronto Press, 1973, microfiche v.101).

47. Ibid.

48. Ibid., April 13, 1908, p. 60 (Toronto: University of Toronto Press, 1973, microfiche v.102).

49. Ibid., April 14, 1908, p. 68 (Toronto: University of Toronto Press, 1973, microfiche v.103).

50. *Report of Mr. W.L. Mackenzie King on his Mission to England in Connection with the Immigration of Asiatics into Canada.* June 1908. p. 5. Accessed January 9, 2012, at http://gateway.proquest.com/openurl?url_ver=Z39.88-2004&res_dat=xri:hcpp-us&rft_dat=xri:hcpp:fulltext:1908-009943:5.

51. Ibid.

52. Ibid., p. 4. Accessed January 9, 2012, at http://gateway.proquest.com/openurl?url_ver=Z39.88-2004&res_dat=xri:hcpp-us&rft_dat=xri:hcpp:fulltext:1908-009943:4.

53. Ibid., p. 6. Accessed January 9, 2012, at http://gateway.proquest.com/openurl?url_ver=Z39.88-2004&res_dat=xri:hcpp-us&rft_dat=xri:hcpp:fulltext:1908-009943:6.

54. Ibid.

55. Ibid.
56. Ibid., p. 7. Accessed January 9, 2012, at http://gateway.proquest.com/openurl?url_ver=Z39.88-2004&res_dat=xri:hcpp-us&rft_dat=xri:hcpp:fulltext:1908-009943:7.
57. Ibid.
58. Ibid., p. 4. Accessed January 9, 2012, at http://gateway.proquest.com/openurl?url_ver=Z39.88-2004&res_dat=xri:hcpp-us&rft_dat=xri:hcpp:fulltext:1908-009943:4.

SIX: THE INDISPENSABLE MAN

1. NA, FO 371/274, Foreign Office: Political Departments: General Correspondence from 1906–1966. Japan. Code 23 File 22241-30377, pp. 396–7.
2. Government of Canada, Sessional Paper, 74f, W.L. Mackenzie King, *Losses Sustained by the Chinese Population of Vancouver, B.C., on the Occasion of the Riots in that City in September, 1907* (Ottawa: S.E. Dawson, 1908) pp. 10 and 12.
3. W.L. Mackenzie King, *The Mackenzie King Diaries, 1893–1931,* "Private Diary, International Relations, Missions to the Orient; India, China and Japan, Chinese Mission, Negotiations at Peking, October 30, 1908–May 7, 1909," March 19, 1909, p. 97 (Toronto: University of Toronto Press, 1973, microfiche v.119).
4. Government of Canada, Sessional Paper, 74f, p. 15.
5. Government of Canada, Sessional Paper 36b, *Report by W.L. Mackenzie King, C.M.G., deputy minister of labour, on the need for the suppression of the opium traffic in Canada* (Ottawa: S.E. Dawson, Printer to the King's most Excellent Majesty, 1908) pp. 12–3.
6. Government of Canada, *Official Report of the Debates of the House of Commons* (Ottawa: S.E. Dawson, Printer to the King's Most Excellent Majesty, 1908), July 10, 1908, p. 12550, and *An Act of the Parliament of the United Kingdom and Ireland* (Ottawa: S.E. Dawson, 1908) July 20, 1908, p. 441.
7. LAC, Mackenzie King Diary, May 4, 1908. Accessed October 8, 2009, at www.collectionscanada.gc.ca/databases/king/001059-119.02-e.php?&page_id_nbr=4497&interval=20PHPSESSID=2opg654d9bs4k3rjhnjeau88a1.
8. LAC, Mackenzie King Diary, August 29, 1908. Accessed October 8, 2009, at www.collectionscanada.gc.ca/databases/king/001059-119.02-e.php?&page_id_nbr=4509&interval=20PHPSESSID=2opg654d9bs4k3rjhnjeau88a1.
9. LAC, Mackenzie King Diary, September 9, 1908. Accessed October 8, 2009, at www.collectionscanada.gc.ca/databases/king/001059-119.02-e.php?&page_id_nbr=4521&interval=20PHPSESSID=2opg654d9bs4k3rjhnjeau88a1.
10. Mackenzie King, *The Mackenzie King Diaries, 1893–1931,* "Mission to China, October 30, 1908–May 7, 1909," Oct. 30–Dec. 6, 1908, p. 2 (Toronto: University of Toronto Press, 1973, microfiche v.104).
11. Ibid., October 30–December 6, 1908, p. 12 (Toronto: University of Toronto Press, 1973, microfiche v.104).
12. Ibid., p. 6 (Toronto: University of Toronto Press, 1973, microfiche v.104).

13. Ibid., p. 7 (Toronto: University of Toronto Press, 1973, microfiche v.104).

14. Ibid., p. 21 (Toronto: University of Toronto Press, 1973, microfiche v.104).

15. Ibid., pp. 11–3 (Toronto: University of Toronto Press, 1973, microfiche v.104).

16. LAC, Mackenzie King Diary, December 3, 1908. Accessed October 8, 2009, at www.collectionscanada.gc.ca/databases/king/001059-119.02-e.php?&page_id_nbr=4535&interval=20PHPSESSID=rgi3sm8e5r4e3im6ir3prsru85.

17. Ibid., December 2, 1908.

18. Mackenzie King, *Mackenzie King Diaries, 1893–1931*, "Mission to China, October 30, 1908–May 7, 1909," December 13, 1908, p. 27 (Toronto: University of Toronto Press, 1973, microfiche v.105).

19. Ibid., December 16, 1908, pp. 38–9 (Toronto: University of Toronto Press, 1973, microfiche v.105).

20. Ibid., December 23, 1908, pp. 53–4 (Toronto: University of Toronto Press, 1973, microfiche v.105).

21. Ibid., December 23, 1908, p. 70 (Toronto: University of Toronto Press, 1973, microfiche v.105).

22. Ibid., December 25, 1908, p. 88 (Toronto: University of Toronto Press, 1973, microfiche v.106).

23. Ibid.

24. Ibid., December 23, 1908, p. 54 (Toronto: University of Toronto Press, 1973, microfiche v.105). In this, he had in mind both questions connected with limiting opium traffic and removing any misunderstanding about the deportation of Indians to British Honduras. Canada had begun deporting Indians for the crime of destitution. There was some concern that if this was done in large numbers it would be received poorly in India. See Henry Ferns and Bernard Ostry, *The Age of Mackenzie King* (Toronto: James Lorimer and Company, 1976) p. 88.

25. Mackenzie King, *Mackenzie King Diaries, 1893–1931*, "Mission to China, October 30, 1908–May 7, 1909," December 23, 1908, p. 56 (Toronto: University of Toronto Press, 1973, microfiche v.105).

26. Ibid., December 24, 1908, p. 73 (Toronto: University of Toronto Press, 1973, microfiche v.105).

27. King describes his use of these documents while sailing for India and the institutional character which produced them. Mackenzie King, *Mackenzie King Diaries, 1893–1931*, "Mission to China, October 30, 1908–May 7, 1909," January 13, 1908, pp. 155–6 (Toronto: University of Toronto Press, 1973, microfiche v.107).

28. Ibid., December 25, 1908, pp. 76 and 89 (Toronto: University of Toronto Press, 1973, microfiche v.106).

29. Ibid., December 25, 1908, p. 77 (Toronto: University of Toronto Press, 1973, microfiche v.106).

30. Ibid., December 25, 1908, p. 78 (Toronto: University of Toronto Press, 1973, microfiche v.106).

31. Ibid., December 25, 1908, p. 86 (Toronto: University of Toronto Press, 1973, microfiche v.106).

32. Ibid.

33. Ibid., December 28, 1908, p. 95 (Toronto: University of Toronto Press, 1973, microfiche v.106).

34. Ibid., December 28, 1908, p. 96 (Toronto: University of Toronto Press, 1973, microfiche v.106).

35. Ibid., December 28, 1908, p. 106 (Toronto: University of Toronto Press, 1973, microfiche v.106).

36. Ibid., December 28, 1908, p. 107 (Toronto: University of Toronto Press, 1973, microfiche v.106).

37. Ibid.

38. Ibid., December 28, 1908, p. 108 (Toronto: University of Toronto Press, 1973, microfiche v.106).

39. Ibid., December 28, 1908, p. 103 (Toronto: University of Toronto Press, 1973, microfiche v.106).

40. Ibid., December 28, 1908, p. 117 (Toronto: University of Toronto Press, 1973, microfiche v.106).

41. Ibid.

42. Ibid., December 29, 1908, pp. 114–5 (Toronto: University of Toronto Press, 1973, microfiche v.106).

43. King misquoted Browning in his diary, but it is clear he was referring to Robert Browning's poem "Rabbi Ben Ezra."

44. Mackenzie King, *Mackenzie King Diaries, 1893–1931*, "Mission to China, October 30, 1908–May 7, 1909," December 29, 1908, p. 116 (Toronto: University of Toronto Press, 1973, microfiche v.106).

SEVEN: THE JOURNEY TO INDIA

1. W.L. Mackenzie King, *The Mackenzie King Diaries, 1893–1931*, "Private Diary, International Relations, Mission to China, October 30, 1908–May 7, 1909," December 31, 1908, p. 124 (Toronto: University of Toronto Press, 1973, microfiche v.106).

2. Ibid., December 31, 1908, pp. 124–5 (Toronto: University of Toronto Press, 1973, microfiche v.106 and 107).

3. Ibid., January 1, 1909, p. 126 (Toronto: University of Toronto Press, 1973, microfiche v.107).

4. W.S. Lilly, *India and its Problems* (London: Sands & Co., 1902) pp. 241–2.

5. Mackenzie King, *Mackenzie King Diaries, 1893–1931*, "Mission to China, October 30, 1908–May 7, 1909," January 2–6, 1909, p. 128 (Toronto: University of Toronto Press, 1973, microfiche v.107).

6. Ibid., January 15, 1909, p. 164 (Toronto: University of Toronto Press, 1973, microfiche v.107).

7. Ibid., January 2–6, 1909, p. 131 (Toronto: University of Toronto Press, 1973, microfiche v.107).

8. Ibid.

9. Ibid., January 2–6, 1909, p. 132 (Toronto: University of Toronto Press, 1973, microfiche v.107).

10. Ibid., January 2–6, 1909, p. 133 (Toronto: University of Toronto Press, 1973, microfiche v.107).

11. Ibid.

12. Ibid.

13. Ibid., January 7, 1909, p. 134 (Toronto: University of Toronto Press, 1973, microfiche v.107).

14. Ibid.

15. For more on the pervasiveness of this outlook, see Edward W. Said, *Orientalism*, 25th Anniversary Edition (New York: Vintage Books, 2003).

16. Mackenzie King, *Mackenzie King Diaries, 1893–1931*, "Mission to China, October 30, 1908–May 7, 1909," January 16, 1909, p. 165. (Toronto: University of Toronto Press, 1973, microfiche v.107).

17. Ibid., January 16, 1909, p. 166 (Toronto: University of Toronto Press, 1973, microfiche v.107).

18. Ibid., January 18, 1909, p. 185 (Toronto: University of Toronto Press, 1973, microfiche v.108).

19. Ibid., January 18, 1909, p. 187 (Toronto: University of Toronto Press, 1973, microfiche v.108).

20. Ibid., January 19, 1909, p. 197 (Toronto: University of Toronto Press, 1973, microfiche v.108).

21. Ibid., January 19, 1909, p. 206 (Toronto: University of Toronto Press, 1973, microfiche v.108).

22. Ibid., January 21, 1909, p. 241 (Toronto: University of Toronto Press, 1973, microfiche v.109).

23. Ibid., January 21, 1909, p. 242 (Toronto: University of Toronto Press, 1973, microfiche v.109).

24. Ibid., January 20, 1909, p. 210 (Toronto: University of Toronto Press, 1973, microfiche v.108).

25. Ibid., January 21, 1909, p. 219 (Toronto: University of Toronto Press, 1973, microfiche v.109).

26. Surendranath Banerjea, *A Nation in Making: Being the Reminiscences of Fifty Years of Public Life* (Bombay: Oxford University Press, 1963) pp. 25–8.

27. Mackenzie King, *Mackenzie King Diaries, 1893–1931*, "Mission to China, October 30, 1908–May 7, 1909," January 21, 1909, p. 229 (Toronto: University of Toronto Press, 1973, microfiche v.109).

28. Ibid., January 21, 1909, p. 231 (Toronto: University of Toronto Press, 1973, microfiche v.109).

29. Ibid., January 21, 1909, p. 233 (Toronto: University of Toronto Press, 1973, microfiche v.109).

30. Ibid.

31. Ibid., January 24, 1909, p. 259 (Toronto: University of Toronto Press, 1973, microfiche v.109).

32. Ibid., January 25, 1909, p. 262 (Toronto: University of Toronto Press, 1973, microfiche v.109).

33. Ibid., January 25, 1909, p. 264 (Toronto: University of Toronto Press, 1973, microfiche v.109).

34. Ibid., January 25, 1909, p. 267 (Toronto: University of Toronto Press, 1973, microfiche v.109).

35. Ibid., January 26, 1909, pp. 272–3 (Toronto: University of Toronto Press, 1973, microfiche v.109).

36. Ibid., February 2, 1909, p. 293 (Toronto: University of Toronto Press, 1973, microfiche v.110).

EIGHT: DIPLOMACY IN CHINA

1. International Opium Commission, "Report of The International Opium Commission," in *The Lancet* 174 (4499), November 1909, p. 1510.

2. W.L. Mackenzie King, *The Mackenzie King Diaries, 1893–1931*, "Private Diary, International Relations, Mission to China, October 30, 1908–May 7, 1909," February 5, 1909, p. 298 (Toronto: University of Toronto Press, 1973, microfiche v.110).

3. Ibid., February 13, 1909, p. 314 (Toronto: University of Toronto Press, 1973, microfiche v.110).

4. Ibid., February 14, 1909, p. 316 (Toronto: University of Toronto Press, 1973, microfiche v.110).

5. Ibid., February 15, 1909, p. 318 (Toronto: University of Toronto Press, 1973, microfiche v.110).

6. King kept a diary of his outward journey and of his return and a special volume on the immigration negotiations at Peking. The International Opium Commission at Shanghai may be found at W.L. Mackenzie King, *The Mackenzie King Diaries, 1893–1931*, "Private Diary, International Relations, Missions to the Orient; India, China and Japan, Shanghai–Ottawa, October 30, 1908–May 7, 1909," February 16, 1909, p. 1 (Toronto: University of Toronto Press, 1973, microfiche v.111).

7. David Edward Owen, *British Opium Policy in China and India* (New Haven, CT: Yale University Press, 1934) pp. 336–7.

8. W.L. Mackenzie King, *The Mackenzie King Diaries, 1893–1931*, "Private Diary, International Relations, Missions to the Orient; India, China and Japan, Shanghai–Ottawa, October 30, 1908–May 7, 1909," February 16, 1909, p. 6 (Toronto: University of Toronto Press, 1973, microfiche v.111).

9. Ibid., February 16, 1909, p. 7 (Toronto: University of Toronto Press, 1973, microfiche v.111).

10. Ibid., February 18, 1909, p. 17 (Toronto: University of Toronto Press, 1973, microfiche v.111).

11. Ibid., February 21, 1909, p. 37 (Toronto: University of Toronto Press, 1973, microfiche v.112).

12. Ibid., February 22, 1909, pp. 44–5 (Toronto: University of Toronto Press, 1973, microfiche v.112).

13. Ibid., February 23, 1909, p. 55 (Toronto: University of Toronto Press, 1973, microfiche v.112).

14. Ibid., February 19, 1909, p. 27 (Toronto: University of Toronto Press, 1973, microfiche v.111).

15. Ibid., February 20, 1909, p. 29 (Toronto: University of Toronto Press, 1973, microfiche v.111).

16. Ibid., February 21, 1909, p. 42 (Toronto: University of Toronto Press, 1973, microfiche v.112).

17. Ibid., February 22, 1909, p. 50 (Toronto: University of Toronto Press, 1973, microfiche v.112).

18. Ibid., February 28, 1909, p. 76 (Toronto: University of Toronto Press, 1973, microfiche v.112).

19. Mackenzie King, *Mackenzie King Diaries, 1893–1931*, "Missions to the Orient; India, China and Japan, Chinese Mission, Negotiations at Peking, October 30, 1908–May 7, 1909," March 6, 1909, p. 2 (Toronto: University of Toronto Press, 1973, microfiche v.117).

20. For the details of the rumours about the Chinese royal family that reached King while he was in Peking, see W.L. Mackenzie King, *The Mackenzie King Diaries, 1893–1931*, "Private Diary, International Relations, Missions to the Orient; India, China and Japan, Shanghai–Ottawa, October 30, 1908–May 7, 1909," March 12, 1909, pp. 129–32 (Toronto: University of Toronto Press, 1973, microfiche v.114).

21. W.L. Mackenzie King, *The Mackenzie King Diaries, 1893–1931*, "Private Diary, International Relations, Missions to the Orient; India, China and Japan, Chinese Mission, Negotiations at Peking, October 30, 1908–May 7, 1909," March 6, 1909, p. 7 (Toronto: University of Toronto Press, 1973, microfiche v.117).

22. For more on Canada's trade relations with China and the role of the trade commissioner in Shanghai, see John D. Meehan, *Chasing the Dragon in Shanghai: Canada's Early Relations with China, 1858–1952* (Vancouver: University of British Columbia Press, 2011), and Mackenzie King, *Mackenzie King Diaries, 1893–1931*, "Missions to the Orient; India, China and Japan, Chinese Mission, Negotiations at Peking, October 30, 1908–May 7, 1909," March 9, 1909, p. 7 (Toronto: University of Toronto Press, 1973, microfiche v.117).

23. Mackenzie King, *Mackenzie King Diaries, 1893–1931*, "Missions to the Orient; India, China and Japan, Chinese Mission, Negotiations at Peking, October 30, 1908–May 7, 1909," March 9, 1909, p. 21 (Toronto: University of Toronto Press, 1973, microfiche v.117).

24. Ibid., March 9, 1909, p. 23 (Toronto: University of Toronto Press, 1973, microfiche v.117).

25. Ibid., March 9, 1909, p. 25 (Toronto: University of Toronto Press, 1973, microfiche v.117).

26. Ibid., March 9, 1909, p. 28 (Toronto: University of Toronto Press, 1973, microfiche v.118).

27. Mackenzie King, *Mackenzie King Diaries, 1893–1931*, "Missions to the Orient; India, China and Japan, Shanghai—Ottawa, October 30, 1908–May 7, 1909," March 4, 1909, p. 102 (Toronto: University of Toronto Press, 1973, microfiche v.113).

28. Mackenzie King, *Mackenzie King Diaries, 1893–1931*, "Missions to the Orient; India, China and Japan, Chinese Mission, Negotiations at Peking, October 30, 1908–May 7, 1909," March 9, 1909, p. 43 (Toronto: University of Toronto Press, 1973, microfiche v.118).

29. Ibid., March 9, 1909, p. 51 (Toronto: University of Toronto Press, 1973, microfiche v.118).

30. Ibid., March 10, 1909, p. 56 (Toronto: University of Toronto Press, 1973, microfiche v.118).

31. Ibid., March 10, 1909, p. 59 (Toronto: University of Toronto Press, 1973, microfiche v.118).

32. Mackenzie King, *Mackenzie King Diaries, 1893–1931*, "Missions to the Orient; India, China and Japan, Shanghai–Ottawa, October 30, 1908–May 7, 1909," March 11, 1909, p. 120 (Toronto: University of Toronto Press, 1973, microfiche v.113).

33. Mackenzie King, *Mackenzie King Diaries, 1893–1931*, "Missions to the Orient; India, China and Japan, Chinese Mission, Negotiations at Peking, October 30, 1908–May 7, 1909," March 17 1909, pp. 80–2 (Toronto: University of Toronto Press, 1973, microfiche v.119.

34. Ibid., March 17, 1909, p. 75 (Toronto: University of Toronto Press, 1973, microfiche v.119).

35. Ibid., March 17, 1909, p. 80 (Toronto: University of Toronto Press, 1973, microfiche v.119).

36. Ibid., March 17, 1909, p. 81 (Toronto: University of Toronto Press, 1973, microfiche v.119).

37. Ibid., March 19, 1909, p. 86 (Toronto: University of Toronto Press, 1973, microfiche v.119).

38. Ibid., March 24, 1909, p. 105 (Toronto: University of Toronto Press, 1973, microfiche v.119).

CONCLUSION: CLOSING THE CIRCLE

1. W.L. Mackenzie King, *The Mackenzie King Diaries, 1893–1931*, "Private Diary, International Relations, Missions to the Orient; India, China and Japan, Shanghai–Ottawa, October 30, 1908–May 7, 1909," April 5, 1909, p. 194 (Toronto: University of Toronto Press, 1973, microfiche v.115).

2. Ibid., April 10, 1909, p. 202 (Toronto: University of Toronto Press, 1973, microfiche v.115).

3. Ibid., April 6, 1909, p. 199 (Toronto: University of Toronto Press, 1973, microfiche v.115).

4. Ibid., April 13, 1909, p. 210 (Toronto: University of Toronto Press, 1973, microfiche v.115).

5. Ibid., April 16, 1909, p. 232 (Toronto: University of Toronto Press, 1973, microfiche v.116).

6. Ibid., April 16, 1909, p. 235 (Toronto: University of Toronto Press, 1973, microfiche v.116).

7. Ibid., April 17, 1909, p. 242 (Toronto: University of Toronto Press, 1973, microfiche v.116).

8. Yanosuke Iwasaki was the fourth governor of the Bank of Japan and the brother of the founder of Mitsubishi. He died on March 25, 1908. It is not clear which son was getting married—the eldest, Koyata, or another.

9. Mackenzie King, *Mackenzie King Diaries, 1893–1931*, "Missions to the Orient; India, China and Japan, Shanghai—Ottawa, October 30, 1908–May 7, 1909," April 18, 1909, p. 252 (Toronto: University of Toronto Press, 1973, microfiche v.116).

10. Ibid., April 18, 1909, p. 245 (Toronto: University of Toronto Press, 1973, microfiche v.116).

11. Ibid., April 20, 1909, p. 260 (Toronto: University of Toronto Press, 1973, microfiche v.116).

12. Ibid., April 24–30, 1909, p. 264 (Toronto: University of Toronto Press, 1973, microfiche v.116).

13. Ibid., April 24–30, 1909, p. 270 (Toronto: University of Toronto Press, 1973, microfiche v.116).

14. Ibid., May1, 1909, p. 273 (Toronto: University of Toronto Press, 1973, microfiche v.116).

15. Gore Vidal, *Empire: A Novel* (New York: Vintage Books, 2000), ebook: WorldCat.

16. Julie Gilmour, "'And who is my neighbor?' Refugees, Public Opinion, and Policy in Canada since 1900," in *Canada Among Nations 2008: 100 Years of Canadian Foreign Policy*, Robert Bothwell and Jean Daudelin eds. (Montreal and Kingston: McGill-Queen's University Press, 2009) pp. 159–82.

17. Thank you to Robert Bothwell for spotting this diary entry that provides such direct evidence of the link between the two stages of King's career. LAC, William Lyon Mackenzie King Diary, 24 October, 1935, p. 865. Accessed June 29, 2012, at www.collectionscanada.gc.ca/databases/king/001059-119.02-e.php?&page_id_nbr=16487&interval=20&&&&PHPSESSID=sueqh5c810f7jiuckes82btp01.

ACKNOWLEDGMENTS

This book was written with the generous support of the L.R. Wilson Institute of Canadian History and H.V. Nelles at McMaster University. I am also grateful to the Social Services and Humanities Research Council and Roberto Perin at Glendon College, York University, who provided me with a community during my postdoctoral fellowship, and to Trinity College at the University of Toronto for giving me an office in which to work. In addition, this book would not, indeed could not, have been written without the help of a number of generous scholars, archivists, and friends. I have great respect for the work of the archivists and the staff of Library and Archives Canada, the National Archives of the United Kingdom, the US National Archives, the Library of Congress, the City of Vancouver Archives, and Robarts Library at the University of Toronto, and I am grateful for the materials and assistance they each provided during my research. This book greatly benefited from the support and encouragement I received from Patricia Roy, Henry Yu, John Price, Aya Fujiwara, Yukari Takai, Laura Madokoro, David Webster, Sam-Chin Li, and John Meehan, who helped me get my feet wet in Canada's history in the Pacific. A special thanks must go to the team at Penguin Canada, who turned the manuscript into a far better book than it otherwise might have been. Thanks to publishing director

Diane Turbide, production editor Sandra Tooze, and particularly to line and copy editor Tara Tovell, who took great care with my words and made sure that the book communicated my ideas effectively. I owe a great debt to Jeff Kilpatrick for reading my work and pushing me to improve. And finally, I am beholden once again to the editors of the History of Canada series, Robert Bothwell and Margaret MacMillan, who suggested I do this in the first place.

INDEX